Conflict & Cooperation

To Marilyn,
with much appreciation
and affection, for all that
you do.
Peter.
1/08

Syracuse Studies on Peace and Conflict Resolution

Louis Kriesberg, Series Editor

Other titles in Syracuse Studies on Peace and Conflict Resolution

Conflict & Cooperation

Christian-Muslim Relations in Contemporary Egypt

PETER E. MAKARI

 SYRACUSE UNIVERSITY PRESS

The paper used in this publication meets the minimum requirements of
American National Standard for Information Sciences—Permanence of
Paper for Printed Library Materials, ANSI Z39.48–1984.∞™

For a listing of books published and distributed by Syracuse University Press,
visit our Web site at SyracuseUniversityPress.syr.edu

ISBN-13: 978-0-8156-3144-6
ISBN-10: 0-8156-3144-8

Library of Congress Cataloging-in-Publication Data

Makari, Peter E.

　Conflict and cooperation : Christian-Muslim relations in contemporary egypt / Peter E. Makari. — 1st
ed.

　　p. cm.

　Includes bibliographical references (p.　　　) and index.

　ISBN 978-0-8156-3144-6 (hardcover : alk. paper)

　1. Egypt—Ethnic relations.   2. Copts—Egypt.   3. Religion and state—Egypt.   4. Islam and politics
Egypt.   5. Civil society—Egypt.   I. Title.

DT71.M35 2007

261.2'70962—dc22

2007022142

Manufactured in the United States of America

It is with great joy that I dedicate this book

to our two young daughters, Deborah Noor and Sarah Eve,

who have tolerated with loving acceptance

the time I have spent working on it.

The spirit they have exhibited toward me

during the countless hours of my work on this project

is an inspiration for the ideal of human love.

• • •

Peter E. Makari received his Ph.D. from New York University in 2003 in politics, with a concentration in Middle East studies. He also earned an M.A. from the American University in Cairo in Middle East studies. Peter works as executive for the Middle East and Europe with the Common Global Ministries Board of the United Church of Christ and Christian Church (Disciples of Christ). He is Egyptian American and has lived extensively in the Middle East, including Egypt and Cyprus.

Contents

Table

A Note on the Text

In transliterating Arabic words, I have chosen to follow the style adopted by the *Middle East Journal,* that is, that of the *International Journal of Middle East Studies,* but without diacritical marks. In some cases, especially regarding names, I have diverged from that practice in favor of more commonly known English spellings and have deferred to individuals' preferences on the English rendering of their names when known. Special difficulty concerns the transliteration of the Arabic letter ج because, while normally carrying the value of the English *j,* in Cairean pronunciation it has the value of a hard *g.* In most cases, I have followed *IJMES* style; however, in some cases because of more common local usage, I have favored the use of *g.*

As for translation of many Arabic sources not available in English, I have attempted to come as close to the meaning of the original as possible without being overly stylistic. Gender-specific references in translation reflect the original. I alone bear responsibility for any errors in translation of the Arabic texts.

Regarding dates, I have chosen to use the Common Era (c.e.) as the principal point of reference, and not the *Hijra* calendar. I recognize that the basis for the Common Era is Christian, but its use should not be interpreted as exclusivist. Dates before the Common Era are designated b.c.e.

Acknowledgments

This book is the outgrowth of my doctoral research, which spanned successive stages of my life; I started it in my bachelorhood, continued it in marriage, and completed it in the early childhood of our two daughters. I am exceedingly grateful to my mother and father, who afforded me many opportunities to encounter the wider world during my formative years. To my wife, Amany, I am deeply thankful for her constant support and encouragement throughout the time this project has taken to complete. Deborah and Sarah have inspired me in their own ways.

Too many people and experiences to name or recognize here have played essential roles in shaping my intellectual development and my thinking and understanding on many matters—particularly Egyptian politics, society, and religion, both Christian and Muslim. Many contributed significantly in sincere and personal ways to my understanding of interfaith relations in Egypt, and it would be unfair to attempt to name them. I am particularly grateful to all those who agreed to be interviewed for this project; their insight and frankness in conversation have added much to the outcome of this research.

Certainly not least, I owe a great deal to Professor Farhad Kazemi, who saw me through important stages of this project as a faithful adviser, offering encouragement, guidance, and motivation when I needed each.

As for the preparation of this manuscript for publication, I appreciate the enthusiasm of the Syracuse University Press and its acquisitions editor, Michael O'Conner, for seeing value in pursuing this project. In particular, I am grateful to the editor with whom I worked most closely, Glenn Wright, for his persistence and patience with me, as well as his encouragement. Syracuse University Press shared with me the comments and challenges of two anonymous readers—comments that enabled what I hope are helpful revisions of this text, and better problematization and analysis of the issues at stake. Carolyn Russ served as an outstanding—and interested—copy editor, tightening language, checking for consistency, and asking me helpful and important questions of clarification about this text.

An earlier, and briefer, version of chapter 2 appeared in the *International Review of Mission* (vol. 89, no. 352, January 2000), and its editor's permission to publish it here, with expansion and added analysis, is appreciated.

I am also grateful for the sabbatical time afforded me by Common Global Ministries of the United Church of Christ and Christian Church (Disciples of Christ) in late summer 2006, during which I was able to revise, update, and format this manuscript for its publication by Syracuse University Press.

Despite the input and influence of so many, I bear unique responsibility for the content of this text, including any errors herein.

Introduction

Recently, much has been suggested and written about conflict between and among peoples of different faiths and communities. The prevailing popular explanation for the current international situation of a "clash of civilizations," as proposed by Samuel Huntington in his landmark article and book, fails in its inability to capture much of the nuance that is the fodder of daily interaction among peoples, institutions, and nations. There can be no denying the reality of conflict in the world, but parallel with conflict are uncountable efforts and unquantified energies intent upon better relationships: cooperation and tolerance.

In the wake of September 11, 2001, and the continuation of struggle in the Middle East, it seems especially appropriate—and perhaps essential—to attempt to capture some of that nuance. The experience of contemporary Egypt can serve as a laboratory for such a task. The last two decades of the twentieth century provide a context replete with examples of interfaith and intercommunal interaction, both positive and negative. Without suggesting that Egypt's experience can be generalized to the entire Middle East, or to other places where more than one religious community reside, it is possible to learn from that experience in order to better understand how communities defined by religion can and do interact when options for change are limited.

This book seeks to describe the prevailing dynamics of Christian-Muslim communal relations in the contemporary Egyptian context. At the same time, it aims to present and analyze how these dynamics are manifested in rhetorical and actual cooperation or conflict at different social and political levels, particularly in times of apparently heightened sectarian crisis. The focus is on cooperation, even in the context of conflict, because harmonious relations do exist but are routinely overlooked—to the detriment of a more complete understanding of reality, not just in Egypt, nor only in the Middle East, but in many places of multiple communities.

An increasingly large body of literature is becoming available on the issue of tolerance as debates over characteristics of civil society continue. In the Arab world, where the issue of tolerance has a distinctively religious overtone, new literature appears on coexistence and social relations from a theoretical point of view, with a specific focus on the politics of sectarian interaction. Two examples are Milad Hanna's *Qubul al-akhar* (Acceptance of the Other) and 'Abd al-'Aziz bin 'Uthman at-Tawijri's *al-Hiwar min ajl it-ta'ayush* (Dialogue for the Sake of Coexistence). These books are illustrative of the proliferation of such topics written in Arabic for Middle Eastern audiences. The issue is clearly prominent in the minds of many, and even among people whose field is not necessarily the social sciences (Milad Hanna is a professor of engineering and has served in Parliament).

To define tolerance as a positive and active expression of accepting the presence and identity of some Other, even if that Other's beliefs or views are somehow different than, or even opposed to, one's own, is to understand tolerance as an attempt to overcome differences. This definition leads to the conclusion that such an attempt is a social initiative that results in constructive community building. Such a definition, though, may be too restrictive, especially in environments where there is a particularly high potential for intercommunal tension. Tolerance in such cases may be better defined as simply coexisting peacefully, without entering into dialogue or actively attempting to seek ways of cooperation. Acceptance of the Other's presence, and not seeking the Other's exclusion, may then be a minimalist definition.

A crucial factor in determining which definition is to be used is the level of political and social activity examined. There is obviously a close interrelation. Here, since we are focusing on socially and politically active groups and people, it is more useful, and practical, to adopt the stricter and more "active" definition. This book considers the actors who are more prominent socially and politically and therefore have a high level of activity, either tolerant or not, according to the former definition. It would not be helpful simply to use a minimalist definition as a gauge in considering them.

The book aims to describe Christian-Muslim dynamics in Egypt in light of a discussion of communal relations, tolerance, and civil society, focusing on the relevant literature and the prevailing currents. Those actors whose attitudes of tolerance are most (or least) closely in line with this definition (either rhetorically or de facto) are also those actors who are most active socially and politically. Given the reintroduction of the importance of religion in Middle Eastern (not to mention other regions) identity over the past twenty-five to thirty years, the issue of sectarian relations has been prominent in political rhetoric. While the politicization of religion is not a brand-new phenomenon, it has become an increasingly powerful mobilizing force. At many levels, the rhetoric of political religion has replaced, or at least joined in prominence, other discourse of the public economy and other matters of national concern. These expectations are tested through an examination of several examples of actors in Egyptian politics and society.

This research also provides access for the English reader to some of the existing literature and trends current in Egypt today, mostly expressed in Arabic. While there has been a steady supply of new and relevant writings in Arabic, the body of literature in English on current relations and trends is limited. In addition to this linguistic access to current literature, I have relied also upon personal access to some key political, religious, and social figures who were willing to express their views clearly and without hesitation.

It is perhaps informative for the contemporary discussion to examine Christian-Muslim relations as they exist at different levels of Egyptian polity and society, during the period of the Mubarak presidency (1981–present). Analysis and documentation of examples of the rhetoric and fact of communal cooperation between the two religious communities in Egypt is presented in order to offer insight into these different levels, all of which contribute to the sociopolitical fabric.

One group's tolerance of the other is considered to be an aspect of these communal dynamics, although it is not measured in a quantified method as such. One of the difficulties of such a study is that concepts such as tolerance and acceptance are not easily quantifiable. To attempt to devise a metric would be quite complicated and could detract from the analysis that is possible through observation and collection of data. Even so, the segments of society that this book considers are identified and analyzed in a way that shows the characteristics of tolerance, through examples of cooperation or conflict.

These segments or levels include the governmental and legal policies that deal with the relationship between Muslims and Copts in Egypt. This case takes into consideration the official position of the Egyptian government and how government officials have responded during different phases of the relationship between Christians and Muslims. Through reading reports and articles in the major Egyptian press, especially *al-Ahram*, the semiofficial newspaper, the government's positions can be determined. This reading is supplemented by analyses of the government's positions, available in books and articles. Official rhetoric of "national dialogue" and "national unity," as is demonstrated, is an attempt to break down barriers; yet it highlights differences and is often in contradiction with a growing political awareness of a need to seek legitimacy in religion, exemplified by increased religious programming on government-controlled television and broadcasts of national leaders performing their religious duties.

A second segment is that of official religion and the relationship between official religious bodies. This case necessarily includes prominent religious institutions and personalities, for example, al-Azhar University and its rector *(sheikh al-Azhar)*; Dar al-Ifta' (the Islamic Office of Religious Pronouncements) and its head, the mufti; the pope of the Coptic Orthodox Church; and the head of the Protestant Churches of Egypt. These institutions and individuals have been quite active in fostering better relationships between the faith communities, and they have attempted to translate this rhetoric into action. Statements made independent of such dialogue can also give a sense of the how consistent positions stated in and out of dialogue are.

A third level is that of political parties. The rhetoric of some political parties, specifically the ruling party, supports dialogue and improved congeniality. Other parties, or would-be parties, such as the Muslim Brotherhood and the Islamic Group *(al-jama'a al-islamiyya,* which is not legally a party but which is aligned closely with the Labor Party), have a stronger Islamic bent. Still others, such as Hizb al-Wasat (the Centrist Party), which was denied party status after application through the normal channels, call for recognition of Egypt's Islamic culture and, at the same time, work for reconciliation of Egypt's citizens. Given their particular ideologies, it is important to delve further into the positions of the Labor Party and of Hizb al-Wasat on intercommunal relations and cooperation. The controversy that has arisen over the creation of the latter, a party with Christian and Muslim membership, has been great, partly because of the idea that political alliances have been sought between Christians and former Muslim Brotherhood leaders. The fact that this party has not yet been allowed to participate raises other issues of religious tolerance, since it is widely believed that the government has not granted Hizb al-Wasat proper party status because of some of its leaders' former ties to the Muslim Brotherhood. For the examination and analysis of party positions, party platforms are cited as primary sources.

A fourth segment is the nongovernmental organization sector. NGOs, some of which are religiously based or have a distinctly religious tint, offer a clue into cooperation at the more grassroots level. They also can offer insight into a segment that includes institutions some of which often cooperate with the government and others that offer a different, and sometimes opposing, point of view. Their work in fostering better intercommunal relations figures critically in the nonofficial and less political or apolitical social segment of Egypt's society.

Here, a note on sources is in order. The number of sources is necessarily large and the kinds of sources vast. For the chapter on relations at an official level, laws and court decisions cannot be considered in isolation; some relevant laws have been on the books since the Ottoman period and are referred to irregularly. Officially sponsored programs of national dialogue between Christians and Muslims, a rhetoric of reconciliation and national unity, and efforts to seal the national fabric have been prominent as well. Commissioned texts and speeches in this regard are considered as primary and informative sources. I contend that the rhetoric expressed in official oration and the texts published for public consumption encourage and attempt to foster a vibrant spirit of tolerance.

At the level of official religion, primary sources such as the material and tracts published by al-Azhar and the Coptic Orthodox papacy, for example, will be important in evaluating the spirit of tolerance they encourage. Records of proceedings of interfaith dialogue meetings between Islamic leaders (*shaikh al-Azhar*, the mufti) and Christian heads (Pope Shenouda III, the late Rev. Samuel Habib, and Catholic leaders) are invaluable. In addition, interviews with the current *shaikh al-Azhar*, Muhammad Sayyid Tantawi, and Christian leaders of the Coptic Orthodox and Protestant churches are drawn upon.

For the discussion of parties, a greater reliance on written texts and platforms is necessary, especially in the case of the Muslim Brotherhood. In my presentation of Hizb al-Wasat, I rely both on party documents and interviews with a party founder and other leaders. Rafiq Habib is a prominent Christian writer and thinker who was also a founding member of this party.

Finally, on the NGOs, I necessarily rely on personal interviews with and documents produced by the NGOs themselves.

I have used three main types of sources. First, through interviews with leaders in several of these sectors, I was able to enter into discussion about the state of intercommunal relations in Egypt, the individual's views on tolerance (and necessarily those of the organization or association he represents), and how his institution expresses its view on tolerance as it strives to attain its main goal. Through contacts I made while living in Egypt, I was able to interview the grand *shaikh* of al-Azhar, Muhammad Sayyid Tantawi; Christian leaders from the Orthodox, Protestant, and Catholic communities; Rafiq Habib, one of the founders of Hizb al-Wasat; and Saad Eddin Ibrahim, founder of the Ibn Khaldun Center for Development Studies. These figures are important for they are from the various segments this study analyzes. They are prominent in their communities and are in position to form public opinion.

I am confident that the conversations that comprised the essence of the interviews were authentic and honest; this is verifiable by public statements and positions made over the course of time. It is therefore helpful to support such data through compilation and analysis of a second kind of source, that is, primary sources such as party platforms, speeches, official documents, and books and articles written by key individuals at the various levels. As readers progress through this book, they will be able to identify quotations from primary sources in each area. Finally, as a second level of authentication, independent reports on the institutions in question are invaluable. With these three types of sources, a fair representation of the institutions being examined is reasonably expected.

It should be made clear that the project is undertaken from a historical point of view, documenting recent trends in Christian-Muslim relations rather than attempting to measure in a scientific way levels of tolerance and cooperation. This approach is more feasible since the intangible and abstract concepts involved are not easily quantified. Rather than becoming entangled in defining and using methods of quantification and statistical comparison, although such an approach would no doubt be of value for other kinds of projects, this volume is intended to describe and analyze the contemporary period in terms of Christian-Muslim relationships. Statistical analysis would perhaps detract from this description of an activity that can lead to better management and even resolution of conflict. This description and analysis thus seeks to fill a void in the popular literature, which tends to focus prominently on tensions and crises. The opportunity to seek better relationships between Christians and Muslims in Egypt is an activity that is carried out through the strong convictions of many in important positions. Their efforts deserve attention, as does the context in which they are exerting those efforts.

Such a project necessarily faces problems. One such problem is how to select the cases, especially when venturing beyond the official institutional levels. Especially in the NGO sector, in which there are literally thousands of organizations, it can be challenging to select ones to examine. While the NGOs selected may not be representative, they are especially important for the work they have done in the area of interreligious dialogue and cooperation, and for their visibility in society. A second difficulty is how to approach the question of grass-roots relations. It would be quite problematic to attempt to determine a random and representative sample of the population and devise a set of questions that the sample would be expected to answer truthfully with a perfect stranger, even if that stranger is of Egyptian heritage and speaks Arabic. Given the overwhelming difficulties in selecting such a sample, and the lack of ability to verify the responses, I determined early on that an analytical discussion of the grass roots would be beyond the scope of this project. A third, and related, difficulty is how to treat individuals' anecdotal comments and opinions that indicate a genuine suspicion and even fear of the other community. Such comments surfaced with some frequency among Christians, in particular, when discussing possible future scenarios, especially the regional resurgence of Islam as a political force. Such views cannot be ignored, and in fact they point to a greater need for intercommunal communication and interaction, especially among the moderates of both faith communities who are working actively, but perhaps less visibly, for better relations. Such comments of concern have reinforced my own conviction that the current "clash" is not between the West and the East, or between Christianity and Islam, but rather between the more conservative and extreme elements of all religions and civilizations that adopt exclusivist claims and intolerant attitudes toward the Other, and the moderates/progressives who actively seek reconciliation, peace, and justice for all and who are tolerant and accepting of the Other. The former have come to control the public discourse and debate in ways that suppress the voice of the latter, leading to a sense of frustration and even despair, reflected in the comments of some individuals. This book may help to ensure that the voices of those working positively to nurture toleration and full citizenship are given a hearing.

Conflict & Cooperation

1

Civil Society, Citizenship, and Tolerance

The spring of 2005 was a watershed moment in the Middle East for the perceived thawing of hardened political practices that had until then excluded a wide swath of the citizenry. Elections were held in Iraq, in Palestine, and in Lebanon, all in radically different circumstances. In Iraq, the overthrown regime of Saddam Hussain was replaced by a new and different composition of leadership, under the watchful eye of Washington and surrounded by a pervasive, but questionably effective, U.S. military presence; under occupation, Palestinians chose a leader to succeed the late Yasir Arafat, whose character as a symbol of the Palestinian struggle had become an unsurpassable barrier to progress in the peace process to Israel and the United States; and the Lebanese-Syrian knot had become loosened following the assassination of former prime minister Rafiq Hariri and popular demands for complete Syrian withdrawal. These events were hailed by governments around the world for the new inclusion of the masses in the shaping of their nations' political futures.

Egypt, long seen as the leader in the Arab world, did not sit on the sidelines. On February 26, 2005, President Hosni Mubarak announced that, after four six-year terms in Egypt's highest office, he would propose a change to the Constitution to allow for presidential elections to include multiple candidates, rather than the simple referendum that he had always won with affirmations of 90 percent and higher. Popular demands for change were symbolized in the slogan *"Kifaya,"* an Arabic word meaning "enough," signaling opposition to an unchallenged fifth term for the president. More significantly, the challenge signaled "enough" of a system that perpetuated such stasis, including the continued imposition of emergency laws imposed since President Anwar as-Sadat's assassination in October 1981 by members of a militant Islamic group, Islamic Jihad.

The Kifaya movement, a secular and populist configuration, was not satisfied with the proposed constitutional change because it would essentially give power to the ruling National Democratic Party to determine who could run against the president in the elections. Interestingly, the very popular Muslim Brotherhood joined the Kifaya movement in opposing the proposed change because of the likelihood that it would continue to be excluded from the process, as it had been for decades, despite its activities, its organization, and its widespread popular support. Both Kifaya and the Muslim Brotherhood boycotted the May 2005 referendum that submitted the constitutional change to the people for approval.

The November/December parliamentary elections, which spanned three rounds, brought about a major shift in the composition in Parliament, with nearly one-quarter of the seats now held by members of the Muslim Brotherhood, candidates who had run as independents because their associational affiliation would have disqualified them. Many observers of the region delved again into the question of the political participation of Islamic groups, especially as the Muslim Brotherhood gained representation and Hamas[1] emerged as a clear majority following parliamentary elections in Palestine.

Earlier in 2005, a relatively long period of quiet was broken by suicide bombings by members of an Islamic group. Between 1997, when a group of German tourists were attacked in Luxor, and the spring of 2005, there had not been a major attack. Two attacks, separated by just weeks, served as a reminder that some Islamic groups still might resort to violence, even though the motives for these two incidents were not determined. The culprits were identified, however, and in an *al-Ahram Weekly* profile of Shubra al-Khaima, the industrial district of Cairo from which the assailants came, sectarian issues were raised:

---

1. *Hamas* is an acronym for the Arabic name Harakat al-muquwama al-Islamiyya (Islamic Resistance Movement); the acronym itself translates as "zeal."

Shubra and its environs are famous for their multi-sectarianism. This basically means that the population of the neighborhood includes a large number of Copts living aside Muslims. The fact that this is reiterated *ad nauseum* [sic] whenever anyone says "Shubra" hints at the tension beneath. It's not as if people cease to remember that they are Muslim or Copt, they never do, they are consciously aware of that. You see it in signs here and there. A photo might celebrate the co-existence of Markaz Israa Al-Tibi across the street from Maktabat Al-'Ahd Al-Gadid. But the fact that they had to name them Israa and Ahd Gadid, to invoke Muhammad's nocturnal journey to Jerusalem and Christ's New Testament, in itself suggests the discomfort lurking beneath the co-existence and the need to emphasize and uphold a religious identity. (Elbendary 2005, 23)

This confluence of events, prominently featuring civil society and sectarian politics, points to an issue that persists in contemporary Egypt: Christian-Muslim relations. Over the course of more than fourteen centuries, Christians and Muslims have lived together in Egypt, and not once has their relationship degenerated into a sectarian civil war. There have been periods of heightened tension and periods marked by cooperation. The period of the Mubarak presidency has been, in many ways, emblematic of the nature of the relationships that have existed over time. The case of Egypt is often the starting point of accounts of the history of Islamism in the twentieth century. International media often focus on the tension between the two communities, with particular attention to violence perpetrated by Islamic groups against the government, against Egyptian Christians, and against foreign tourists. The rise of Islamic extremism is a phenomenon that has attracted the world's attention and ire. Egypt, therefore, is a case worthy of attention.

The reality of sectarian strife, however, is not the whole picture. The period of the Mubarak presidency to date has also demonstrated to the world that Egypt's religiously defined communities can and do interact positively. Perhaps especially when matters of potential or real conflict arise, efforts are made to ensure that sectarian crises do not mushroom. Three particular situations illustrate this point: a conference on Middle

East minorities that included the Copts of Egypt as a minority; new U.S. legislation to monitor international religious freedom; and a violent attack on Christians in an Upper Egyptian village. In all three cases, tension and efforts to reconcile reflected a tenuous reality in Christian-Muslim relations. Greater crises were averted because of the history of relationship that the communities enjoy, but singular events threatened the stability of the relationships.

Christian-Muslim relations in Egypt, of course, are not singularly defined. There are multiple actors and multiple dynamics that must always be considered. This multiplicity of relationships complicates analysis but better represents reality. While some actors are hostile, others are working for reconciliation, and still others carry on with their lives aware and in tune, but not actively engaging this issue. This book focuses on those who have been working on reconciliation and amelioration of relationships.

To what extent do the two religious communities coexist and cooperate, and what happens when there is strife? The debate continues about the place of Islamic law, or *shari'a*, in Egypt's Constitution and what that means for the Christian population. Are Christians and Muslims equal citizens? Clearly, there are no simple answers to such questions, but there are concrete and observable examples of cooperation in many sociopolitical settings. A study of these settings illustrates ways that intercommunal conflict can be managed, if not resolved, and offers lessons about the complex history of Christian-Muslim relations in the Egyptian context. Such lessons may offer positive insights to the so-called West, where the liberal tradition has its roots but where challenges to living it out are presented by new and different demographic profiles in an increasingly pluralistic religious landscape.

The study begins with an examination of theoretical aspects of civil society, toleration, and citizenship. The issue of the presence and impact of civil society is one that has been debated in the context of the Middle East. It is often coupled with a discussion of democratization and citizenship because "the voluntary associations and individuals [with] common interests and objectives outside the realm of the state . . . are supposed to provide checks and balances on state power, and to press for particular programs and reforms. . . . In short, it is the sphere of citizens and citizenship" (Zubaida 2001, 21).

According to Partha Chatterjee, there is an important distinction between "civil society" and "political society." Chatterjee considers civil society to be based on a Western political model of individual participation, while in political society, individuals "do not relate to the state as citizens, but as loosely or tightly formed groupings with communal and corporate interests, making claims on the state for rights and services . . . [who] constitute a population to be managed and controlled" (quoted in Zubaida 2001, 21). The distinction is evident throughout this study of Egypt.

Theoretical Aspects

Citizens and Citizenship

The concepts of citizen and citizenship have been discussed as far back as Aristotle; in ca. 334 B.C.E., he wrote in *The Politics*, "Now, in general, a citizen is one who both shares in the government and also in his turn submits to be governed; their condition, it is true, is different in different states; the best is that in which a man is enabled to choose and to persevere in a course of virtue during his whole life, both in his public and private state" (quoted in Clarke 1994, 46).

Aristotle's definition reveals two aspects of citizenship. The first part is a legal definition, establishing a formal relationship between the person and government. The second part is a social relationship in which the citizen is called to act in a virtuous manner. Aristotle also distinguishes between the public and private spheres, touching on the dichotomy of state and civil society.

In current politics, commonly held ideas of citizenship are derived from the theoretical framework of liberalism. In its political form, liberal theory ascribes to individuals' "power in their own lives and an equal say in how government is run" (Spinner 1994, 3). At its fundamental level, citizenship is "concerned with social relationships between people, and relations between people and the . . . institutions they have created" (Twine 1994, 9). Especially relevant in this time of optimism for political reform, this idea also asserts that each citizen is protected from arbitrary actions of others and from the government. Fundamentally, the theory ideally protects each citizen from tyranny and accords equal rights to all. Religion, for liberals, is not a reason for discriminatory treatment of a person by the government or by another person. Religious toleration is an extension of the idea of liberty in thought and expression (Spinner 1994, 3–4).

Liberal theory has not avoided important criticisms in terms of citizenship and personal identity. Liberal theory treats the individual as an independent actor without taking into account certain other factors or associations that contribute to that individual's identity in larger politics and society, such as identification with a particular nation—indeed, being a citizen of a particular nation—or race, ethnicity, or religion. Even though each individual ought to be accorded the same rights and protection, these associations often play a role in the extent to which a person enjoys citizenship. Association with groups, actively or passively, may prove to be a barrier to the full benefits and responsibilities of citizenship. The logical conclusion of this failure of liberalism to recognize such groups "may mean the end of those smaller cultures that exist precariously, or this refusal may relegate their members to the margin of society, to be constant victims of discrimination and racism" (Spinner 1994, 10).

This conclusion can have serious consequences for a country like Egypt, in which religious identity is very important and is by no means a neutral aspect of one's identity. Christians and Muslims, Egypt's two main religious communities, have experienced tension as a result of their confessional differences. A model that takes group identity into account would therefore be more descriptively accurate in considering Egyptian political culture, especially since the 1970s. Sectarian conflict exists, and by its mere existence it negates the liberal concept of religious tolerance. The real focus is not on each individual but rather on the group.

Having noted the distinction between legal citizenship and social citizenship, legal citizenship can be defined as how citizenship is determined from a juridical perspective. The status of citizenship is determined in a particular nation by that nation's body of laws or constitution. In addition, the rights to which a citizen is entitled are explicitly or implicitly stated in the nation's body of laws. The legal citizenship status of a person in a nation is therefore quite important in determining the extent to which that person can be included in the political activities of the nation. Pranger (1968, 9) defines national citizenship as "basic membership in a nation state—a status which gives the occupants freedom in the sense that they are full members with special rights and duties denied to others." In the same vein, Post and Rosenblum (2002, 10) tell us that "citizens are presumptively equal, and for this reason birthright citizenship has nothing to do with merit or ability. . . . Exclusion from citizenship is demeaning, of course, an injurious mark of public disrespect, but inclusion per se does not have the opposite, positive significance."

The other side of citizenship is social citizenship: how members of society include or exclude others and allow others to enjoy the rights to which they are entitled. The legal definition of citizenship has merit with respect to the courts and entitlement from the nation. The social definition has merit in the activities of daily life and in interaction among people. These two aspects of citizenship are clearly complementary and equally significant.

Seligman relies on T. H. Marshall to describe three aspects of citizenship—civil, political, and social—in a concise and helpful manner:

> "The civil element is composed of the rights necessary for individual freedom—liberty of person, freedom of speech, thought and faith, the right to own property and to conclude valid contracts, and the right to justice [that is] the right to defend and assert all one's rights on term of equality with others by due process of law." The political element comprises "the right to participate in the exercise of political power as a member of the body invested with political authority or as an elector of the members of such body." And the social component includes "the right to a modicum of economic welfare and security [and the] right to share to the full in the social heritage, and to live the life of a civilized being according to the standards prevailing in society." (Seligman 1997, 3)

These aspects of citizenship are particularly helpful in the case of Egypt and its sectarian divisions, where the concept of social citizenship is especially relevant. It may be helpful to keep in mind that it makes a difference whether one gives priority to one's identity as a citizen or as a member of a group, since "citizenship should be modeled to fit people's religious identity, not vice versa" (Kymlicka 1996, 100). Kymlicka writes that citizenship includes "qualities and attitudes of citizens; for example their sense of identity, and how they view potentially competing forms of national, regional, ethnic, or religious identities; [and] their ability to tolerate and work together with others who are different from themselves" (quoted in Miller 2002, 379).

The case of Egypt's Christians and Muslims brings the discussion of legal and social citizenship into bold relief.

Ideas of Tolerance

The concept of tolerance is related to citizenship but does not have the same legalistic overtones. Like citizenship, tolerance has a dichotomous nature, encompassing both political and social components. *The Oxford English Dictionary* defines *tolerance* in several ways, the primary being "the action of allowing; permission granted by authority; a license to actions, practices, or conscience." A second definition, one especially relevant to our discussion, is "the allowance, with or without limitations, by the ruling power of the exercise of religion otherwise than in the form officially established or recognized." Rawls associates the principle of toleration "with the idea of freedom of conscience" (quoted in Kymlicka 1996, 82). The Egyptian case illuminates the nexus of freedom to express one's religious identity and the extent to which one can do so and be tolerated. Tolerance "can be seen as a matter of policy, that is, as an official stance on the part of political authority with regard to some particular domain of actions, practices, or beliefs" (McClure 1990, 362). This definition of political tolerance seems to go beyond a legal definition of citizenship because it seems to describe a stance taken by the authority that is not necessarily tied to the constitution or set of laws. Taken to an extreme, political tolerance could allow for actions to take place even if they are in conflict with the letter of the law, so long as they are not disruptive.

Alternatively, "implicit in the broader connotation, [tolerance] might also be understood as a social virtue, that is, an element of what might be called a political or civic culture" (McClure 1990, 362–63). This social aspect also includes the adoption of a neutral stance toward actions that do not offend without interference, but, like social citizenship, occur at the level of society, and not at the level of the state or the courts. In the case of religious identity in Egypt, there is an apparent conflict—one that is debated in a lively way—between the legal toleration of non-Muslims and this social toleration. "People can coherently think that a certain outlook or attitude is deeply wrong and that the flourishing of such an attitude should be tolerated if they also hold another substantive value in favor of the autonomy or independence of other believers" (Williams 1996, 25).

Michael Walzer (1997, 2) defines toleration as what is made possible by "the peaceful coexistence of groups of people with different histories, cultures and identities," which he asserts to be a good thing. Walzer recognizes that a group's "primary aim is to sustain a way of life among their own members, to reproduce their culture or faith in successive generations" (10), a concept of particular importance to Egypt's Christians as they attempt to ensure their presence for the future.

Instead of settling on a single definition of toleration, Walzer (1997, 10–11) sets up a continuum ranging from "a resigned acceptance of difference for the sake of peace" to a "passive relaxed, benignly indifferent [attitude] to difference" to "a principled recognition that the 'others' have rights even if they exercise those rights in unattractive ways" to "openness to others" and finally to an "enthusiastic endorsement of difference." Walzer asserts something more ideal, however, that "to tolerate someone else is an act of power; to be tolerated is an acceptance of weakness. We should aim at something better than this combination, something beyond toleration, something like mutual respect" (52). Finally, Walzer asserts that "the point of toleration is not, and never was, to abolish 'us' and them' . . . but to ensure their continuing peaceful coexistence and interaction" (92). However, "toleration brings an end to persecution and fearfulness, but it is not a formula for social harmony" (98).

Discourse on tolerance has focused on questions of religion. In *Tracts*, John Locke defended imposed ceremonies of the Anglican Church. John Rawls, in *A Theory of Justice*, expresses the idea of "generaliz[ing] the principle of religious toleration to a social form, thereby arriving at equal liberty in public institutions" (quoted in McClure 1990, 364). Williams (1996, 18) points out, "In matters of religion, for instance (which, historically, was the first area in which the idea of toleration was used), the need for toleration arises because one of the groups, at least, thinks that the other is blasphemously, disastrously, or obscenely wrong."

While the matter of individual and group tolerance is critical in our discussion, the thrust of this project is more heavily weighted toward groups, at least as is manifested through various institutions. Kymlicka (1996, 87) discusses the millet system of the Ottoman Empire as a group manifestation of individual rights, and indeed as an alternative to the strict focus on the individual. He goes on to criticize the millet system, saying that "a milletlike system can be seen as a sort of hypercommunitarianism. It assumes that people's religious affiliation is so profoundly constitutive of who they are that their overriding interest is in protecting and advancing that identity, and that they have no interest in being able to stand back and assess that identity. Hence the millet system limits people's ability to revise their fundamental ends and prevents others from trying to promote such revision" (89).

While it may be argued that Egyptians' religious identity is indeed central to their understanding of themselves and others, relying exclusively on a millet system to determine social and political rights and legal status "limits the right of individuals to revise their conceptions of the good" (Kymlicka 1996, 91–92) because the focus is not on the individual but rather on the group. It is possible to "ensure tolerance *between* groups without protecting tolerance of individual dissent *within* each group" (93; emphasis in original).

Civil Society in Egypt

A look at civil society in Egypt is informed by the parameters offered by Post and Rosenblum (2002, 3): "The elements of civil society range from groups based on religion and ethnicity to more fluid voluntary associations organized around ideology, professionalism, social activities or the pursuit of money, status, interest, or power."

Jürgen Habermas proposed a wide space for civil society, including "virtually all non-violent associational activity between individual citizens and the state." Recognizing multiple layers of individual identity, he asserts that "the rise of new forms of mediating institutions . . . was predicated on the ability to move between, to negotiate and identify with more than one set of role identities and status positions" (quoted in Seligman 1997, 58).

Civil Society and Democratization

The debate over civil society as it relates to democratization in the Middle East has been expressed quite adequately in a paper by Michael Hudson, several critiques, and Hudson's response that appeared in the winter 1996 issue of *Contention*. Hudson (1996, 89) presents the view that in the Middle East, there has been clear "antidemocratic behavior. The logic of mutually perceived, zero-sum hostility between a government and a powerful opposition force seems to override adherence by either one to non-violent, liberal procedures." Hudson is also very critical of the concept of civil society with regard to the Middle East, "given its Western origin," noting that "in Egypt . . . the 'march to democracy' has . . . been a case of 'one step forward, two steps back'" (93–94). However, according to Saad Eddin Ibrahim, a prominent Egyptian social scientist, and others (S. Ibrahim et al. 1999, 15), Egypt has gone through a process during the Mubarak presidency that represents "liberalization without democratization," the latter process being one that has failed in its realization but that has taken place because of the presence of a vital civil society for the past two hundred years. Civil society in Egypt has, according to these social scientists,

> been engaged in a three-way dialectic—with the state, traditional forces [defined as defenders of "cultural authenticity" and national dignity . . . suspicious, if not outright hostile, to organizations, values, and practices of civil society], and external Western forces. [There has been a] continuous encroachment of both the traditional forces and the external factors in the state-civil society interaction." (S. Ibrahim et al. 1999, 15)

While much of the debate around the existence of civil society, or lack thereof, in the Arab world has focused on the process of democratization, other important discussants have accepted that the concept of civil society can be applied in the Middle East and have centered their discussion on the question of inclusion or exclusion of Islamic organizations and groups in the realm of civil society, given Islam's political significance throughout the 1980s and 1990s. While "Islamic currents speak with different voices on social and political issues—and some keep silent, sticking to talk of morality, virtue, and piety," it is important to recognize that some feel that "political Islam, in itself, is no longer the major issue in Middle East politics," which are "authoritarian and arbitrary government—and its converse, 'democratization'—as well as the economic and welfare problems threatening the masses in most countries with poverty and degraded environments" (Zubaida 2001, 21). Political Islam is an important, perhaps crucial, part of the political equation, locally in Egypt, regionally in the Middle East and North Africa, and indeed, as demonstrated by September 11, 2001, and its fallout, in the international community.

A concentrated focus in the literature on the Middle East has been on the rise and prominence of an Islamic "awakening." This awakening, strengthened by the results of the 1967 war, has been manifested especially prominently in the last quarter century, since the establishment of the Islamic Republic of Iran.

The inclusion of Islamists in civil society has also been debated. At least two facets are identified in the activities of the Islamic parties and organizations: a strong, and sometimes violent, opposition to the government, and the provision of badly needed social services to complement and supplement those offered by the government. The argument that includes in civil society those groups involved in the second category of activities is convincing. As for the first, they are often discounted because they do not "play by the rules." If, however, they add a voice to the debate on societal issues and concerns, then they should be included in the picture.

The stumbling block for the inclusion of the more radicalized Islamists in the framework of a civil society on the one hand, and as legalized players in the political arena on the other, is their tendency to hold a less tolerant point of view with regard to other Muslims and non-Muslims who do not conform to their beliefs. A distinction must be made between a government's tolerance of such groups and their categorization as a valid part of the social context. Walzer (1997, 9) suggests, in the context of governmental toleration of parties, that it is not "intolerant of difference to ban a programmatically antidemocratic party from participating in democratic elections; it is merely prudent" (9). He, too, makes a distinction between toleration and inclusion in the political process and in social intercourse, as his "concern, then, is with toleration when the differences at issue are cultural, religious, and way-of-life differences" (9). More explicitly, he states, "What separation [between 'church and state'] means in their case [the case of religious movements outside the body politic] is that they are confined to civil society: they can preach and write and meet; they are permitted only a sectarian existence" (82).

In her logical and orderly discussion of the history of civil society, Schwedler (1995, 6) reaches the important conclusion that, in the modern, liberal discussion, "civil society represents two ideals: first, the rights of each member of a community or nation to interact with a representative government; and, second, the establishment of a set of rules of acceptable, tolerant behavior between civil society and the state as well as within civil society. In particular, tolerance toward those with different views is paramount."

Schwedler's conclusion is particularly relevant to this discussion of tolerance in Egypt, specifically with regard to sectarian categorization of groups.

In one particularly helpful set of minimum criteria for determining the presence of civil society, Mustafa Kamal al-Sayyid (1993, 230) puts forward three components that must be present: "the presence of formal organizations of various types among different social groups and classes; an ethic of tolerance and acceptance by the majority of minority legitimate rights, no matter how such minorities are defined; and limitations on arbitrary exercise of state authority." While not a comprehensive or exhaustive list, this set makes a contribution to the larger discussion of the civil society debate. The first two criteria, and particularly the second, focus on some of the relevant issues of this study.

Tolerance and Toleration

Tolerance in the liberal sense of the word has been defined as "respect for people as human beings, that is, respecting their choices freely (so long as they do not harm others)." It is not something that is exercised purely for one's own benefit or for the sake of one's interests (Cohen-Almagor

1994, 20–21). In al-Sayyid's criteria, tolerance is a particularly important element in defining civil society. Based on these understandings, tolerance is an essential factor in positive and constructive communal relations and management of potential or real conflict. Civil society, then, is a crucial element for the formation and maintenance of a peaceful and harmonious community. For the Middle East, long torn by intra- and inter-state conflict, tolerance and the encouragement of a strong and vibrant civil society would go a long way toward reducing social and communal tensions, as well as regional conflict. The absence or presence of tolerance in Egyptian society varies from one sociopolitical and socioeconomic level to another, from one party to another, and from one group to another. Without generalizing about society as a whole, it is possible to study different levels and groups of association to see what kinds of tolerance they exhibit and how they translate those into practice.

The Question of Identity

Theoretical paradigms dealing with ethnicity and ethnic relations can inform an examination of relations between Egypt's Christians and Muslims. Fredrik Barth, in his introductory essay to *Ethnic Groups and Boundaries: The Sociological Organization of Cultural Difference,* notes previous anthropological use of the term "ethnic group" to refer to self-perpetuation, cultural homogeneity, communal interaction, and identification of self and other. Barth (1969, 10–11) objects to this ideal definition because it "prevents us from understanding the phenomenon of ethnic groups and their place in society and culture." Such ideal approaches can be problematic because Egyptian society is arguably not heterogeneous. Clearly, though, aspects of the criteria used to identify ethnic communities described above can be applied to the two basic religious communities in Egypt.

Barth (1969, 13–14) discusses issues of particular relevance to the Egyptian case, concentrating on the use of "ethnic identities to categorize themselves and others for purposes of interaction." The possibility of establishing and maintaining social boundaries is based on recognition of similarities or differences in "shared understandings, . . . criteria for judgment of value and performance, and . . . interaction [in] sectors of assumed common understanding and mutual interest" (15). The greater the interaction between groups, the less their distinguishing differences persist, or at least the more likely there is to be prescribed structures of interaction which "allow for articulation in some sectors, . . . and prevent . . . interaction in other[s], and thus insulating parts of the cultures from confrontation and modification" (16).

Lisa Schirch (2001, 149) draws three conclusions regarding identity and its role in conflict situations: "One, people have a human need to define themselves in relation to others. Two, people are willing to both kill and die defending certain sociocultural identities. And three, people's understanding of who they are is often based on perceptions and constructions of an adversarial 'other.'"

Schirch (2001, 150) goes on to point out that "individuals and groups search for cognitive consistency by ignoring or rejecting information that contradicts their worldview . . . in shaping perceptions of . . . the 'other.'" Her prescription for resolution of conflict is an approach that rehumanizes the "other" in a way that strips it of its dehumanized identity and seeks aspects of identity that are shared (Schirch 2001, 152). In his important work *Interfaith Dialogue and Peacebuilding,* David Smock (2002, 130) writes, "A central goal [of dialogue] should be to address misperceptions and to break down stereotypes that each group holds regarding the other."

These theoretical structures are helpful because they can be applied directly to the interrelations between Egypt's two religious and social communities, in which there is a numerical (and arguably social and political) majority-minority dynamic and where the "member of the minority, looking to be tolerated by [the majority, which] . . . no longer require[s the minority's] toleration" (Walzer 1997, 24). In this power dynamic, though, "to be the object of tolerance is a welcome improvement on being the object of intolerance, but typically people do not wish themselves or their actions to be the object of either" (Horton 1996, 35). Williams (1996, 18–19) negates this power relationship, however, by proposing a more egalitarian approach to the parties involved: "We may think of toleration as an attitude that a more powerful group, or a majority, has (or fails to have) toward a less powerful group or a minority. . . . [T]oleration is a matter of the attitudes of any group to another and does not concern only the relations of the more powerful to the less powerful."

Egypt's Christians and Muslims do maintain boundaries, yet members of each claim that both communities are integral to the national fabric and that there is no difference between the two. While matters of personal faith are certainly not part of the issue, social (and political) manifestations of the faith communities are.

Discussing minorities and political security, Barth (1969, 36) writes: "In most political regimes, however, where people live under a greater threat of arbitrariness and violence outside their primary community, the insecurity itself acts as a constraint on inter-ethnic contacts." In classical Islam, such division between the primary community (governing Muslims) and other communities (the non-Muslim governed) is manifested in the category of *ahl adh-dhimma* ("protected people"), living under an Islamic government. These protected people "paid tribute to the Islamic government in exchange for the right of limited freedom. Christians, for example, were allowed to govern their own affairs in family and commercial law, provided these created no conflict with Muslims. They were allowed to worship, so long as their public displays did not disturb the peace of Islam" (Kelsay 2002, 304–5).

Some writers have suggested a similar relationship in contemporary Egypt, thus relegating Christians to a status of citizenship not in parity with their Muslim compatriots. On this point, too, there is debate. One side may be summarized as follows: "As we move into the modern period, we do better, in fact, to think of [Christians and others] as recognized minorities" (Kelsay 2002, 305) in the Islamic world. Others have rejected this notion: "The key question is whether civility and the acceptance of the other is any less prevalent in Islamic traditions than in other great monotheistic religions" (Kazemi 2002, 324).

The debate over the nature of the relationship between Muslims and non-Muslims is central for this study. What is the definition of community in Egypt? Is it the community of Egyptians, or is it defined in terms of religious affiliation? How do groups relate to each other? Harel (1996, 121) explains that "modern societies . . . regard equality of some sort as a prerequisite for membership. . . . Denying equality is therefore interpreted in modern societies as a denial of membership itself." Kazemi (2002, 328–29) emphatically asserts the varying degrees of intolerance that exist in the

Middle East: "Clearly, many militant Islamic groups have negative perceptions of both religious minorities and secularists. This perception is
nurtured, however, in a larger environment where even the moderate pro-
Western regimes do not fully appreciate the fundamental right of religious
freedom."

There are, of course, further questions worthy of examination. Walzer
(1997, 25) writes that "toleration in nation-states is commonly focused not
on groups but on their individual participants, who are generally conceived
stereotypically, first as citizens, then as members of this or that minority."

A central question, then, is how an individual member of one group
regards an individual member of the other group, or the entire group, and
how the two perspectives affect relations. This question is not only important for the Other but also for the self, as "some people seek escape from
the confines of religious or ethnic membership, claiming to be citizens only,
whereas others want to be recognized and tolerated precisely as members
of an organized community of religious believers" (Walzer 1997, 86).

In the context of Egypt, for example, an Egyptian Christian might
not be able to exhibit tolerant behavior toward an Egyptian Muslim if the
Christian only sees the Muslim as a member of the Muslim community,
which the Christian might define by a set of preconceptions. Ronald Fisher
(2001, 32) puts it clearly: "Among the most pervasive cognitive errors that
individuals, and thereby groups, involved in destructive conflict make are
misattributions about the characteristics and motives of the other side." It
would rule out the possibility of the Christian engaging in a relationship
with the Muslim as an individual with similar interests and aspirations.
That is not to say that trust is something one can expect in a relationship;
risk is more a part of individual relations than of group relations, where
the latter is premised upon certain role expectations (Seligman 1997, 63).
Even so, "relationship issues (e.g., misperceptions, mistrust, and frustrated
basic needs) must be addressed through innovative, mutually agreeable
solutions, developed through joint interaction, in order to reach a lasting
resolution" (Fisher 2001, 28).

The case of Egypt is particularly illustrative. As Fisher (2001, 25)
points out, "One of the most serious global problems facing the world . . .
is how to manage destructive and protracted conflict between groups with

differing identities who are interacting within the same political system or geographic region." In addition to the fact that Egypt has been an important leader of the Arab world and that its population is by far the largest of the Arab Middle East, the debate over the existence of civil society there has become quite intense, especially in regard to the question of intercommunal relations between Muslims and Christians, religious communities that have coexisted for almost fourteen centuries.

It is not enough, however, to say that the Muslim and Christian communities have coexisted. They have, indeed, been engaged in close cooperation throughout history, and bitter conflict as well, a reality that can be attributed at least in part to historical circumstance. At the same time, there is a reality of individual "trust . . . being replaced by . . . forms of solidarity . . . oriented not toward the agentic or intentional self but toward group loyalties" (Seligman 1997, 155). Seligman further argues that "as people return more and more to group-based identities . . . , we may well ask if, in some cases, . . . risk is not giving way to danger . . . ?" (172).

While putting aside Seligman's historical argument of the shift from group to individual and back to group agency through the centuries in predominantly Western societies, there is significant value in his social relational analysis for this subject.

The core of the problem is that tolerance is not universal at all levels of society. In addition, rhetoric is not always consistent with practice. Therefore, one cannot simply conclude that a society as a whole is either tolerant or not. There are certainly different components of society that have various views with respect to the Other. At the same time, the question is not simply reducible to "an ethic of tolerance and acceptance by the majority of minority rights." If a society as a whole is to demonstrate elements of tolerance, then the same ethic of tolerance and acceptance must be held by the minority toward the majority. Surely, the majority has an advantage of numbers, which is often parlayed into political strength, but at the same time a spirit of tolerance is desired, if not required, of all groups toward each other.

The matter of majority-minority relations in Egypt is not one of political party alliances, or even of ethnicity. The majority of the population (about 90 percent) is Sunni Muslim, and the significant minority (about 10 percent, depending on the source) is Christian (overwhelmingly Coptic Orthodox, but with a visible Protestant community and a small yet active Catholic population). Here, the communities are defined in terms of quantitative majorities and minorities. Many might prefer the argument that all Egyptians are of one ethnic heritage, stating in support of that assertion that it is virtually impossible to differentiate between a Muslim and a Christian based simply on appearance. Muslims and Christians have lived together in Egypt for nearly fourteen centuries; factors such as religious conversion, intermarriage, intercommunal exchange of ideas and traditions, and general social interrelations have made what once may have been two distinct communities (a debatable proposition in itself) virtually indistinguishable.

The Arabic Discourse

Much has been written in Arabic on civil society and citizenship, and on tolerance and acceptance of the Other. Tolerance, narrowly defined, can be less inclusive than acceptance as a concept. Toleration means to recognize the Other's difference in a way that is distant, even perhaps with a hostile attitude, but not confrontationally. Acceptance means to recognize the Other's difference and adopt a more open attitude toward the Other, despite the differences.

In her discussion of civil society in the Arab world, Amani Kandil proposes that religion has played a central role in the establishment of civil society.

> The foundational and motivational bases for the development of the voluntary sector are represented in the heavenly [or "monotheistic"] faiths. . . . If religion played, and continues to play, an essential role in pushing charity and voluntary work in most regions of the world, it has taken on some particularities in the Arab world. This result is natural in light of the knowledge that a unique and common culture unites the Arab world, and the weight of the religious facet is raised up to a great extent. (Kandil 1994, 27)

Kandil highlights the role of religion in the Middle East and, more than that, the critical link between religion and civil society. She proposes that religion has been one of the basic motivations for the establishment of voluntary associations in the region, and a basic element for holding together a sociopolitical sector that is extragovernmental. This sector is not only engaged with its constituent community in the faith-nurturing aspect of religion, but it is also active in services and social programs that are derived from interpretations of faith. With regard to social services and charity, Kandil elucidates these religious sources as follows:

> If we focus on Islam—in its status as the religion of the great majority in the Arab world—we find that it motivates giving and volunteerism in order to help others, within its cornerstones and basic principles. Among the most important of these is the *zakat* ["almsgiving"], one of the basic pillars of Islam, and charity giving, which is mentioned thirty times in the Qur'an. The aims of *zakat* and charity giving are to promote helping others monetarily, through one's efforts, and in all manifestations of support. This idea is reflected in what is called the philosophy of social responsibility. (Kandil 1994, 27–28)

Kandil is referring mainly to charity and voluntary associations, but, to stress the point, she is also referring to the bases for civil society and the role that religion has played in its development in the Arab world.

While accepting the notion that organizations based on religion can be part of civil society, Ibrahim poses some basic questions:

> The question of whether religious-based political parties could be part of civil society is as overtly academic as the same question with regard to primordially based associations. In both cases, the ultimate answer is an empirical one. So long as such parties and associations accept the principle of pluralism and observe a modicum of civility in behavior toward the "other," then they remain integral parts of civil society. . . . There is nothing intrinsically Islamic which is in contradiction with the codes of civil society or the principles of democracy. (S. Ibrahim 1995, 52)

The inclusion (or exclusion) of religious-based parties in civil society is an essential matter for this study. Having accepted that there is a civil society sector in Egypt, and concluding that religiously oriented associations have a legitimate place in civil society, the question that arises concerns the "modicum of civility in behavior toward the 'other.' "

Through Egyptian and Arab Eyes

To gain a better understanding of how relations between religious communities are couched in contextualized expression, the perspectives of widely read Egyptian intellectuals are helpful. Tariq al-Bishri is a prominent historian and lawyer in Egypt who has written extensively on citizenship and the relationship between Christians and Muslims in fostering a more viable and inclusive state. In his studied estimation, "The most dangerous of divisions from which we suffer is the division between the Islamic current and the Arab nationalist current. . . . Many of us [in the Arab and Islamic world] assert this division without recognizing its strangeness or its danger, and even without recognizing it" (al-Bishri 1998b, 83).

In this regard, al-Bishri (1998b, 25) discusses the principle of citizenship by asking, "Among the resident population, upon whom is accorded on the land of the state the full rights and responsibilities of citizen? Is a preference given to one political group? Does one sect of the different sects of the populations bear more of those rights? To what degree?"

In the balance of his chapter, al-Bishri outlines some of the contemporary Islamic thinkers' conclusions on the rights of non-Muslims in an Islamic state, according to *shari'a*. For example, he notes Muhammad Fathi 'Uthman's suggestion that Muslims and non-Muslims must have the same opportunity to enjoy the same rights, in equality, including positions of authority, such as "vice minister, judge, or military officer." In proposing a dialogue to discuss this issue, 'Uthman expressed his belief that the "issue is one of political, social, and economic position, and an important issue at that" (al-Bishri 1998b, 27). Al-Bishri also points out the position of al-Ghazali, who asserted a *dhimma* (protected) status for non-Muslims, particularly Jews and Christians (29). He goes on to examine variations on the theme of *dhimma* and concludes the chapter with an assertion by 'Umar at-Tilmisani, quoted in an article in *ad-Da'wa*, an Islamic newspaper, regarding the contemporary situation in Egypt and the possibility of implementing this kind of *dhimma* principle in actual legal practice: "The state of affairs in Egypt from all points of view does not deserve all of these agitations. . . . Are the Muslims of Egypt so stupid as to wrong their nation with their own hands? To hurt themselves by themselves? I do not think so. [Egypt's Muslims] remain at the height of reason" (48).

Al-Bishri's writings are also important for his extensive treatment and practically authoritative tomes on the contemporary history of Egyptian nationalism and the inclusion of both Christians and Muslims in that context. A thinker who examines the issue diligently and comprehensively, al-Bishri is certainly a respected voice among intellectuals. He is no doubt a nationalist and, on top of that, one who recognizes and is proud of the Arab and Islamic influences on Egyptian culture. He writes:

> We speak about Egyptianness with reference to the unity of the members of the nation [al-umma]. We speak of Arabness meaning Arab unity in the appropriate organizational structure in the appropriate political and historical conditions. We speak of the nation [al-watan] to mean the fraternity among citizens by the scales of equality and participation. We speak of independence to mean the foreign military evacuation and the discontinuation of foreign influence in the political and economic destinies of the nation [al-watan]. We exert our efforts in the creation of the practical context in which to achieve what we are singing [i.e., advocating], in an environment of the most complete inclusiveness for Egypt, guaranteeing equality among citizens. (al-Bishri 1998a, 99)

Al-Bishri has a very complete and thorough knowledge of shari'a and demonstrates his mastery of its historical and contemporary interpretation. His own commitment to an inclusive nation is clear, and his contribution to the literature cannot be minimized.

In the contemporary debate, another prominent voice, also coming from the legal profession, Muhammad Sa'id al-'Ashmawi, has contributed to the question of Christians as dhimmiyyin by denying that they comprise any other category than full citizen. His article "Copts Are Not Ahl adh-Dhimma" was written in response to the debate over their minority status (see chapter 7). One who has served as a judge and counsel for Egypt's Court of Cassation, as well as professor of Islamic law and comparative law, 'Ashmawi's positions are controversial but widely read, published in numerous books and newspapers. His criticisms and alternative perspectives have been described as follows:

> Insisting upon a liberal interpretation of Islamic teaching and the tenets of the faith, Judge Muhammad Said al-Ashmawi and Ambassador Husein Ahmad Amin, in their writings of the last dozen or so years, challenge—and indeed refute—the claim of the fundamentalists to the monopoly of interpreting Islam. In certain instances, they successfully question the quality of the fundamentalists' Islamic scholarship and peculiar interpretation and view of Islam, the faith and the law (Sharia) in their own terms and on their own chosen ground. (Vatikiotis 1991, 502)

'Ashmawi wrote an article regarding religion and politics and submitted it to *al-Ahram*, but it was not published. The article treats the historical relationship in Islam between religious and political aspects of the religion, including the way that Muslims and non-Muslims interact. He focuses on "People of the Book" (Jews and Christians) as they enter into contractual relationships, and investigates the jurisprudential principle that there is no contractual obligation on a Muslim imposed by a non-Muslim, relating the example of interfaith marriage. His conclusion is one of challenge, that "Islam truly is in need of searching for a secure relationship in society and for the requisite rules for national fraternity and human peace. Without exhibiting these rules or these relationships, society will remain in a state of worry and suspicion; fraternity, hope, and peace only a wish" (al-'Ashmawi 1989a, 244).

'Ashmawi may be seen by some as an extreme Islamist because of his calls for implementation of the Islamic *shari'a* and for the installation of an Islamic government. It is important to keep in mind his conception of an Islamic government, however, before rushing to any conclusions.

> Islam does not define any shape for government or system of governance, except that it prescribes the basis for government as being fairness. In the noble *hadith*, "Governance can continue in polytheism, but it cannot continue if unjust." Justice is therefore the basis of rule. *Any government that acts for the sake of achieving political justice, social justice,*

and juridical justice is an Islamic government, in word and in deed, in state-
ment and in fact. (al-'Ashmawi 1989b, 120; emphasis in original)

'Ashmawi is therefore a proponent of just rule and fair treatment of the
citizens of the country. This principle is discussed in his article on the status of the Copts in Egypt that appeared in the March 13, 1995, issue of
Rose El Yossef. In that article, "The Copts Are Not *Ahl adh-Dhimma,*" he
recounts the historical development of the Egyptian state through various
Islamic periods. He also treats the development of the idea of citizenship
through Western development, focusing particularly on the philosophy of
the French Constitution and the importance it gives to human rights. After
treating the history of the nation-state, he defines citizenship as "the principle that links each individual to his nation and what calls together the
loyalty of citizens and states. . . . The idea spread to the Middle East where
it began in Egypt first when Muhammad 'Ali established a civil state" (al-
'Ashmawi 1995, 63). 'Ashmawi had developed the idea of citizenship in
his book *Usul ash-shari'a* (Bases of Islamic Law). With respect to classical
Islamic terms, such as *ahl adh-dhimma,* he concludes:

> With these contemporary concepts, and humanism, those who use
> old terminology such as *ahl adh-dhimma* and "They have the rights
> we have, and the responsibilities we bear" [*lahum ma lana wa 'alay-*
> *him ma 'alayna*], are living in a different time and residing in a differ-
> ent place. They are backward in their analysis and extreme in their
> prioritization.
>
> The Copts of Egypt are citizens, just as Muslims, fully equal.
> They enjoy their rights and know their responsibilities, based upon
> the Constitution, the basic rule of the state, which defines rights and
> responsibilities for all. As for references to them as *ahl adh-dhimma* or
> "They have the rights we have and the responsibilities we bear," they
> are uses of expressions lost in time and exempt from development,
> having become—in current thought—void of content and empty of
> meaning. The Copts are not in anyone's protection [*dhimma*]. . . . Use
> of these borrowed expressions, with no understanding or awareness
> of their meaning, subverts the Constitution, scatters the law, and
> throws national unity into crisis.

> Those who reemploy the language of the past to rule the present, threatening the nation and committing treason against the citizens, they are the sect of political Islam contravening, through their slogans, ideas, and actions, the idea of the state, the principle of citizenship, and the system of human rights. (al-'Ashmawi 1995, 63)

It would be easy to continue to quote 'Ashmawi's eloquent, and very accessible, argument. The point is, however, that 'Ashmawi has attempted to take the idea of citizenship and compare it to classical Islamic ideas that some say roughly correlate to the liberal model, and has refuted such correlations categorically. The article is important because it puts 'Ashmawi in a camp that is clearly liberal, but does so in a way that expresses the authenticity of the liberal model, even against the backdrop of a strong Islamic current.

Gudrun Kramer makes a particularly helpful observation about this debate:

> The status of non-Muslims in a Muslim or Islamic society is therefore a very sensitive issue and it is not surprising that it has become strongly politicized. This is a debate in which the stakes, both real and symbolic, are very clear and which has seen the participation, in the past and in the present, of 'ulama', both traditional and reformist, 'enlightened' intellectuals and militant absolutists, defenders of the government and their opponents, indigenous and immigrant non-Muslims, foreign observers and Orientalists. This debate illustrates, possibly better than others, the logic and modalities of the Islamic reform movement, as well as its limits and limitations. (Kramer 1998, 34)

This politicization is reflected in the passages cited from al-Bishri and 'Ashmawi. They are Muslims who are not only eager to engage in the ongoing dialectic but are also nationalists committed to the unity of the population. From their legal backgrounds, they are able to write in a way that is analytical and convincing; from their Muslim faith and discourse, they are able to engage authentically in the debate.

A third jurist who has been a part of the debate is Edwar Ghali ad-Dahabi. His contributions on Christian-Muslim relations are examined in chapter 3, but at least one is worth noting here, especially in light of 'Ashmawi's article. In his book *Mua'malat ghair al-Muslimin fi'l-mujtama' al-islami* (Treatment of Non-Muslims in Islamic Society), ad-Dahabi commits an entire section to the rights of non-Muslims. In the first chapter of the section, he treats the rule "They have the rights we have, and the responsibilities we bear" as the basis for the legal rights of non-Muslims:

> The general juridical rule that defines the place of non-Muslims residing in Islamic society is "They have the rights we have, and the responsibilities we bear." Since the dawn of Islam and over the course of fourteen centuries—with the exception of some eras of weakness and failing—Muslims have remained faithful to this rule and have given it a place of precise implementation in all their interactions with non-Muslims in general and people of the book in particular. There is no doubt that a religion that assumes such a rule is truly a religion of justice and equality. (ad-Dahabi 1993, 91–92)

It is interesting that ad-Dahabi chose this particular rule as a starting point, especially in light of the fact that such a prominent Muslim reformer as 'Ashmawi wrote against the use of "antiquated terminology."

Obviously, the debate over the rights and responsibilities of Muslims and non-Muslims in Egypt has been filled with passion and much logical reasoning. To some extent, it is a reaction to the quite tangible reemergence of a radical element, often referred to as political Islam. Nevertheless, it is a debate that is long-standing within Islam and is playing out in the situation of modern Egypt. Many have entered into the debate, and a resolution is likely not forthcoming. Clearly, though, various actors in the political and social realm in Egypt today have approached the questions, and with vibrant rhetoric.

Germane also is the explicatory work of Milad Hanna, an Egyptian Christian who has served in Parliament, first as an elected member and later as an appointee (see chapter 3 regarding parliamentary apointment). His book *Qubul al-akhar* (which he states is the best translation of "tolerance") is a discussion of one of the central principles in the civil society discourse. It is particularly relevant that, in the early chapters of the book, Hanna discusses the role of religion in the formation of social relations:

In Egypt, for example, religious association is just about the strongest of associations or main elements in the "formation of associational feelings" from the point of departure of prevailing concepts. Religion is tied to all facets of earthly life and the afterlife. Thus, religious organizations are effective and influential in society. . . . This is in contrast to the nations of Western civilization which consider, with the spread of Renaissance values and the separation of religion from the state, that religion is a personal matter and not societal. (Hanna 1998, 25)

Hanna therefore sets up a contrast between the civilizations of the West and the East and asserts the importance of religion in a person's identity in Egypt. Based upon the idea of religion as perhaps the most important associational reference, he continues, "Religion is linked to spiritual belonging, and thus benefits [the faithful person] and strengthens him. It is also linked to national belonging, and is perhaps sometimes an alternative to it. Thus, religion gives its believer—in addition to spiritual fullness—a sense of distinction and pride, a sense that he is better than the 'other'" (Hanna 1998, 25).

Hanna's book is a history of the theory of liberalism and the discourse on civil society, with the conclusion that social democracy is the path that will lead in Egypt to a vibrant tolerance. His final chapter is an exposition of that vision, in which he proposes that Egypt is a model of tolerance (Hanna 1998, 149). In Egypt today, one may find the whole range of opinions on tolerance, from the fully accepting to the extremely intolerant.

Some Perspectives on Dialogue

The matter of interreligious dialogue, particularly as dialogue relates to tolerance and acceptance of the Other, can help to inform an in-depth examination of the Egyptian context. The Huntingtonian model of civilizational clash proposes civilizational boundaries along lines defined by Western liberalism and Eastern religion.

Western concepts differ fundamentally from those prevalent in other civilizations. Western ideas of individualism, liberalism, constitutionalism, human rights, equality, liberty, the rule of law, democracy, free markets, the separation of church and state, often have little resonance in Islamic, Confucian, Japanese, Hindu, Buddhist or Orthodox cultures. . . . The central axis of world politics in the future is likely to be, in Kishore Mahbubani's phrase, the conflict between "the West and the Rest" and the responses of non-Western civilizations to Western power and values. (Huntington 1993, 40–41)

Arab intellectuals have posited a variety of responses to this thesis from their context. For example, Tarek Mitri, a Lebanese who has taught, served as minister of culture, and been actively involved in interreligious dialogue internationally and regionally through the Arab Group for Muslim-Christian Dialogue, proposes:

The clash between the "West and the rest," we are told, is religious to the extent that religions shape civilizations and they do so significantly. It is political as long as politics is determined by civilizational affinities instead of ideological options. This discourse is nourished by what is called the regained vigour of religions. But when we observe the relationship between nationalism, ethnicism and religion, we see the latter functioning as a sort of diacritical mark. *There are conflicts between communities that have a religious past, but the religious content is of no relevance. A religion in which people have little or no faith continues to define a community in which they have much faith.* (Mitri 1999, 78; emphasis added)

The assertion that religion often defines a conflict even if faith is removed from the equation is important and applicable in the case of Egypt, where sectarian conflict is often the result of a commercial argument or economic disagreement. Smock (2002, 3) confirms this idea in the international arena when he writes, "With regrettable frequency, religion is a factor in international conflict. Rarely is religion the principal cause of conflict, even when the opposing groups . . . are differentiated by religious identities. But religion is nevertheless a contributing factor to conflict."

Local conflict often takes on the same flavor. When such differences are crystallized around the rallying point of religious identification, they often get out of control as more and more members of the parties' "religious" communities become involved.

Mitri goes on, however, to elucidate a further role that religion can, and indeed does, play within communities.

> Yet, there are cases, such as in the Muslim World, where religion is not only the mark of a group identity, for its content is part of its self-image. In other words, religion does not define borders between groups only. It draws their internal landscape as well. However, in a religiously pluralist context, whether rooted in ancient or more recent history, a secularist option continues to be widespread. Religions are seen as divisive and their manifestation, beyond the private sphere, are not conducive to peaceful and harmonious living together. Such an assumption is, more than ever before, questionable. (Mitri 1999, 78)

Mitri's identification of religion's historical role in conflict is critical. He goes on, though, to advocate for productive and effective interfaith dialogue. Mitri identifies three central themes that need to be addressed in that dialogue. The first is "the role of religion in the present conflicts between, and within, nations." The second is in relation to human rights, and the third concerns the future of the world and the role of religions (Mitri 1999, 84–85).

'Abd al-'Aziz bin 'Uthman at-Tawijri (1998, 75) proposes that dialogue's goal is coexistence (at-ta'ayush, used in the title of his book): "Coexistence is the principal axis for the matter of this study." In his book, he proposes that Islam inherently requires coexistence with other faiths and civilizations. He suggests that the Golden Rule for all the monotheistic faiths to follow is spelled out clearly in the Qur'an: "Say, 'O People of the Book! Come to common terms as between us and you: That we worship none but God; That we associate no partners with Him; That we erect not, from among ourselves, lords and patrons other than God' " (Qur'an 3:64).

At-Tawijri (1998, 95) concludes this description and summarizes his position by stating that "coexistence of religious faiths, therefore, is [to be pursued] for the sake of God alone, and no one else, and for the sake of free and dignified human life, in the shadow of faith, goodwill, and virtue. In it is the interest of all humanity in all circumstances."

Sa'ud al-Mawla (1996, 32) proposes that "dialogue for us is at the heart of our belief. It is at the core of natural human life, Christian and Muslim alike." Recognizing that dialogue and the possibility for tension-free co-existence have been challenged by violence in the name of religion and by Islamic movements in the Middle East, al-Mawla also points out that "contemporary political movements have in fact posed questions about dialogue and citizenship, democracy and freedom, coexistence and the civil state. They have done so with boldness and realism which have characterized the Arab Islamic movements, in concept and in practice" (29).

His point is that the Arab Islamic movements need to be considered in the discussion as well.

In keeping the ultimate goals of dialogue in mind, Smock (2002, 130) asserts, "The dialogue process should aim at building relationships between participating individuals and between communities, both within the dialogue setting and over the long term." Muhammad as-Sammak, a prominent Lebanese journalist and influential intellectual (also a part of the Arab Group for Muslim-Christian Dialogue), writes, "The goal of dialogue is not to convince the other to refrain from being himself. The goal is the opposite: the attempt to discover the other and his profundity, to enable him to share his own thoughts and experiences, and to complement his faith in truth, and then moving from there to cooperation. The work of accomplishing that with love in itself brings out the manifestations of relationships with the other" (as-Sammak 1998, 92).

Discussion of the advantages and critiques of dialogue will be postponed to chapter 3, but dialogue clearly can have a positive role.

Setting the Stage

With the theoretical groundwork laid, the case of contemporary Egypt can now become illustrated and illustrative. The historical record shows that, in the late twentieth century, sectarian conflict increased in Egypt. Such a turn in relations would seem to have negative implications for the strength of civil society, citizenship, and toleration in the country. The rise of Islamist movements and the importance of religion as a primary identifying characteristic by Egypt's citizens have necessarily contributed to the deterioration of relations between members of the two faith groups. At the same time, they have had political repercussions. A governmental initiative called al-Hiwar al-Watani (National Dialogue) was launched in 1994 to reconcile Muslims and Christians in the sociopolitical context. Even though the initiative never picked up momentum and was shut down in 1996, it demonstrates the importance the government placed on maintaining peaceful and amicable relations between Muslims and Christians. At the same time, while government tolerance of political parties and organizations with an Islamic bent decreased significantly, the government itself became more conscious of the image it was projecting and intentionally began to demonstrate a more Islamic image, albeit quite moderate.

Programs of Christian-Muslim dialogue are not uncommon in the Arab world, especially in Lebanon and Egypt, where the non-Muslim community is significant. For example, the Arab Group for Muslim-Christian Dialogue is a region-wide organization made up of intellectuals, journalists, clergy, and other influential personalities who discuss together issues of the day and concepts of particular relevance. Such programs are encouraged as well in non-Arab Western countries where migration of Muslims has led to the establishment of a not-insignificant Muslim population. In Egypt, such dialogue programs occur at several levels, including the official governmental level and among nongovernmental organizations (NGOs). Their emergence and continuation have demonstrated that a spirit of sectarian tension is not as widely pervasive as media accounts might suggest. These initiatives have brought to the forefront a significant segment of society that is not only tolerant but is also active in fostering a spirit of tolerance among the religious communities.

These tensions and positive initiatives must be considered in tandem. Due to the existence of both tensions and cooperation, it is impossible to categorize the whole of a society as tolerant or intolerant.

This book examines various segments of contemporary Egyptian society in terms of the level of intercommunal cooperation exhibited and manifested in their rhetoric and activity. A key element of these case studies is an examination of the various segments' positions and rhetoric on tolerance. Such results are useful in determining to what extent the Egyptian polity and society (not just the government) are serious about equal levels of citizenship and participation for all Egyptians. If a significant portion of political and societal actors are indeed serious, then their actions will go a long way to marginalize the more extremist trends that have become manifest in society. If, on the other hand, a spirit of intolerance is prevalent among important sectors of society, then sectarian conflict will continue to pervade Egyptian society. The priority that various actors give to cooperation, not based uniquely upon their rhetoric, will determine the extent to which sectarian relations are harmonious.

Several segments of society have recognizable positions on the issue of religious tolerance. These segments actively express their positions in terms of clear political and social activity. Their social and political expressions, either tolerant or intolerant, have significant impact on intersectarian cooperation or conflict, depending on the position. Their statements are significant because of the high prominence or level of political or social activity the segments represent. Since these segments are to such a large extent in the forefront, or in the headlines, they affect public thought and discourse.

These expressions vary in type. One is purely rhetorical, yet it carries weight merely because it is the official position of a particular actor, be it official government, official religion, party, or NGO. Rarely, though, is such rhetoric isolated; some form of action often accompanies it. If tolerant, perhaps such action would be a visit to a leader of another faith on the occasion of a religious holiday, or perhaps coparticipation in a seminar in which the topic is a particularly relevant social or political issue. Another expression might be the establishment of an association or political party with both Christians and Muslims in the core group, whose aim is something other than religious tolerance; through the expression of tolerance, a larger message is conveyed.

There is an underlying relationship between expressions of tolerance and the prevailing social and political context. Expressions of tolerance come in more than one form but, at a minimum, include explicitly pronounced rhetoric and social or political action. The prevailing social or political climate may include a time of particularly strong feelings of national unity or, conversely, a time when a particular debate divides society (such as debate over personal status laws or the minority status of Egypt's Christians). In such times, expressions of tolerance (or intolerance, and everything along the full continuum) have a special meaning. Generally speaking, there is tension between various segments of Egyptian society:

some foster intolerance through their actions, and others are firmly committed to strong relationships. It may be argued that the various segments attempt to be proactive in their tolerance (or intolerance), but given the social or political context, they are often reactive. It is in times of elevated tension, following an ideological or physical attack on national unity and communal harmony, for example, that a strong reactive response comes to attempt to patch things up and restore the spirit of cooperation that is desired by the latter segments. It is in such times that a special degree of clarity exists to evaluate segments on the tolerance continuum.

The manifestations of these actors' positions not only contribute to the prevailing political culture (either positively or negatively), but they also further the public debate on this important issue. Unfortunately, the radicalization of some segments has caused a decrease in popular feeling that the Other is tolerant.

The narrative of "national unity" is one that governments and advocates of dialogue commonly employ, not just in Egypt but in other Arab countries such as Lebanon where there is a diverse population. The basic concept is that, despite internal diversity (which may be racial, ethnic, or religious), the nation is defined by its all-inclusive nature and the rights and responsibilities incumbent upon each person. In the case of interreligious relations, the national government purports to represent the many faith communities of its citizens. This narrative has been an effective rhetorical tool and has had important and positive policy implications. Even so, efforts to preserve national unity can lead to especially harsh treatment of those who challenge its veracity, and those who may challenge its desirability. Such consequences of making national unity a priority can have the unintended result of fostering blame and anger of one community toward another, if the other is seen as culpable or indirectly responsible for the maltreatment of the one.

Acknowledging the more extreme character of certain segments, the two social communities examined in the following pages are not internally homogeneous. There are spectra of positions within each community, from liberal to extremely conservative, from secular to religious, from tolerant to intolerant. Along these spectra in the Christian and Muslim communities of Egypt are actors who find greater proximity of outlook across communal lines than within their own communities. In many instances, liberal Muslims and liberal Christians, for example, cooperate more easily than liberal and conservative members of either group. However, communal identification still plays an important role in determining some limits.

It follows that the various groups along the spectra have differing motivations for, interests in, and commitments to social relations. If the social fabric is simplified and represented by quadrants divided by communal affiliation on one axis and a liberal-extremist continuum on the other, often the liberal segments of the Muslim and Christian communities work together to seek greater social harmony between the two communities. Their efforts have often been hindered, and even stymied, by the disruptive role of each more extreme contingent (but more tangibly on the part of the Islamic extremists). Such a disruptive role can and does have lasting effects on the public's approach to communal relations.

Herein, a deliberate focus is placed on intercommunal toleration in order to demonstrate that such positive relations pervade many settings of the Egyptian sociopolitical horizon. Extremism—and particularly Islamic extremism—is not treated to the extent that it perhaps deserves given its prominence in much literature and impact in the world. Extremism in Egypt has informed much about the country's contemporary history, and any serious reader should seek any of a myriad of volumes on its impact. Likewise, any serious reader should not rely solely on those volumes to understand social-political interaction in today's Egypt.

The government may not officially recognize some of these extreme segments; in fact, they may be illegal. Even so, their inclusion in the debate and framework of discussion is valuable, and they are included in different ways herein. In considering would-be parties or established movements that have not realized government approval for their existence, actors have been identified that attempt to make a contribution to the political and social debate. Their exclusion by the ruling party or government should not exclude them from legitimate consideration. Their existence and message are realities that cannot be ignored; their message may be more expressive because of controversy surrounding them. They deserve careful attention, especially if they have something to add to the debate on our topic of intercommunal relations.

Plan of the Book

Chapter 2 chronicles Egypt's religious history and focuses on the historical relationship between Christians and Muslims. Naturally, it is not a detailed examination, but it sets the stage for the rest of the study. The following four chapters examine the period of the Mubarak presidency, focusing on expressions of Christian-Muslim cooperation at the levels of government (chapter 3), official religion (chapter 4), political party (chapter 5), and nongovernmental organization (chapter 6). Chapter 7 examines three important cases during the Mubarak presidency in which religious overtones set the stage for confrontation and cooperation.

While the focus of the book is on examples and incidents of cooperation, one should not be lulled into a false sense that the state of affairs in Egypt is harmonious. In fact, it is perhaps because of the heightened level of recent tension that so much attention has been paid to advancing the cause of national unity, with a specific focus on relations between Christians and Muslims. Understanding the complex dynamics involved in the relationship between Egypt's Christians and its Muslims can only be informed by an historical overview.

2

Aigyptos, Misr

A History of Intercommunal Relations in Egypt

Egypt's civilization can be traced back ten thousand years. It is among the oldest nations in the world. The Greek historian and traveler Herodotus not only visited Egypt but also made it a subject of his *History*. One of his most famous quotations from that work, "Egypt is the gift of the Nile," signified Egypt's dependence on this source of water and life over its thousands of years of existence. Much has been written about Egypt during its many periods of history, from the many pharaonic dynasties to the Greek period, the Roman period to the Islamic period, the Napoleonic expeditions, the British colonial years, and the revolution of the Free Officers and after. Histories and accounts range from archaeology to sociology, economics to politics, language and art to science. The many volumes on Egypt are impressive, and the stories they tell are just as impressive.

The course of history in Egypt has been turbulent, and that is just as true today as it has been for many centuries. Political and social struggle has been as much a part of Egypt's history as the more glorious grandeur of its ancient civilization. While many of the more popular accounts of ancient history focus on Egypt's grand past, discussions of contemporary Egypt seem to focus more upon the difficulties of economic development, criticism of the postrevolutionary regime, and the recurrence of social tensions, including the conflict between the government and opposition groups, which include the so-called Islamist opposition. Religion as a social dynamic is in no way a characteristic unique to contemporary Egypt, as it has been both a unifying and divisive force in many places in many eras of history. The case of Egypt today is compelling because society has been challenged by sectarianism. The threat of a Christian-Muslim divide in Egypt during the last three decades of the twentieth century brought the country to the verge of civil strife. Even so, Egypt has never fallen victim to a civil war. This apparent social and political cohesion can be attributed to strong rulers and regimes, and recognition of methods of controlling societal discord that have been challenged in today's context. The increase in societal discord along religious lines has become more apparent since Anwar as-Sadat's regime, when religious opposition was allowed to express itself overtly. Culminating in two tragic episodes in al-Kusheh in the late 1990s, religion has played a particularly important part in defining Egypt's societal and political dynamics.

In the context of religious sectarianism in Egypt, numerous books, articles, and tracts have appeared in Egyptian bookstores, media, and streets, discussing religion and its role in various facets of life. They have been extremely popular, a fact that has encouraged more to be written and offered for consumption. The mere fashion of concentrating on religion within the public discourse has contributed to the polarization of society along religious lines. This polarization has coincided with the renewed interest in Islamic alternatives of expression that first reappeared in society after the Arab defeat in the 1967 war with Israel and later was given new energy by the successful revolution in Iran, which brought an Islamic regime to power. Kazemi and Norton (1996, 108) identify these as the first two of five historical events in the last third of the twentieth century to "have had a significant impact on the psyche and consciousness of the Muslim masses, further increasing the appeal of Islamists in the Middle East." The other three they enumerate are "the Soviet occupation of Afghanistan, the allied Gulf War against Iraq, and the Bosnian debacle." Kazemi and Norton also name societal transformation as important, including "significant demographic shifts and important population increases, rapid urbanization, increasing youthfulness of the population, greater access to education increasingly among women as well as men, widespread access to alternative sources of information through the electronic and print media, and a major increase in travel both internally and abroad" (109–10). In their analysis, "the accumulated impact of these developments has propelled the Middle East into an era of mass politics" (Kazemi and Norton 1996, 110).

With this polarization within Egypt, feelings of distrust and even fear of other faiths have surfaced among the Muslim and Christian communities.

These sentiments locally and regionally, combined with events of recent decades on the international level, have exacerbated the level of suspicion between the groups. One contributing factor may have been the fall of Communism in the Soviet Union and Eastern Europe and the consequent end of the cold war. Some have postulated that with the loss of such an enemy, the United States needed to identify another enemy in order to justify its military spending and maintain its military capabilities, and, perhaps more basically, to keep itself in competition with an Other to demonstrate its power. A common theory is that terrorism has become that new international enemy of democracy. Most often, terrorism is associated with persons from the Middle East or the parts of Asia that are more heavily populated with Muslims, and the coverage in the American media and images on U.S. television reinforce that association. Events such as the bombings of the World Trade Center, the Federal Building in Oklahoma City, and the USS *Cole,* as well as the bombings of trains and buses in Madrid and London, together with responses to the military campaigns in Afghanistan and Iraq, have further bolstered the argument that terrorism is the new Western enemy.

Many resources have been committed both in Egypt and other parts of the world to describe the resurgence of religion as a social movement and, indeed, in a negative way. Beyond that, manifestations of Islam have been identified both in Egypt and abroad as reasons for societal discord, and social discord certainly exists.

Nonetheless, religion has contributed to social participation and cooperation between Christians and Muslims in contemporary Egypt. Important levels of dialogue and interaction are often overlooked when it is easier to concentrate on tension and division.

Overview of Egypt's Demographics, Geography, and Society

Islam became the majority religion in Egypt by the end of the tenth century and remains so to this day. According to the 1976 census, the percentage of Christians in Egypt was 6.2 percent. Many Christians feel this representation is not accurate; the Orthodox Church claimed an unofficial membership of 8 million, or nearly 22 percent of the population of 36.6 million, also in 1976 (Ansari 1984, 399). Christians have suggested reasons for the discrepancy, including a governmental interest in reducing the percentage of Copts to a minimum so that the government is not perceived as discriminating in government jobs and scholarships, and the possibility that people with names commonly Muslim and Christian are regularly counted as Muslim (Pennington 1982, 158–59).

Geographically, it is estimated that about 60 percent of all Copts live in Upper (southern) Egypt. More than half of this number live in the three provinces of Assiut, Minia, and Suhaj, where the 1976 census indicates that the Christian community "is much larger than the national average . . . reaching 20 per cent, 19.4 per cent and 14.6 per cent respectively" (Kepel 1986, 157). Historically, because of its greater distance from the capital, Upper Egypt had been less impacted by the state, yielding to private interests; it was based more on social patterns of family and tribe; and it was more prone to violent resolution of conflict. These characteristics persist today, especially away from the main cities. Communal tension has roots and history in the south, to the extent that some Christians proposed a Coptic secession from Egypt to form an independent state—a proposal that was rejected (Kepel 2002, 285). About one-quarter of Egypt's Christians live in Cairo, and 6 percent in Alexandria.

The social status of Egypt's Christians, commonly referred to as Copts, is not different from that of their Muslim neighbors. They are well-integrated and do not enjoy any privileged status, nor are they particularly worse off. In the countryside, the majority of Christians are peasants, as are Muslims. In the cities, the Copts are represented at all levels of income. They range in occupation from *zabbalin* (garbage collectors), providing this necessary service to the city of Cairo and profiting from it; to owners and employees of businesses; to professionals, including teachers, lawyers, engineers, pharmacists (upwards of 80 percent of the pharmacists in Cairo are Copts), and doctors (Pennington 1982, 159).

Population statistics, geographic distribution, and social status of minorities in the Middle East are difficult to measure, given the infrequency and problematic nature of censuses and the interest that diverse actors have in the results. One trend is of particular concern here, and that is Christian emigration from the Middle East. It is attributed to push-and-pull factors such as social, and sometimes legislative, discrimination in societies that are more and more influenced by Islamic extremism, the worsening economic situation throughout the region, including high unemployment rates, and at least a perception of lack of opportunity for social advancement. Other factors include the hope for integration into a "Christian" country in the West and for employment opportunities, and a desire to strengthen the tie to family members who have already emigrated. These, among other factors, have contributed to a quantitatively smaller Christian presence in the Middle East, a trend that has also affected Egypt.

A History of Religious Interaction in Egypt

Identification of important milestones in the development of the religious culture in Egypt helps set the stage for a focus on contemporary Christian-Muslim relations during the Mubarak presidency.

From Christianity to Islam

Prior to, during, and following the introduction of Christianity into Egypt in the first century C.E., Egypt was part of the Greco-Roman Empire, known as Byzantium. From as early as the seventh century B.C.E., Greeks and Jews had inhabited Egypt. Alexandria was its capital and center of culture and art. Most rural Egyptians, though, spoke their own language, Coptic, which had developed from the ancient Egyptian tongue. The Egyptian people lived and carried on relatively separately from either the Jewish or the Greek communities of the urban centers, and according to some historians, the rural and urban cultures and communities "had coexisted in mutual incomprehension . . . since the conquests of Alexander the Great" (Kennedy 1986, 4). It was not until the sixth century that the rural culture and language would come to dominate in many areas, because of a decline in urban population.

In 30 B.C.E., Egypt became a province of the Roman Empire. Because the Romans had such extensive contact with the Greek world, it was not difficult for Rome to assume political sovereignty among Egypt's ruling elite (Gabra 1993, 14). Egypt at that time was properly called "Aigyptos," attributable to the influence of the Greek language on Egypt's own history and culture. A *gypt*, anglicized as "Copt," was then one who was from Aigyptos, an Egyptian. The Coptic language, which was already used in the rural communities and villages of Egypt, was based on both the Greek alphabet (with four additional characters) and the ancient Egyptian language, or hieroglyphics, the picture writing of the ancient Egyptians. It was only after the penetration of the Arabic language, following *al-fath al-'arabi* (or the "opening" of Egypt to the Muslim armies coming from the Arabian Peninsula), that the word *gypt* took on a new connotation, one that remains today.

Historically, Egypt was among the first places to be introduced to Christianity, in the first century C.E. In the early years of Christian expansion, and by those who were Jesus' contemporaries, tradition holds that Egypt was brought the new religion by St. Mark the Evangelist in about 68 C.E. Coptic Christians regard St. Mark as the first of a line of patriarchs, Pope Shenouda III being the current and 117th in that line. Alternatively, it has been argued that, by the time St. Mark arrived in Egypt, there was already a community among the Jewish segment of society in Alexandria that had accepted the new faith (Gabra 1993, 19). The church St. Mark is said to have established in Alexandria is the Coptic Orthodox Church, today the largest Christian church in the Middle East. There are significant numbers of Coptic Orthodox believers living outside of Egypt, the great majority of whom are Egyptian emigrants or from emigrant families. They comprise a well-organized community in the United States and elsewhere.

From the time of the influx of the Arabic language until today, the word "Copt" usually refers to Egyptian Christians, particularly Orthodox Christians. In Arabic, the word *qibti* was originally borrowed from the Coptic language. By the seventh century, most of Egypt's population, the Copts, was Christian. In 642, the Arab armies, under the leadership of 'Amr ibn al-'As, invaded Egypt, bringing with them the Arabic language and Islam. After less than three centuries, the Christians no longer were a majority, most of Egypt's population having converted to Islam. The word "Copt" has remained in Arabic usage, but since the Arab invasion, it has referred to those Egyptians who did not convert to Islam, i.e., the Christian population, and today, primarily the Orthodox. The Coptic language faded as Arabic replaced it in administration and then daily life, first in the cities and later in the villages.

The Christian population in Egypt today consists of members of the Coptic Orthodox Church, the Coptic Catholic Church, and sixteen recognized Protestant denominations.

The Coptic Orthodox Church is the historic, and national, church of Egypt and is deeply tied to a monastic tradition of spiritual growth and preparation for ministry for monks and nuns, a tradition that continues to thrive. It is by far the largest church in Egypt and has a clear ecclesial hierarchy, with the pope (also called patriarch) at the top. Orthodox membership may include up to 95 percent of Egypt's Christian population.

The Coptic Catholic Church is also hierarchical in structure, with a patriarch of its own, and has a special relationship with the Vatican that gives the Coptic Catholic Church an international connection. Taken as a whole, though, the Catholic population in Egypt is very small.

There are sixteen officially recognized Protestant denominations, the largest of which is the Evangelical Presbyterian Church. They use Arabic (not Coptic) in worship. Established as a result of missionary movements, the Protestant churches have ties with church denominations outside of Egypt, but their membership is authentically Egyptian. Historical and contemporary tensions among the Christian communities exist over doctrine, social motivation, and political agenda.

In early times, the two Christian communities (the Greeks and the Egyptians) debated Jesus' nature. At the Council of Chalcedon in 451 C.E., two families of churches emerged from the council, representing the diphysite and monophysite schools, the Greek Orthodox Church holding firm on the duality of Christ's nature and the Eastern (or Oriental) churches, including the Syrian, Armenian, and Coptic Orthodox churches expressing the unity of Christ's two natures. The importance of this aspect of Egypt's social dichotomy, according to Hugh Kennedy, is that the division between the ruling class of Greek Orthodox and the majority Coptic Orthodox population further alienated the people from the rulers. This alienation occurred "both culturally and because the church they were devoted to was regarded as heretical and subject to dire official sanctions" (Kennedy 1986, 5) Some historians assert that the ecclesial divisions occurring over the nature of Christ had more to do with an acute feeling of Egyptian nationalism, as it related to the church, than strong theological positions that supported one side of the debate over another.

The tension between Egyptian Christians and oppressive Roman rule was great, to the extent that a sense of nationalism was tied to the Egyptian practice of religion. The Patriarch of the See of St. Mark was a leader of Christian thought, both theologically and philosophically (S. Ibrahim 1996a, 7). Even so, independence from the Byzantine Empire was a hope that was not realized, and persecution continued. Efforts of the Byzantine rulers to synthesize beliefs in order to establish a kind of reconciliation between the two worlds were not successful, and the Coptic Orthodox pope was forced to escape to the desert, priests and bishops left their churches and communities, and a large number of Egyptians were forced to deny their faith in order to save their lives (S. Ibrahim 1996a, 7–8).

The Byzantine rule was therefore a time of great tension between the rulers and the indigenous Egyptians, to an important degree over faith and philosophy. The economic situation in Egypt did not help to establish the Byzantine period as particularly flourishing, either. It is a commonly held view, then, that due to an alienation from Roman rule, the Egyptians did not offer resistance to the Arab invasion, carried out by the troops of a single commander, 'Amr ibn al-'As, completed by the autumn of 642 c.e. after defeating the Byzantine forces in Heliopolis and then proceeding on to Alexandria.

The Early Islamic Period

With the expulsion of the Byzantines complete and administration in the hands of the Arabs, the Copts were again allowed rights (Kennedy 1986, 64–66). Among these rights were the right to choose their church leader and for clergy to practice their clerical and pastoral duties, and the right to regain possession and ownership of church buildings, which meant that repairs could be made to make them again functional (Malaty 1993, 104).

The situation in Egypt had thus radically changed for the better with respect to religious freedoms. This sense of freedom made it possible for Copts to accept the new rulers, without feeling pressure to announce any change in religious affiliation. That is not to say, however, that there was complete satisfaction with the new Arab ruling party. Between 725 and 773, there were at least six documented rebellions against the regime in which the Copts were defeated, and, as a result, many converted to Islam (S. Ibrahim 1996a, 8). The process of conversion to Islam among Christians was slower in Egypt than in other centers such as Iraq and Iran, however. In fact, "Muslims remained a small ruling group among a largely Coptic population until Fatimid times [established in 972]" (Kennedy 1986, 202). Even so, the first twenty years of the Fatimid rule were characterized by many freedoms for the Copts: worship, church and monastery construction and renovation, artistic expression, political position, and professional advancement (Malaty 1993, 120).

Such openness and tolerance came to an end during the rule of the caliph al-Hakim, who ruled from 996 to 1020 and was known for his particularly harsh treatment of all of his subjects, Christian and Muslim alike. With regard to the Copts, he required them to wear dark-colored clothes, and he destroyed their churches and property. It was during al-Hakim's caliphate that many Copts were forced to convert to Islam. His successor, az-Zahir, recognized the forced nature of many of the conversions to Islam and allowed people to convert back to Christianity, declaring that religious conversion is a matter of will, not of force (Malaty 1993, 121–23).

Saad Eddin Ibrahim identifies three factors in the process of the Arabization of Egypt. The first factor was the waves of migration of Arabs from the Arabian Peninsula to Egypt, especially between the seventh and thirteenth centuries, which were influenced by higher birth rates among Arabs, and the appointment of rulers for Egypt and the large number of people who came with them. The second factor was the spread of Islam, including conversion among Egyptians. Some of the reasons for conversion included sincere acceptance of the new faith, conversion after suffering (particularly economically through high taxes) under Arab rule, and the desire to gain equal footing socially and politically with Muslim copatriots. The third factor was the Arabic language. Arabic was slow to overtake the Coptic language in Egypt, but even with Copts serving in governmental positions, the isolation of Coptic to monasteries and ecclesial life was inevitable for many reasons: decrees made Arabic the official language of the *diwan* (court); children were taught Arabic to ensure their ability to hold

government positions; governmental tolerance of Copts and encouragement of full social integration meant that senior officials adopted Arabic
names and titles; and, finally, a papal decree by Pope Gabriel II (r. 1131-
1145) called for the use of Arabic along with Coptic in liturgy since so few
of the worshipping faithful understood Coptic (S. Ibrahim 1996a, 8).

For a number of centuries, there was relative harmony between
the Christian and Muslim populations of Egypt. For the periods of rule
through the Fatimid era, that is, until 1171, the Christians were afforded a
high degree of tolerance and respect (Mainardus 1977, 8–9). The following
two periods, the successive reigns of the Ayyubids (1171-1250) and Mamlukes (1250-1517), marked an important contrast, and this deviation from
the good relations the two faith communities had enjoyed was at least
partially attributable to the Crusades.

The Impact of the Crusades

It is important to precede a discussion of the effects of the Crusades with
a word about Salah ad-din al-Ayyubi, who became the head of the Egyptian government, though not the head of state, since Salah ad-Din was
not the caliph. While he is best known for taking Jerusalem from the Crusader armies in 1187, his rule marked an important highlight in Christian-
Muslim relations. Among other things, he honored the relationships and
contracts that were made with non-Muslims, namely, the Christians living
within his span of rule (Hodgson 1974a, 268). His position among Copts
is best related by Malaty, who writes, "In Salah El Din's era stability and
justice were restored along with generosity and abundance which made
all Egyptians, Christians and Muslims, cherish him and become loyal to
him" (Malaty 1993, 131). Some of the reasons for his popularity among
Christians were that sectarian conflict came to a halt for the time being
during Salah ad-Din's rule; he lifted some of the taxes that Copts were
uniquely required to pay; he appointed Copts to high governmental positions, including one as his own private secretary; and he returned confis-
cated property to their Coptic owners. As a result of the good relations that
were prevalent, two Copts accepted Salah ad-Din's request to design the
Citadel in Cairo, which served as the main government office until 1874
(Malaty 1993, 131–32). Salah ad-Din's rule was marked by reconciliation

and cohesiveness among people. The Crusades nevertheless had a major impact on such internal dynamics.

The paths of the first, second, and third Crusades included Turkey and the lands of the Fertile Crescent (Syria, Lebanon, and Palestine), but the fourth Crusade (1202–4) targeted Egypt more directly than the others in an attempt to break up the Islamic dynasty there (Queller 2001, 1160–61). Even so, the Crusader wars had a particularly negative impact on the relations between Copts and Muslims. Tadros Malaty, a Coptic historian, sees the Copts as "victims of all these raids" because "as the Muslims saw the invaders carrying crosses on their chests, they assumed that the Copts would side with the invaders . . . [and] the Latins [Catholic Crusaders] viewed the Copts (mia-[mono]physites) as outcast schism [sic] and in general worse than heretics in their view" (Malaty 1993, 129). As a result of the latter perspective, the Crusaders who controlled Jerusalem prohibited Coptic Christians from making pilgrimages there, a fact that increased the already wide gap between the Copts and the Crusaders (Malaty 1993, 129–30).

Some of Ibrahim's conclusions as to the result of the Crusades upon Christian-Muslim relations in Egypt are especially relevant. First, he notes that Muslim tolerance not only of Western but also of Eastern Christians (including the Copts) decreased. This intolerance can be attributed to the intensity of the wars waged by the Crusaders, which "awakened the dormant spirit of *jihad* (holy struggle)" within Muslims. The second conclusion, which supports Malaty's idea that the Copts suffered from both sides, is that the Crusaders treated all local populations the same, both Muslims and Eastern Christians, denying rights to all, a particularly important shift because the Muslim rulers had allowed Copts local rights. Third, as a result of the Crusaders' efforts to divide the Ethiopian church from the Egyptian church in order to ally themselves with the Ethiopian ruling family, pressure was placed on the Coptic church of Egypt and therefore involved the Coptic church in the nationalistic struggle the Egyptians faced with the Crusaders (S. Ibrahim 1996a, 9).

The Mamluke and Ottoman Periods

The Mamluke rule (1250–1517) was significant because Egypt was freed of the presence and influence of the Crusaders. For peasant Copts, who made up the greatest portion of the Coptic population, a weakening economy meant that the degree of freedom they enjoyed was greatly reduced. Other Copts were in important government positions, close to the sultan, able to become very rich and own a great deal of property, including land and slaves. The position of Copts in the bureaucracy created tensions because of the wealth they were able to amass and because of the development of an Islamic middle and intellectual class who aspired to such positions. Tensions during the Mamluke period were particularly high because the Islamic middle class felt that it could not break into the Coptic-dominated bureaucracy. The Copts dominated the clerical positions, and the Mamlukes tried to balance the Muslim and Christian employees as they attempted to consolidate their power (S. Ibrahim 1996a, 9). Tension between the communities therefore reached a high point. The Mamluke period came to an end in 1517 with the Ottoman invasion of Egypt.

The Ottoman period meant that the center of power with regard to Egypt was no longer located locally, and no ruling class per se existed in Egypt; Egypt became a state within the much more expansive Ottoman Empire. The Ottoman Empire was characterized by a political and religious alliance that made the empire strong. The empire, according to Marshall Hodgson, was based on a rather equal status for rulers and religious authorities. Despite the fact that the *'ulama'* were under control of the state, "they brought the Shari'ah into the centre of state life" (Hodgson 1974b, 105). In the Ottoman structure of the *shari'a,* millets were organized. Millets were groups of religious minorities that were offered *dhimmi* status by the state. They were under the jurisdiction of their priests and rabbis. Again according to Hodgson, the Coptic Christians were among the larger faith communities that were allowed to exist under their own religious authority, "but heretics in their midst were left to the mercies of the established bishops that they rejected, who were granted both ecclesiastical and civil judicial authority over them. The only legal way out of a resented jurisdiction would be conversion to Islam" (Hodgson 1974b, 125).

From three different sources, it is possible to summarize the situation of the Copts under Ottoman rule until Muhammad 'Ali. Malaty, the Coptic historian, describes the Ottoman rulers levying heavy taxes upon the Copts, forcing Christianity out of Nubia (southern Egypt) through terrorism and stealing, imprisoning Pope Mark IV, requiring Copts to wear distinctive dress, and, finally, creating an atmosphere of insecurity that was experienced by both Muslims and Christians (Malaty 1993, 150–52). The English traveler and observer of Egypt Edward William Lane (1973, 552) writes in his classic work, "From the [mid-fourteenth century], the Copts continued subject to more or less oppression, until the succession of Mohammad 'Alee Basha, under whose tolerant though severe sway nothing more was extracted from the Christian than the Muslim, except . . . exemption from military service."

Finally, Ibrahim describes the beginning of Ottoman rule in Egypt as marginalizing the Copts, removing them from administration, where they had played a prominent part until Ottoman times. Later, some Copts gained positions of wealth and status, but "the peasants and agricultural labourers, Coptic and Muslim, continued to live together in poverty and oppression" (S. Ibrahim 1996a, 10).

With the reign of Muhammad 'Ali, a new era was ushered in. Muhammad 'Ali ruled Egypt for the remarkable period of forty-three years (1805–1848). Even though Muhammad 'Ali was an Ottoman Turk, his reign was characterized by the separation of Egypt from Turkey. Themes of independence and modernization marked his rule. In terms of intercommunal relations, P. J. Vatikiotis writes:

> A feature of the Pasha's insistence upon public order and security
> was his policy of religious toleration. Christian—Armenians, Copts,
> Greeks, and other Europeans—held key posts in his administration.
> Although throughout his reign the Sharia Courts (Islamic religious
> courts) remained the sole judicial system in the country, he initiated
> the study of French-modeled civil, criminal, and commercial codes,
> which were to be adopted later under his successors. (Vatikiotis 1991,
> 63–64)

Muhammad 'Ali's successors were his progeny, Ibrahim (r. 1848–1849), 'Abbas I (r. 1849–1854), Sa'id (r. 1854–1863), and Isma'il (r. 1863–1879). The single most important law enacted during the rule of any of these five men was the Hamayouni Decree, which is still in effect today. Enacted during Sa'id Pasha's rule in 1856, the law reflected the movement to legislate equality among peoples, revoking any sort of discrimination based upon ethnicity, race, or religion. This law was in response to inequality that existed between the Muslim and non-Muslim communities. With respect to these communities, the decree reestablished Coptic personal status independence from the implementation of *shari'a;* allowed for the formation of councils that would have sole responsibility for church financial matters and be allowed to discuss personal status matters; provided a process for requests to be presented by the pope to the sultan for church building and repair (this process has recently been changed by President Husni Mubarak); allowed for the freedom to express and practice one's faith; made discrimination in hiring illegal; ended the exclusion of non-Muslims from the military; and legislated inclusive religious languages in the legal codes (S. Ibrahim 1996a, 11). Clearly, this law had important implications for the legal relationship between Muslims and non-Muslims. The fact that this decree is still a basis for religious tolerance and mutual acceptance is evidence of the transcendent principles it represented.

The Hamayouni Decree laid the way for even greater tolerance at many levels of society, including the official level. Malaty recounts that the next ruler, Isma'il Pasha, was "the most tolerant ruler of Mohammad Ali's family [because he] appointed the Copt Wasif Bey Azmi his chief-protocol, and Abd-Allah Bey Serour governor of Qalubia province" and regularly implemented the Hamayouni Decree's call to recruit Copts into the army (Malaty 1993, 175).

Protestant Missionaries and Their Impact

In the first decades of the second half of the nineteenth century, the Christian community in Egypt (and elsewhere) was exposed to a new kind of Christianity. Today, the largest Protestant church in Egypt, and in fact in the Middle East, is the Coptic Evangelical (Presbyterian) Church. It was founded in March 1854, growing out of missionary efforts of the United Presbyterian Church of the United States. The missionaries went to Egypt with the goal of converting Muslims to Christianity. The establishment of the Egyptian Presbyterian church came about, however, as a result of the conversion of Orthodox Christians who had become disenchanted with the hierarchy of their own church and the fact that Coptic, a language not understood by ordinary people, was still used as the language of the mass. Thus, a sort of Protestant reformation took place within Egypt. The Orthodox Church underwent a self-evaluation and considered using Arabic more prominently in the mass. It also began to emphasize social services and educational institutions in its local ministry, which previously had focused on monastic life. In a similar sense, then, the Orthodox Church experienced a counterreformation as well.

Twentieth-Century Egyptian Nationalism

In the first quarter of the twentieth century, Egyptian nationalism developed at a considerable rate. Egypt was still under the colonial rule of the British and part of the Ottoman Empire. It therefore was pulled between Europe and the West on the one hand, and Islam and the East on the other.

This period was marked by the ideas of Muhammad 'Abdu, who "insisted on retaining the essentially Islamic character of Egyptian society while at the same time permitting it to accept the beliefs of a secular ethic to guide its social and political conduct" (Vatikiotis 1991, 196). His ideas influenced Mustafa Kamil, a leader in the National Party (al-Hizb al-Watani) who mixed secular and Islamic themes and called above all for British evacuation from Egypt (Vatikiotis 1991, 204–5). Islamic nationalism, then, was an important trend in the early 1900s. The Islamic aspect of this ideology had alienated many Copts, and the creation of the Egypt Party (Hizb Misr) was a reaction by Copts to the National Party. In 1908, a Copt, Butros Ghali Pasha, was chosen as prime minister. While the selection was based on merit, his appointment exacerbated the tension between Copts and Muslims. Less than two years later, in February 1910, an extremist member of the National Party assassinated Butros Ghali (El-Feki 1988, 39–40).

A Coptic congress was convened in Assiut to defend the rights of Copts. The delegates to the conference called for the observation of Sunday as a national day of rest, an end to discrimination in the appointment of civil servants, and governmental financial support for Christian schools (Pennington 1982, 160). None of these demands was officially acknowledged, but a Muslim congress was held later in the same year in reaction.

With World War I, confessional sentiment became of secondary importance, and nationalist feelings emerged dominant. The national cause was supported by Christians and Muslims alike for several reasons. First, the Ottoman Empire was broken up, and the idea of pan-Islamism was, for the time being, destroyed. Second, the intellectual climate was more liberal. Third, the Wafd Party made national unity based on a secular ideology central to its platform, one which gained widespread appeal (Pennington 1982, 161). The Wafd Party leadership comprised Muslims and Christians and dominated the Parliament. There was always a number of Copts in Parliament and the cabinet. A prominent member of the Wafd Party, Makram 'Ebeid, a Copt, was very close to the party leader, Sa'ad Zaghlul.

The Wafd Party was named for the delegation *(wafd)* that had hoped to attend the Paris peace talks in 1919 to discuss Egyptian independence. After negotiations with the British, Egyptian independence was declared almost three years later (Vatikiotis 1991, 260–72). With the emergence of secular nationalism, higher levels of tolerance and cooperation existed because the struggle was no longer between religious communities in Egypt but against a foreign colonizer.

February 28, 1922, marked Egypt's conditional independence from England. Independence was conditional because the British decree claimed discretion over four matters: security of British communications in Egypt, defense of Egypt if a foreign power threatened aggression, protection of foreign interests and minorities in Egypt, and the issue of the Sudan (Vatikiotis 1991, 273). Because of the third condition, some nationalist Muslims felt that the Wafd was controlled by Copts and that it had agreed to these four matters to ensure their protection in the case of sectarian conflict.

In the following year, a constitution was promulgated by the Egyptian government, yet it still had to be approved by the British. One of the issues at stake in the drafting of the constitution was representation of religious minorities in government. This issue and the issue of the need for British protection of minorities were debated extensively, both in Parliament and among Copts. The Constitution of 1923 was clear on one important matter: that Islam would be the official religion of the state. This article was included despite strong support for the separation of religion and politics.

While this article did not make Egypt a theocracy, "the fact [is] that the much vaunted guarantees of freedom of worship and equality were not inviolable and were not taken seriously" (Carter 1986, 133). The debate on guaranteed representation of minorities in Parliament ended in defeat for its proponents. While Copts wanted representation, many did not consider themselves a minority and therefore considered that such a guarantee would confirm a second-class status they did not desire. By defeating the proposal, those who supported nationalism and secularism emerged victorious (Carter 1986, 141). Such issues in the wake of independence were divisive. After an intense period of national unity, the reality of state building caused tensions that would only grow.

In 1928, an organization that would signal the reemergence of an Islamic ideology was established. The Muslim Brotherhood was founded by Hassan al-Banna in Isma'iliyya. The Brotherhood remains on the Egyptian political scene to the present day. Its establishment marked a break from the secular model of politics that had been promulgated as it called for an Islamic society and polity. It rejected European liberalism as the basis for Egypt's government and society as well (Vatikiotis 1991, 319). The Muslim Brotherhood's establishment not only represented a return to sectarian ideas but also came at a time when the Wafd Party was beginning to experience internal strife.

In the mid-1940s, according to El-Feki's account in chapter 4 of his *al-Aqbat fi's-siyasa al-misriyya* (The Copts in Egyptian Politics), an internal power struggle eventually resulted in the breaking away of some of its Coptic leadership from the Wafd. The tensions between the monarch and the ruling Wafd Party were enough to break up the party. Between 1937 and 1942, Makram 'Ebeid was the number-two man in the Wafd, second to Mustafa an-Nahhas. King Faruq and 'Ali Maher, the prime minister, wanted to reduce the power held by the party and did so by stressing an Islamic ideology, designed to divide the party. An-Nahhas's failure to name Makram 'Ebeid party secretary or prime minister despite his superior qualifications was seen by 'Ebeid as sectarian politics. In 1942, 'Ebeid resigned from the Wafd Party. He formed the Wafdist Bloc (al-Kutla al-Wafdiyya) as a splinter party, taking with him a number of prominent Copts from the Wafd Party.

As a result of this crisis, the Wafd lost much of its power. Its liberal and secular ideology had been challenged constantly since the debates over the constitution in 1923. The king's advocacy of an Islamic polity, due to his desire to be a new *khalifa,* or head of an Islamic nation, also played a part in the destruction of the liberal ideology during this period.

The constitution that was drafted and approved included an article that officially established Egypt as an Islamic state and did not recognize Egypt's significant non-Muslim population. While the Constitution did not restrict citizenship to Muslims, this article did erect a barrier between the two religious communities in Egypt, especially after the struggle for independence that transcended religious identity in focusing on the national cause. Non-Muslims were, however, tolerated at a political level even though they were not part of the majority and state religion.

The 1952 Coup and the Nasir Era

The Free Officers' coup of 1952 was meant primarily to overthrow the monarchy, seen as both corrupt and controlled by the British government, despite the declaration of Egypt's independence in 1922. The coup's success and the subsequent ascension to power of the military elite headed by Jamal 'abd an-Nasir (Gamal Abd al-Nasser) meant an essential transformation of the government and the administration. In one important sense, the new ideology of the Free Officers brought significant change, not only for Egypt but also for the Arab world. Nasir's ideology was closely aligned with an Arab identity, but with a socialist bent. He envisioned the unification of Arab countries and the consolidation of their power to stand up against the West, which the Arabs felt was continuing to exercise colonial power. Equally significant had been the establishment of the state of Israel and the Palestine wars in 1948. Perceived to have been created by the West through the United Nations in the heart of the Arab world, displacing Arabs without any apparent reason, Israel was a rallying point for all Arab states on which to unify. Politically and economically, Nasir was a pioneer in the creation of the Non-Aligned Movement, the idea of which was that the countries of the so-called Third World not be pawns in the emerging cold war between the United States and the Soviet Union.

A significant act by the new government was to undertake major reforms at al-Azhar, placing it effectively under state control and thus asserting control over the message it could disseminate. With this action, according to Kepel, the government "deprived it of its credibility. The ulemas found themselves no longer effective in their traditional role as intermediaries between the state and the people, preaching obedience to the regime while remaining free to criticize it and make it promote justice. . . . A vacuum had been created, to be filled by anyone ready to question the state and criticize governments in the name of Islam, whether that person had received clerical training or not" (Kepel 2002, 53).

The National Charter (al-Mithaq) was accepted by Parliament on June 30, 1962. It spelled out the direction Egypt would take politically, economically, and socially, identifying Arab socialism as the true path to regaining Egypt's greatness. There is no doubt that this document, written by Nasir himself, was particularly revealing of his thought and vision. What is relevant to this study are the references to religion. Of course, Arab socialism was, as the name suggests, quite secular in nature, but the document acknowledges the importance of Islam in Arab history and, implicitly, the multiconfessional community that is Egypt.

Chapter 3 of the charter, "The Roots of the Struggle," juxtaposes Arab and Islamic history with Western and Christian history, but it emphasizes the Egyptian role more than the Islamic role in the struggle.

> In the history of Islam, the Egyptian people guided by the message of Mohamed, assumed the main role in defence of civilization of mankind. . . . [The Egyptian people] made of their noble university Al Azhar, a stronghold of resistance against the colonial and reactionary factors of weakness and discrimination imposed by the Ottoman Caliphate in the name of religion, while in fact, religion is incompatible with such factors. (United Arabic Republic 1962, 17–18)

While religion was not by any means a central part of Nasir's ideology, he was able to use it to consolidate his leadership position, criticizing illegitimate usages of religion.

Later in the Charter, Nasir discusses social freedoms that each Egyptian has the right to enjoy. One of those freedoms is religion: "The freedom of religious belief must be regarded as sacred in our new free life. . . . The essence of religion does not conflict with the facts of our life. . . . All religions contain a message of progress. . . . The essence of all religions is to assert man's right to life and to freedom" (United Arabic Republic, 75).

Nasir thought that religion, if practiced in a way that neither interfered with other people's freedoms nor obstructed the progress of the nation, was a positive element of a person's character. He denounced reactionary religion as a hindrance to the national project. In this way, the Charter stated a very tolerant position with respect to religion in general, not just the minority Christianity but Islam as well.

Citizenship was not determined by religion; the national program outlined by Nasir was secular, yet tolerant of most manifestations of religion. To this end, Nasir harshly suppressed the Muslim Brotherhood, which was opposed to his secular program, and he had Sayyid Qutb, one of its leaders and ideologues, executed in 1966. The church enjoyed freedoms it had not in the recent past, but it did not play a particularly political role (Pennington 1982, 165–66).

The 1967 defeat by Israel came as unexpectedly to Muslims as it did to Christians. The defeat itself, many have argued, played a critical role in the reemergence of religious sentiment in Egypt, as Egyptians felt they were being punished for their lack of faith. With the defeat and the emergence of some more militant religious groups, both Christian and Muslim, sectarian conflict also increased after the defeat. This emergence can partly be attributed to the defeat itself, but some argue that a deeper cause was "disappointment with and the insecurity felt under the Nasser regime" (Vatikiotis 1991, 420). President Nasir died in September 1970, and Anwar as-Sadat, Nasir's vice president, was confirmed almost immediately as president. The period of his presidency lasted eleven years and ended when he was killed by Khalid al-Islambuli, a member of Islamic Jihad.

Sadat and the Conflicts of Religion

One of Sadat's early acts was the release of Nasir's political prisoners, including members of the Muslim Brotherhood and other Islamic organizations. He took this measure to gain their support against the Left, the Nasirites. Sadat's policy of *infitah* (opening) was both an economically and politically motivated policy. Very simply, economically he wanted to gain the support of the West, for he saw that neither nonalignment nor alliance with the Soviet bloc was advantageous for Egypt's needs. Politically, he attempted to allow greater freedom, including freedom of the press and freedom of association. This latter freedom included allowing Islamic groups to form and exist. However, "by encouraging the Islamists, Sadat gave up the Egyptian state's monopoly on ideology, as well as the strategy of containing religion on which his predecessor had relied" (Kepel 2002, 65).

Islam, for Sadat, was a means of legitimization. He was often shown on television praying on Fridays, demonstrating his faith. He also called himself *ra'is al-mu'minin* (president/head of the faithful). While making frequent rhetorical reference to Egypt's pharaonic history to stress the common history of Muslim and Christian Egyptians, his presidency was a time during which sectarian conflict was fostered.

The 1970s witnessed a high level of sectarian strife with the emergence of Islamic groups like at-Takfir wa'l-Hijra. Such groups attempted to bomb churches. Additionally, simple property disputes escalated to become religious conflicts between Christian and Muslim families.[1] It is ironic that many of the extremist Muslims, whom Sadat allowed to be openly expressive of their political and social views, accused the regime of favoring Christians and accused the Christians of being in league with the administration and the Israeli Jews, with whom Sadat eventually signed the Camp David accords.

In 1971, one year after his rise to the presidency, Sadat promulgated a "permanent constitution" that declared that "the Shari'a constituted *one of the sources* of legislation." In 1979, this clause was amended to make the *shari'a* the *principal* source of legislation. The actual text of the amendment reads, "Islam is the religion of the state, Arabic is its official language and principles of Islamic laws are the main sources of legislation" (Ansari 1984, 401).

During his presidency, Sadat described conspiracies in which the Copts were allegedly involved, thus affecting the level of legal and social

---

1. For more in-depth accounts of such incidents, see Farah (1986); Pennington (1982, 167–77); and Vatikiotis (1991, 420–24), among others.

citizenship the Copts enjoyed. Sadat accused the Copts of "instigating religious strife to destabilize the country." He also accused Pope Shenouda
of trying to raise Coptic support to defeat the 1979 constitutional amendment that was to be voted on by referendum (Farah 1986, 10). In 1980,
Sadat paid an official visit to the United States, "during which American newspapers had printed full-page advertisements placed by Coptic
emigrants denouncing 'the persecution suffered by Christians in Egypt'"
(Kepel 1986, 159), and Sadat, upon his return to Egypt, implied that the
pope was to blame for Sadat's embarrassment in the United States. As
relations between the church and state worsened, the pope called upon
Christians to fast and pray on several occasions to raise up their condition.
Sadat finally exiled Pope Shenouda to a desert monastery, stripping him
of his temporal power as head of the church. He was not released until
after Sadat was assassinated and Husni Mubarak allowed him to return
to his position.

This personal conflict, combined with several incidents of communal
violence between Christians and Muslims in 1980 and 1981 that resulted
in clashes and some deaths, resulted in the suspension of Pope Shenouda,
as well as other religious leaders, again both Christian and Muslim. On
September 3, 1981, mass arrests of more than fifteen hundred people took
place, thirteen religious organizations were dissolved, and the Muslim
Brotherhood was deemed illegal (Vatikiotis 1991, 423). "One of the pre-
texts for the repressive measures against the Islamicist movement . . . [was
a] slogan like the threat to boycott Coptic shops [which] amounts to a direct attack on Egyptian national unity, which is itself one of the keywords
of state legitimacy" (Kepel 1986, 119).

Sadat's initial strategy of opening up the country to religious organizations had come full circle, with Sadat repressing Christians and Muslims
alike.

Kepel (1986, 165) writes, "In order to establish a confessional balance
in the repression and thus to disarm any potential Muslim solidarity, the
regime [in addition to cracking down on the Islamicists] also dealt heavy
blows to the Coptic church and hierarchy, which were cast as the Christian equivalent not of al-Azhar, which is the institutional reality, but of the
jama'at."

Intercommunal conflict toward the end of Sadat's presidency involved not only Christians and Muslims but also the state. Exactly four months before Sadat's assassination, a prominent and popular *shaikh*, Shaikh Kishk, preached a sermon that highlighted the peak level of conflict that prevailed.

> Since 'Amr Ibn al-'As conquered Egypt, the Christians have lived together with the Muslims without ever having the slightest reason for complaint. . . . Nowhere on earth is there any minority that has been accorded the rights enjoyed by the Christians of Egypt, who occupy so many important posts: ministers, chairmen of the boards of directors of banks, generals, and their pope, who sits on the throne of the Church with all its authority. . . . Who is responsible for this tragedy [of Christian preference by the state]? The prime responsibility lies with al-Azhar! If the youth had found real leaders to guide them, this would not have happened. . . . Look at them, these Copts, so sure of their strength and so honoured! (Kepel 1986, 238–39)

By attacking the Copts, according to Kepel (1986, 240), the Islamists were effectively attacking the state, in part because they could not directly attack it. Sadat did not manage this strategy very well, falling into the trap of responding against both Muslims and Christians and then being killed by a direct attack on him, the personification of the state.

The Mubarak Presidency and Militant Islam

One of the most difficult and pressing problems that Husni Mubarak inherited when he was formally elected president in October 1981 was that of militant Islam. He was committed to a continuation of the policy of *infitah*, while at the same time eager to be a president of reconciliation, even if it meant asserting a strong hand in the process. Mubarak reconciled the political implications of these policies. "The tight repression of the radical Islamist militants who more or less shared the worldview of Sadat's assassins was combined with a relative opening of the political system, which allowed the Muslim Brotherhood and various parties to participate in elections and in parliamentary life" (Kepel 1986, 19).

At the outset of Mubarak's administration, the expectations were high for better communal relations, at least in part through containing Islamic groups, which regularly targeted Egyptian Christians, "whether murders, fires set to their churches, or extortion of funds in the name of *jizya*, the poll tax to which non-Muslims were once subject in the land of Islam and which the modern state had abolished" (Kepel 1986, 19).

In naming his government, Mubarak appointed Fikri Makram 'Ebeid deputy prime minister and a second Copt as minister of state for emigration (Vatikiotis 1991, 439). In 1984 he released the pope from the monastic exile imposed by Sadat, but only after the elections of the same year. By keeping the pope in exile and the Islamists in prison, Mubarak attempted to keep religion out of election politics (Kepel 1986, 245). The first few years of the Mubarak presidency were virtually conflict-free. In the late 1980s and throughout the 1990s, however, there was an increased incidence of sectarian conflict, in part because of a reversal of position, allowing more political debate (Kepel 1986, 245). For example, in 1991 al-Jama'a al-Islamiyya (the Islamic Group) established an Islamic "state" in Imbaba, Cairo, overpowering for a time the state police and implementing its version of Islamic law, including forcing Christians to pay the *jizya*. A strong demonstration of force by the government was required to "retake" Imbaba, and the Islamic Group has not been able to mobilize Cairean masses in a similar way since that time (Kepel 1986, 290–91, 292, 294).

Understanding Egypt's Religious History and National Identity

Relations between the two communities, with respect to their legal and social status at varying times, can be interpreted according to one of five schools of civilizational-historic identification. Each exhibits a different degree of tolerance or acceptance of the (primarily two) religious communities in Egypt.

National history, especially with respect to the relationship between Christians and Muslims, offers a very significant key to understanding citizenship and tolerance in Egypt, both politically and socially. The importance of the question of intercommunal relations in modern Egypt is especially critical since it was in late-nineteenth and twentieth-century

Egypt that the British (i.e., a non-Muslim power) controlled Egyptian politics. Previously, the Ottomans and other Islamic powers ruled in Egypt; Egypt was an Islamic state ruled by foreign powers in the name of Islam. With the arrival of British colonialism (effectively lasting from 1882 to 1952), Egypt came under the control of a non-Islamic, Western liberal state. Egypt's primary political identification during these periods was thus not necessarily Islamic.

As a result of this exposure to Western ideas, several schools of thought concerning Egyptian history and national identity were crystallized. These five organizing references could be classified as the Egyptian, the Mediterranean, the African, the Arab, and the Islamic schools. (Even though some authors, such as B. L. Carter, view the Arab and Islamic schools as one and call it "Arabism," the distinction between the two is sufficiently significant to merit independent classifications.) Most of these schools continue to play a significant role in policy and social relations in Egypt. Depending on which school the regime has identified with, its policies have influenced the degree of legal citizenship and political tolerance exhibited with respect to sectarian relations. In the same manner, the school with which a person or society identifies has influenced the degree of social citizenship and tolerance exhibited.

The Egyptian Identity

The first of the five schools is one based on a national history emphasizing the pharaonic period. National leaders such as Sa'ad Zaghlul and Ahmad Lutfi as-Sayyid attempted to solidify national identity in terms of Egypt's historical roots. Focusing on ancient Egypt, they proposed a link between the ancient and the modern Egyptian polity.

This school found great support in the early 1900s for several reasons, including the discovery of Tutankhamen's tomb in 1922. Muslims and Christians alike took great pride in this past, and Lutfi as-Sayyid, a Muslim, was an enthusiastic proponent of asserting a link between past and present, hypothesizing that the Egyptian character is inextricably tied to ancient Egypt. Christians were particularly drawn to this model, for they legitimately could claim direct descent from the ancient Egyptians. They argued that the Muslims, who had converted to Islam from Christianity at the time of the Islamic invasion of Egypt in 642, intermarried with the conquering army and were therefore not of the same pure descent. They also began to study the Christian period more closely as a link between ancient and modern Egypt.

The core idea of this school is the uniqueness of Egypt as a nation and its long history. B. L. Carter (1986, 95–99) writes, "To establish an inheritance in which Islam and Arab culture played no part was to establish a common ground on which Muslims and Christians could both stand."

This school sees all Egyptians as descendants of ancient Egypt and is therefore very inclusive. Despite the invasion of the Arab armies in the seventh century, Egyptians remained more or less homogeneous.

The Mediterranean Identity

The Mediterranean school is not incompatible with the Egyptian school but adds a greater geographic and cultural range, and in particular, it attempts to link Egyptian and European civilizations. The importance of this school is in its attempt to reject European rational superiority by proposing that Egypt, too, is "rational and intrinsically modern" (Carter 1986, 102). It went further, claiming that Egypt was the link between Eastern and Western civilizations. Important proponents of this school were Taha Hussain and Salama Musa, both of whom were zealous members of the Egyptian school.

This school also has had strong support among Copts, such as Salama Musa. The natural tie between Egyptian Christians and Christian Europe appealed to the Copts. It also affords them an opportunity to claim a closer link to Europe through the Greeks and Romans, who had conquered Egypt, than to the Arabs. Among Muslims, it was naturally less accepted (Carter 1986, 102–4).

This school is perhaps more inclusive than the Egyptian school, as it would accept the Greek and Italian communities that resided in Egypt as part of the society. As long as both Christian and Muslim Egyptians are included as well, then this school should be considered the most liberal of the five.

The African Circle

In writing his *Philosophy of the Revolution*, Jamal 'abd an-Nasir identified three "circles" in which Egypt was situated. They were, in order, the Arab, the African, and the Islamic circles. Nasir wrote,

> As for the Second Circle—the African Continent circle—I should say without the necessity of going into details, that we cannot under any circumstances, even if we wanted to, stand aloof from the terrible and terrifying battle now raging in the heart of that continent between five million whites and two hundred millions Africans. We cannot stand aloof for one important and obvious reason—we ourselves are in Africa.
>
> Surely the people of Africa will continue to look to us—we who are the guardians of the continent's north-eastern gate and constitute the link between Africa and the outside world. (quoted in Mansfield 1969, 114)

The reality, of course, is that Egypt is physically a part of Africa. There is, however, a linguistic barrier between Egypt and the countries of sub-Saharan Africa. Arabic is spoken in Egypt as well as in the countries of North Africa and, at least, northern Sudan, but south of those countries, Arabic is not common. Despite the rhetoric of the *Philosophy of the Revolution*, which was indeed played out as Egypt offered support for African countries' struggles for independence, by the time of the formation of the Organization for African Unity, Nasir had withdrawn Egypt's bid to play a leadership role in Africa (Mansfield 1969, 118). Most Egyptians do not think of themselves as African in the same way that they think of themselves of Arab. Egypt has certainly played a stronger role—from Nasir's time to the present—in Arab issues.

The Arab School

The proponents of the Arab school tend to focus on the years following the Arab conquests in 642. In stressing the cultural and religious links to Egypt's Arab neighbors, this school clearly is opposed to local identification and European regionalism. It concentrated not on Egypt's pharaonic history but instead on a shorter historical time frame. Proponents point to the common language that binds Arab countries together, although not necessarily the Muslim countries that speak languages other than Arabic. Some Arab Christians, in fact, played an important part in disseminating this ideology.

While the Arab school has had a great appeal to Muslim Egyptians because of the emphasis on language and culture, it has not been accepted by many Copts since it denies them a sense of pride in their non-Arab identity and denied them inclusion. Nasir's secular variant of this ideology called for a pan-Arab, secular state in which religion was incidental (Mansfield 1969, 104).

This school is a bit problematic, for while its secular variant views religion with secondary importance and therefore is tolerant, i.e., liberal, the school also reduces the place of Egypt itself in the ideological framework, looking instead toward a larger political and cultural, and certainly geographic, entity. It is therefore inclusive over a greater geographic scale but focuses less on Egypt than on the Arab "nation." In its Egyptian form, it is less inclusive than the first two schools because it ignores Egypt's pre-Islamic history.

Islam

Islam as a national identity is closely related to the Arab identity. The key difference is the centrality of religion instead of language and culture. Instead of a secular state, this school claims that Egypt, with a predominant number of Muslim citizens, is a Muslim country and should be ruled as such. This would mean the implementation of the *shari'a* and a second-class citizenship status for non-Muslims. It also stresses the importance of including Islam in the national educational curriculum.

Clearly, this school has held very little appeal for Copts. One major exception has been people like Makram 'Ebeid, who considered himself "Christian in faith and Muslim in nationality." Many Christians and Muslims viewed this prominent Coptic politician of the first half of the twentieth century as a politico whose rhetoric was sharp. Nonetheless, even this Christian considered himself part of the Muslim nation. Most Copts, however, have strongly opposed this kind of identification for Egypt due to its obvious repercussions for them. Needless to say, such identification has found an almost overwhelming receptivity in recent years with the emergence of Islamic movements and their conservative religious ideologies.

Relatively speaking, and in its extreme form, this school is the least liberal; by nature it is sectarian. Through the application of the *shari'a*, the Copts would be considered *ahl adh-dhimma*. This status would mean that they would have second-class citizenship. Clearly, they would be viewed as a non-Muslim religious group and therefore as a sect. Society as a whole would be defined in sectarian terms. Taken to its extreme, non-Muslims would be at severe disadvantage, denied rights that conflict with Islamic law and forced to pay the *jizya*. The temptation to convert to Islam in order to be accorded full citizenship would be strong. Another option would be to emigrate, thereby relinquishing the right to live in one's own country. The pressure either to become a full part of the Muslim society or leave might be too overwhelming to refuse; taking a stance based on a principle could be dangerous. While unlikely, such a scenario is the logical conclusion of this ideology being played out to its fullest.

Tensions naturally exist between the schools, but the degree of tension varies. For example, the Egyptian school provides the most nationally oriented framework and can be exclusivist in nature. It locates identity through the assertion of a millennia-old nation. It recognizes influence in the national character of the other schools and thus is not in great tension with any of them, to the extent that the other schools are informative and not narrow in focus. Mediterranean identity, on the other hand, claims identity formation by looking northward. There is greater tension between this school and the Arab, Islamic, and African schools, because of the geographic and cultural specificity implied. The Arab school is somewhat, but not entirely, compatible with the Islamic school, but like the Mediterranean school, it is specific in its orientation, increasing tensions between it and the Mediterranean and African schools. Exclusivist adherents to the Islamic school would reject identity formation from non-Muslim societies, i.e., Mediterranean (read Christian) and African (read traditional religion). Finally, the African school, albeit significantly less influential in Egypt than the other four schools, is surely in tension with the Mediterranean school because of the historical colonial relationships that existed between Europe and Africa. It is possibly in greater tension with the Arab and Islamic schools than one might at first suppose, and for some of the same reasons of dominant-subordinate dynamics (the case of the Sudan illustrates these tensions).

Each of these five schools carries an appeal that leaders could use for legitimization and the setting of policies in modern Egypt. Depending on which school is dominant at a particular time, one's perception of Christians and Muslims in the national context can be essentially transformed. Whether one sees the Copts as a minority or as nondistinguishably and fully Egyptian can be determined by the school to which one adheres. These definitions have, therefore, obvious ramifications for policy, ideas of citizenship, and degrees of tolerance in political and social contexts. It is also important to consider that any individual or institution may shift in terms of primary identity given the particular context or indeed over time, or identify with more than one school equally at any given time. It is perhaps, then, impossible to categorize individuals or institutions according to these schools once and for all. In the segments of society examined here, though, it is possible to limit consideration of the schools to the Egyptian, Arab, and religious, including Islamic. Some of the institutions clearly are Christian but may identify in the context of dialogue as Egyptian. Others may think regionally but, in the context of national discourse, identify as Egyptian or specifically Islamic. The schools therefore are helpful in sorting out the primary identities asserted by the individuals and institutions that are the subject of this book.

Beyond the policy implications, which relate directly to the level of government in this study, the school to which an individual or group subscribes has obvious implications for the level of cooperation in which the individual or group is likely to engage. The tensions that exist can be exemplified if we consider Walzer's (1997, 11) continuum of five degrees of toleration, in ascending order of toleration: "a resigned acceptance for the sake of peace. . . . passive, relaxed, benign indifference to difference. . . . a principled recognition that the 'others' have rights even if they exercise those rights in unattractive ways. . . . openness to the others; curiosity; perhaps even respect, a willingness to learn and listen. . . . [and] the enthusiastic endorsement of difference."

This continuum could also extend in the other direction toward intolerance, perhaps starting with an internalized dislike and moving toward closed-mindedness with regard to the Other combined with actions of marginalization, open mistrust and disrespect, and finally zealous actions of hate.

Adherence to one of the five schools mentioned above could prompt a person or group to respond to other people or groups at any point along the continuum described. When the locus of identification of two groups or individuals radically diverges, as is possible with the choice of locus in the range of schools of identification, there is the potential for great intolerance. Intolerance is also possible when one individual or group firmly places identity in one locus and seeks to impose that locus on all others. The schools described are ripe for such tension. Given such possibilities for self-identification, the problem of sectarian strife is manifestly real, but it is neither necessary nor exclusively prevalent.

Conclusions

It should be clear from this historical sketch that there have been periods of better relations and others of heightened tension. Relations can vary at different levels of interaction, at different times, and in different contexts as well. The following chapters investigate various levels of interaction to examine not only the extent of tolerance and acceptance that can emerge but also to see those relations against the backdrop of contemporary events.

3

Ad-Dawla wa'd-Din

The Government's Hopes for Religious Harmony

Religion played an important—indeed, a determining—role in postrevolutionary, twentieth-century Egypt. The presidencies of Jamal 'Abd an-
·Nasir and Anwar as-Sadat were marked by very different approaches to
the question of religion *(ad-din)* and its relationship to the state *(ad-dawla)*,
with significantly different impacts.

In discussing the government's treatment of religion in Egyptian politics and society, it is appropriate to focus on the rhetoric and actions of the
president because, as head of the government, he is considered by much
of the population to be more than a symbolic public character, and more
than the head of one branch of government.

The Historical Presidency

Nasir was an extremely charismatic leader who "haul[ed] the Egyptian
people on to the world stage by the scruff of their necks to play the role
. . . that Egypt's strategic position" called it to play (Mansfield 1969, 246).
Many volumes have been written about his personality and ability to lead
the country for the decade and a half of his premiership. Anwar as-Sadat,
as Nasir's chosen vice president, succeeded Nasir upon his death in 1970,
assuming a public office that had been formulated in a particular way
by Nasir's personality. Although Sadat had very different ideas about international relations and economic policy, his own personal control and
leadership also marked his presidency. Husni Mubarak, who has served
as president longer than either Nasir (1954-70) or Sadat (1970-81), has
made a point of demonstrating a system of checks and balances among
branches of government, but, in the end, it is clear that the chief executive

is first among colleagues, opposition leaders, and citizens. This primacy is illustrated by the fact that Mubarak has never named a vice president. The president and his policies can and do play the central role in national policy formation and implementation.

Nasir did not give religion a central place in the philosophy of the revolution. He did, however, encourage citizens to be faithful people so that they would be of strong moral character. Religion for Nasir was something that should neither interfere with nor obstruct the progress of the nation. Nasir was secular in his political philosophy, but not exclusionary with respect to the place of religion in society. He understood the place of Islam in the fabric of the nation and did not in any way wish to challenge its position. When politicized manifestations of religion, such as the Muslim Brotherhood, began to challenge his program in a way that he felt was an impediment to the nation, he did not restrain his severity in dealing with the Brothers. "The mass public trials of leading Brothers and the common knowledge of tough police repression did nothing to relax the political atmosphere" (Mansfield 1969, 239). Such tensions escalated throughout the 1960s. The 1967 war exacerbated the tensions between secularists and those who espoused a religious ideology; the latter tended to blame the Arab loss in the war upon a lack of centeredness in the nation's faith.

Sadat ascended to the presidency in 1970 and changed the official government's course with respect to religion. He came into office believing that it was important for various voices to be heard. He also released Nasir's political prisoners, including members of the Muslim Brotherhood. The first half of his presidency was marked by an opening up to and acceptance of political-religious influences; by the second half, he viewed radical Islam as a significant challenge that needed to be controlled and, by 1981, even outlawed. In contrast, Sadat made extensive use of "official" Islam through state-controlled media. Kepel (1986, 173) writes, "With Sadat's conquest of power, religious television programmes acquired such enormous importance that a preacher like Sheikh Sha'rawi appeared on television even more than the president himself. . . . But his televised speeches never suggested any challenge to the regime's legitimacy, and he even served as minister of waqfs."

By the end of his presidency, Sadat's confrontation with religion was not limited to the Muslim Brotherhood. He also came into direct conflict with the Coptic Orthodox Church, banning its pope from performing his duties. These two cases of confrontation, with the Muslim Brotherhood and with the Coptic Orthodox Church, demonstrate the extent to which the administration challenged any kind of vocal expression of religion that might have been seen as a threat.

The contrast between Sadat's early presidency and its final years is striking. Sadat's final chapter was written by extremists who assassinated him during the celebrations marking the anniversary of the 1973 war. On Sadat's reviewing stand at that commemoration was Bishop Samuel, a leader within the Coptic Orthodox Church who was very ecumenical and open in his outlook. Sadat surely had invited Bishop Samuel to sit next to him to offer an olive branch to Egypt's Christian community after the confrontations with its pope. Bishop Samuel met the same fate as Sadat that day.

Sadat's assassination at the hands of Muslim radicals was ironic in another sense because, in contrast to Nasir, Sadat was eager to express his faith publicly. Sadat saw himself as *ra'is al-mu'minin* (leader of the faithful). He saw himself as a political and religious leader who was going to bring religion back into the national character. In the end, he expended great efforts to do so, and to create an atmosphere of tolerance and acceptance, especially between the government and religious groups. This openness was perhaps unchecked by meaningful government direction, to the extent that it resulted in religious expression that conflicted with Sadat's idea of the future relationship between state and religion. With Sadat's assassination and Husni Mubarak's ascension to the presidency, a new era began.

Mubarak's Presidency and National Unity

Mubarak's commitment to the continuation of Sadat's economic policy of *infitah* was strong. He also aimed to be a president of reconciliation, especially between Egypt's two main religious communities. The level of religious tension between Christians and Muslims during the better part of the 1980s was relatively low, due in part to the firmness with which the new administration dealt with radical Muslim elements. Immediately after Sadat's assassination, Mubarak imposed a set of emergency laws to have as a tool to control such elements—laws that remain in effect to this day. Later in the decade, radical Islamic groups reemerged on the Egyptian political scene, and sectarian strife increased.

Sectarian strife was evidenced by an increase of conflict and violence in villages between Muslims and Christians, as well as the very public and heated debate over whether Egypt's Christians ought to be considered a minority (see chapter 7). The Mubarak government's rhetoric and actions were attempts to keep the country together and to encourage good relations between Christians and Muslims.

The Mubarak government has gone to great lengths to promote a sentiment of national unity during the years of his presidency. To this end, it is not insignificant that in December 2002, Mubarak issued a decree that made, for the first time in modern history, a national holiday of January 7, Coptic Christmas (*al-Ahram Weekly* 2003). Naturally, it has been important for Mubarak to be seen domestically and internationally as a legitimate president for all Egyptians. Domestically, even though he has been elected to three terms through referenda, as opposed to open multiple-candidate elections, he has tried to ensure the country's unity. He has done this by referring to Egypt's long history as a nation of plural citizenry; by deferring to the courts and the rule of law, especially during his first decade, even though the country remains technically under emergency law; and by asserting a degree of religiosity in the media not only to demonstrate his own faith publicly but also to teach a sort of official Islam to the people, in part at least to attempt to offset the impact more radical elements might have on public sentiments. Kepel (1986, 19) writes that in order "to sanction [the] repression [of the radical Islamists], the state had to seek the support of the *ulema* and ask them for increased Islamic legitimation, thereby distinguishing the 'good Muslims' from the 'extremists.' The dignitaries of al-Azhar thus regained a central position in the politico-religious arena, after years of subordination under Nasser and Sadat."

In the year 1985 alone, state-controlled television broadcast about fourteen thousand hours of Islamic programming (Kepel 2002, 281).

This attempt to counter the impact of more radical elements became a particularly important part of a government campaign following the devastating earthquake of October 1992, when Islamist organizations were able to provide tents, clothes, and food to those who had lost their homes or were afraid to go back into their homes as a result of the earthquake. The Islamist organizations had more provisions available more quickly than the government, and the government was therefore fearful of the effect this efficiency would have in the area of recruiting. "The Brothers were able to contribute thousands of tents to the 50,000 people left homeless by the disaster . . . [which] won them great popularity and visibility, in sharp contrast with the state's ineptitude, and it enabled them to collect substantial new funds, which the government promptly froze" (Kepel 2002, 293).

The "Reading for All" Campaign

One major effort of the Mubarak government has been the "Reading for All" campaign. This effort to provide books of interest to various audiences was established in 1992-93 to encourage not only reading and literacy but also "knowledge and wisdom through the creative energies of the pioneers of Egyptian intellectual renaissance and connect them from generation to generation" (Mubarak 1998). It was Egypt's first lady, Suzanne Mubarak, who took up this cause and has been its chairperson. She has expounded upon her hope that "we verily continue to explode with the light of knowledge for every person. I continue to dream of a book for every citizen and a library in every home" (Mubarak 1998). Through this program, books are introduced through a summer book fair and then are available at bookstores. The books themselves are offered at prices that represent significant government subsidies. For example, a 320-page paperback on social interrelations in Egypt cost two Egyptian pounds (at the time, the equivalent of less than seventy cents). Another 280-page book on a historical period in Egypt's twentieth century sold for roughly the same price.

Examination of the literature that has been included in the Reading for All series, as a clearly government-endorsed effort, can inform us about the government's efforts to maintain and augment Christian-Muslim relations in the 1990s. Three books, representative of the nature of the sociohistoric genre of the series, illustrate how the Mubarak administration has encouraged positive relations through this program.

The first book is part of the historical series chronicling Egyptian history from 1914 to 1921. During this time nationalism was at a high point and national unity was understandably strong because the Egyptian people were engaged in a struggle to eject the English colonial powers from the country. *Thawrat 1919* (The 1919 Revolution) tells the story of Sa'ad Zaghlul's leadership and the efforts of the delegation *(wafd)* to negotiate the independence of Egypt. It is not surprising that this historical period, and particularly the 1919 revolution, was selected for the series. An official presentation of these "glory years" would certainly be designed to stir a sense of Egyptianness that has nothing to do with one's religion but rather everything to do with a sense of belonging to a nation that has gone through a great struggle against a foreign power. National unity is celebrated by introducing the matter, in a slightly veiled way. The conflict with the British was not framed as a religious struggle, that is, Muslim Egypt versus Christian England, but rather an Egypt that was colonized and controlled against a colonizing and controlling foreign power.

The text, not surprisingly, introduces examples of national unity, such as the following section:

> On Friday, December 12, a great number of Muslim and Coptic Egyptian women met at St. Mark's Cathedral to object to the visit of Yussef Wahba Pasha's ministry and the arrival of the Milner Commission. At the head of the group were Huda Sha'arawi, Sharifa Riad, the wife of Mahmud Rifa'at Pasha, the wife of Habib Khiyyat Bey, Ihsan al-Qawsi, the wife of Fahmi Wissa Bey, etc. They issued a statement expressing their opinion of the political situation, the various promises the English had made on the Egyptian question. They ended it by affirming their boycott of the Milner Commission and their objection to its coming, as well as their adherence to full independence. (ar-Rafa'i 1999, 121-22)

This passage illustrates several aspects of the Mubarak strategy to foster national unity: it highlights a meeting during the nationalist struggle in a Cairo setting that would be well-known to a reader at the end of the twentieth century, a setting that happens to be Christian, thus putting the cathedral in the backdrop of nationalism; it shows Christian-Muslim cooperation around a challenge to the nation, identifying Christians and Muslims who are recognizable in the 1990s; it highlights the role of women in social and political activism; and it focuses on unity. All of these elements are employed to inspire such a feeling in the reader.

Such references to Coptic participation in the struggle against the English are scattered throughout the book. Another reference is a section on the Coptic Council's meeting in which it opposed the formation of a government in Egypt that would support the work of the Milner Commission. The entire statement is reproduced, and the closing sentence of the section reads, "The meeting was a marvelous expression of national solidarity" (ar-Rafa'i 1999, 112). Without diminishing the extent to which national unity was prevalent in the early twentieth century, it can easily be argued that the Mubarak government uses such examples to demonstrate Christian-Muslim cooperation and harmony in history, as well as Christian participation, in order to bolster a common national life in the modern period.

A second historical book produced as part of the Reading for All series is *al-Masihiyya wa'l-Islam fi Misr* (Christianity and Islam in Egypt), by Husain Kafafi. A sense of the historical and nationalist tone can be detected in the dedication of the book: "I dedicate this book to the souls of Egypt's martyrs, those who carried the cause of humanity and feelings of faith and unity, even through torture and martyrdom . . . across all eras of victory and servitude to the glorious crossing of October in which Christian and Muslim were killed, without any differentiation" (Kafafi 1998, 9).

The book itself is a religious history of Egypt beginning with the first seven centuries of the Christian Era, passing through various eras of Islamic history, and concluding with "National Unity," a chapter that treats the 1919 revolution.

It is clear from the very first lines of the book that a tone of Egyptian religiosity is to be set, in order to demonstrate that Egyptians are people of faith, no matter what their religion: "Egypt has always been a land of religions, and her people have been raised on and taught the values of faith and unity, from the time of the pharaoh Akhnaton, the first of the unifiers.

Before him, our father Abraham, prophet of God, came to Egypt searching for his wife Sarah after she was kidnapped and sold to the pharaohs of Egypt" (Kafafi 1998, 23).

The title of the first chapter is "Egypt and Christianity," and after listing other prophets and characters from Christianity and Islam, the chapter's first paragraph concludes by saying, "The path of unity continued with the coming of the period of light and salvation when Miriam the Virgin was blessed with her son Jesus Christ, who while still in his cradle began to herald Christianity" (Kafafi 1998, 23).

The author, who is Muslim, dedicates significant effort to recounting Christian history in Egypt in a positive light, by speaking about the period of Roman and Byzantine domination and the persecution under which Christians lived in Egypt, and by targeting the monastic tradition of Christianity in Egypt. Kafafi also dedicates an entire chapter to the Council of Nicaea and the role that the Coptic Church played there. The second two-thirds of the book traces Egypt's Islamic periods, but with an eye to highlighting relationships between Christians and Muslims. In discussing the advent of Islam and thus the advent of the Arabic language, Kafafi (1998, 227) notes that "the advent of Islam to Egypt, and the shift from the Coptic language to Arabic, was easy and smooth, especially because the Coptic and Arabic languages are from one linguistic origin."

Kafafi tries, throughout the book, to show how Egypt's Christians and Muslims share the same fate. If one faith community is persecuted, so is the other; if one enjoys prosperity, so does the other. It is not a zero-sum matter where one community thrives and the other suffers. He is also fair in treating Christian history and Muslim history together. When describing the period of Salah ad-Din al-Ayyubi and the succession of the Coptic papacy during those times, he does this in a way that shows national unity and common sentiment:

Yuhanna VI, the seventy-third pope, . . . remained in the papal seat until his death in 1216, having spent twenty-seven years on the seat. His death had a ring of sadness, as he was loved by Christians and Muslims. By this, we see that the Egyptian people are linked fraternally in good times and bad. In the context of fair governance, things move forward, but in a context of oppression and despotism, we find that oppression is felt by all of Egypt's people, its Muslims and its Christians. This reflects the justice of Salah ad-Din [who ruled when Yuhanna VI was selected, and whose opinion was sought on his selection] in all corners of the country. All of the people were united in facing the common enemy, which was the foreign attacks on Egypt. All Egyptians stood as one, Christians and Muslims. (Kafafi 1998, 254)

In Kafafi's conclusion, he addresses the main objective of his book in a very clear and poignant way:

Now, dear reader, the journey of our seas through the pages of this book approaches its end. It has carried in its essence a message of love and peace to all Egyptians, aiming to confirm at many levels that we do not doubt at all its authentic Egyptianness; for we all plant on this plenteous and good land shade trees of love, dense ears of wheat, and olive branches, and signs of the dove which fill our green pastures. (Kafafi 1998, 319)

The poetry of unity and harmony in a serene nature is the desired message, especially at a time when there has surely been fear and distrust of the Other.

Publishing such a book is an opportunity by the government to get into people's hands the message of communal acceptance and cooperation and the message that all, regardless of religious association, are passing through the difficult times together. Again, by concentrating on the historical periods, the author and publisher can bring across a message of good relations, mutual respect, and commonality of experience in a way that suggests the need to maintain such relations in the present. The analogy is implied: Egypt has been through difficult times before but has survived, and in fact flourished, because of the unity of the nation, particularly across religious lines. In the late 1980s and throughout the 1990s, while Egypt was experiencing another period of tension, one that threatened to become a major crisis drawn along religious lines, it was time once again to revisit what has helped the country to remain strong: national unity.

National unity is the theme of a third book published in the Reading for All series, *an-Namudhij al-misri li'l-wihda al-wataniyya* (The Egyptian Model for National Unity), by Edwar Ghali ad-Dahabi, published in 1998. The book may be more sociological than the first two books, which are more historical in nature, and can thus appeal to a different segment of readership. This book is divided into four parts: "Pluralism in Islamic Society," "Love in the Christian Faith," "The Egyptian People Are of One Race," and "National Unity in the Contemporary History of Egypt." The author writes in support of national unity, and indeed it is a "book for Egypt and for the love of Egypt, for [Egypt] is the beginning and the end, the hope, and the light" (ad-Dahabi 1998, 15). More directly, ad-Dahabi asserts the basis for national unity in his response to the Islamic movements that have challenged national unity through their version of religiosity and to Christians who may have felt animosity toward Muslims out of fear. He writes,

> Proper piety is the fence for national unity. . . . proper piety which flows from a correct understanding of the essence of religion. . . . The true Muslim believes that God created all people from one breath, and that all worshippers are brothers. . . . And the true Christian believes that God is love, and that a human being—created in the image of God—is also love [and] in order to fulfill his religion, must love all people. . . . If we add that all Egyptians—Muslims and Christians— are of one race and one origin, and that they cannot be differentiated by origin, ethnicity, appearance, or lifestyle, then the inevitable conclusion is the establishment of national unity in its most brilliant picture, just as we see it in Egyptian society. (ad-Dahabi 1998, 14-15)

In the first part, ad-Dahabi treats the bases for justice in Islam, the unity of the Islamic faith, and Islam's call for national unity. The latter of these is treated historically, referring to the beginnings of Islam and the importance the prophet Muhammad gave to the "one nation" that included both Muslims and Jews (ad-Dahabi 1998, 33). Citing verses from the Qur'an and examining early Islamic history, ad-Dahabi makes the case for unity among compatriots. In the second part, ad-Dahabi describes

Christianity as the faith of love based upon scripture and then develops this idea by a discussion of the relationship between the believer and the Creator, which is based centrally upon God's love for humanity. Finally, ad-Dahabi discusses love as the sum of all virtues and notes that to know God, a Christian must love his or her neighbor.

The third section of the book focuses upon the Egyptian people and their racial homogeneity, starting with a statement that there is no characteristic that distinguishes one Egyptian from another, from which ad-Dahabi proceeds to contribute to the debate on whether Egyptian Christians are a minority. He concludes that they are not, and supports his conclusion with historical instances of Coptic refusal of such status. (This debate is treated more fully in chapter 7.) He concludes this chapter by demonstrating the fallacy of proposing a Coptic nation.

The fourth and final chapter focuses upon national unity in the contemporary Egyptian context, first by illustrating harmony through four real-life examples. These examples are descriptive of life in villages and cities and how Christians and Muslims indeed do get along in a spirit of neighborly friendship. The next section of the chapter, "Terrorism Will Not Affect National Unity," describes extremist movements in Islam as "without foundation" (ad-Dahabi 1998, 93). The longest single section of the book is the final chapter in this part, "Historical Instances of National Unity." It presents a selection of people and events that illustrate the cause of national unity, including Muslim clerics, Christian leaders, party politicians, and other political and historical figures. The 1919 revolution is a rather long entry, as would be expected given the unifying nature of the episode. Ad-Dahabi concludes the section on the construction and repair of church buildings, a matter of public concern; much attention has been given to the fact that the relevant law on construction and repair of religious buildings remains the Ottoman Hamayouni Decree of 1856, which had required the president's signature in order to proceed. In an attempt to settle the matter, ad-Dahabi writes,

> In an interview with President Husni Mubarak by Ibrahim Nafie [editor-in-chief of *al-Ahram,* Egypt's semiofficial main daily newspaper], [Mubarak] responded to a question about restriction on building

churches by saying, "It has never happened that a request to build a church has been made and we did not consent. I have granted many more permits to build new churches than were issued in the days of Sadat and 'Abd an-Nasir. There have been no problems because we have been able to understand each other. I actually do not see a problem between Muslims and Copts in Egypt. If there is a problem, it is between extremists of both groups. The great majority enjoy a very good relationship. (ad-Dahabi 1998, 129)

In his conclusion, ad-Dahabi sings the praise of national unity in Egypt over the ages and predicts that national unity will prevail. "The people of Egypt will remain, with God's permission, one family, worshipping one God, and offer Him their prayers, in mosques or in churches. Egypt will not succeed except by the cooperation of all of its sons" (ad-Dahabi 1998, 135).

The theme of the three books is national unity, and clearly the tone is one of religious harmony. While the authors of these books are not government officials, it is easily asserted that the positions posited in these works are government positions. Even if we forget government subsidies for the cost of the books, it is enough that Suzanne Mubarak's picture and words of introduction appear on each book. The Reading for All campaign, promoted by the General Egyptian Organization for Books, has succeeded in getting a message of tolerance and acceptance into the hands of the people in an easily accessible way, both economically and by volume.

Such publications have sure value. Not only do they recount Egyptian history and have a positive message of compatriotism, but they also encourage reading. Through the campaign, the Mubarak government has attempted to foster national unity in an accessible way and advance the ideas of the Egyptian school of identity, which highlights a common past, united through struggle and convergent on the timeline of history.

Despite the low cost of the books and their rather widespread availability, they nevertheless remain unavailable to some segments of the population. With a literacy rate in Egypt of less than 65 percent (higher among men than women), not everyone who can afford or find the books is able to read them.

Television

The Mubarak government launched a parallel campaign on its television stations in an effort to counteract the lure of radical Islamic groups. The government has gone to great lengths to project a positive and nonconfrontational kind of Islam through the media, in response to the aggressive acts carried out by what the government refers to as "terrorists," "extremists," or "Islamists." For this reason, the government shows programs about Islam in which the tolerance and acceptance of humanity, particularly non-Muslims, is highlighted.

Government efforts to show religion in a positive light on television have included a weekly show hosted by Shaikh Muhammad Sayyid Tantawi, grand imam of al-Azhar, in the second half of the 1990s, in which he presented a moderate version of Islam. On Fridays, the president is usually shown at prayer in a mosque. If the president is not shown, then another recognizable government figure is shown. A third example of the effort to show religion in a positive light on television is the inclusion of a Christian character or family in a serial. Egyptian serials, usually consisting of twenty to thirty 40-minute episodes, are extremely popular among people of all ages. With the portrayal of Christians in such serials, positive impact may be had. Finally, the government has broadcast important Christian services and masses on television, such as Christmas and Easter. Often, these broadcasts are live. All of these methods are employed by the government to portray religion, both Islam and Christianity, in a moderate and positive light. With access to television a fact among Egyptians in both urban and rural settings, such efforts can reach an audience that may not have access to books for whatever reason, including proximity to bookshops and, more basically, literacy.

The government maintains control of the local television media, even though the number of available channels is expanding. With the rapid increase in the proliferation of satellite dishes and television stations, more and more people are watching nongovernment-controlled media, both Arabic and foreign. This phenomenon can have both a positive and negative impact on the government's efforts to form opinion through television. Nonetheless, the local channels are generally free, so one may assume that most people with televisions have access to them, and thus they have a higher viewership.

"This Is Islam" Booklets

The government has also disseminated its interpretations of Islam through a series of small booklets within the Islamic Cultural Series, published by the Ministry of Religious Endowments *(awqaf)*, called *Hadha huwa al-Islam* (This Is Islam). Many of the booklets treat subjects specific to Islam in order to help Egyptian Muslims understand in a deeper way aspects of their religion. The booklets treat a variety of subjects, with titles such as "The Position of Islam on Family Planning," "Message to Youth," and "The Issue of Faith and Reason." One of the booklets, *Samahat al-Islam wa huquq ghair al-Muslimin* (Islam's Magnanimity and the Rights of Non-Muslims) is especially relevant and illustrative of the nature of the series. A brief 142 pages, it gives a sense of what the Ministry of Religious Endowments, directly responsible for religious matters in Egypt and an important government ministry, has said about Islam in its relationship to other faiths.

Beginning with a section on human fraternity, the booklet goes on to discuss the place of charity and justice in Islam in relation to non-Muslims: "Orthodox Islam has outlined an ideal way to win the friendship of non-Muslims, which results in the spreading of peace, the building of trust, and the dismantling of the barriers of fear that separate Muslims and others" (Egypt 1991, 41).

The booklet outlines the rights and responsibilities of non-Muslims in a way that is clearly egalitarian: "The People of the Book are bound by a primary rule: They enjoy the same rights as Muslims, and have the same responsibilities as Muslims. . . . They are called upon to participate in the single nation. The first right they have is protection from all outside aggression and all domestic oppression" (Egypt 1991, 56).

With regard to freedom of religion, the booklet states, "The freedom of religion is a required right of any human. Acceptance of any religion is not to be forced upon anyone, nor can religion be imposed upon a person by any power, even if that religion is the official religion of the state" (Egypt 1991, 65).

Other sections outline in similar fashion the rights of non-Muslims in the areas of lifestyle, security, education, employment, ownership, and sacred space of worship. The ministry also discusses the importance of dialogue between people of different faiths, as follows: "The call to dialogue between Muslims and non-Muslims flows from the compatriotism that links them, for they live in one nation, all of them enjoying its blessings, each respecting the other's fundamentals" (Egypt 1991, 135).

Even though the book speaks about the *dhimmi* status of non-Muslims, it outlines a program by which Muslims and non-Muslims enjoy the same rights and have the same responsibilities. In conclusion, the ministry states, "Our non-Muslim brothers must know that the path to moderation and conscious knowledge of the supreme interest of the nation is security and safety so that society, and all its members, may live in love and peace" (Egypt 1991, 141).

The Ministry of Religious Endowments has been active in educating Muslims in Egypt about a moderate Islam through such booklets. This one was designed to address questions relating to relations with non-Muslims. In it, one finds allusions to the idea that Egypt is an Islamic state, but one with an emphasis on respect and equality among its citizens. The implication that Egypt is officially Islamic only reinforces a particular identity and the cultural prevalence of Islam in a legal way. By beginning a sentence with "Our non-Muslim brothers," the ministry refers to itself and by implication the government and perhaps society, as well as the reader, as Muslim. This type of reference is problematic, but the themes of national unity and good relations attempt to be conciliatory and unifying, even if they reinforce an idea of dominance.

Public Dialogues

The government has participated in the national dialogue through its endorsement of the Reading for All campaign and has demonstrated its eagerness to portray religion in a positive light through television. Additionally, it has contributed to efforts to foster national unity through its participation in public forums of interfaith dialogue. Such forums are often arranged by several organizations, including Christian and Muslim agencies, churches, and mosques. Often, it is the Ministry of Religious

Endowments that participates, since the themes frequently have had a religious bent. Examining a sampling of statements can clarify the way in which the government has promoted national unity through participation in such public dialogue.

The rhetoric that is employed in such settings is not only heard by those attending the meetings but is also covered by the daily newspapers. The extent of coverage depends on the prominence of the governmental, religious, and intellectual figures participating. In some cases, the main ideas discussed are available within a day or so to the entire country.

It is essential to keep in mind that such public forums are a vehicle for fostering dialogue and are often organized in an academic manner, with different personalities presenting papers. Marc Gopin identifies several critiques of such kinds of dialogue, especially for peacemaking, by stating that they "overemphasize the power of the word over the power of the deed" (2002, 33). He states that formal dialogues favor the better educated (37) and exclude those not present (44), among them those at all other levels who are not involved when "official" dialogue takes place (37). While such a format is less dialogical and more presentational, it has the value of leading to follow-up dialogue, not only among those who attend but also through the media of television and newspaper that cover the event and those who follow the coverage of the event. The format is indeed limiting for more profound dialogue at many levels, but it is presumed that some dialogue not only follows but also precedes the event so that it can take place smoothly and with sufficient publicity for those who participate. As Gopin puts it, "Dialogue should be a subset of a wide range of informal processes that move parties toward a transformation of relationships at a deep level. . . . Interfaith dialogue is good to the degree to which it helps generate good relationships that lead to good deeds, and this in turn will lead to peace and justice" (2002, 44)

Dialogue efforts at the official level can produce such outcomes, if involvement is far reaching and the message is disseminated broadly and received.

The Coptic Evangelical Organization for Social Services (CEOSS), a Protestant development NGO (see chapter 6), organized one such conference in 1994. In that conference, three speakers treated the topic "Religious

Thought and Citizenship." CEOSS's general director, Rev. Samuel Habib, was the first speaker, and the other two were Muhammad 'Ali Mahjub, minister of religious endowments, and Ahmad Kamal Abu al-Majd, a prominent Islamic intellectual and former minister of communications. Mahjub was the only current governmental representative at the forum. He outlined, from an official perspective, some principles of citizenship, based upon Islam and based upon the Egyptian model: "Islam calls for human brotherhood and a strong tie between children of the one nation. This is the essential message of all the heavenly religions. They all call for sincere nation building, without any differentiation. There is no difference in citizenship between one person and another for reasons of religion, color, or belief" (Mahjub 1994, 14).

Based upon this principle of equality, Mahjub went on to discuss Egypt's history of tolerance and acceptance between people of different faiths. He continued by pledging that Egypt would not fall victim to confessional divisions: "Egypt has not known intolerance, and has not differentiated among its people. In today's meeting we see the highest Islamic clergy next to leaders of Christianity. This affirms for us that Egypt has not classified its people by religion or belief. . . . We can say [to the world] that religion calls for national unity, as it deepens the values of national, and human, brotherhood (Mahjub 1994, 14).

It is clear that Mahjub was speaking in a way that is consistent with the goal of such an interfaith event around the topic of citizenship, and in doing so, he put forth the position and rhetoric of the government.

In another such conference, in March 1999, also organized by CEOSS, a similar format was followed, with speakers addressing a particular theme. The title of this conference was "*Haqq al-ikhtalaf*," which can be correctly translated in either of two ways, "the right to differ" or "the right to be different," a subtle distinction of active or passive meaning. The former, the active voice of the verb, implies one's right to offer a different opinion; and the latter, with the passive voice of the verb, implies that a person has the right to be different in ways that are within one's control or beyond it. In this forum, the government representative was Fathi Naguib, the vice minister of justice, whose topic was "An Understanding of Right, and Its Relationship to Duty." He outlined sources of law from an Islamic perspective and described difference as "the nature of things. It is not my place to determine, in my difference with someone else, that my position is better. If I determine who places the boundaries on difference, this means that I have given supremacy to one person over another. It is incumbent upon us to surrender our differences and relegate them to negotiation and dialogue" (F. Naguib 1999, 19).

One of the questions Naguib was asked concerned the application of Islamic law to all of Egypt's citizens, Christian and Muslim. This topic has been one of considerable debate, especially since Egypt's Constitution refers to the *shari'a* as the source of Egyptian law. Naguib's response indicated Islam's universality and the relationship that exists between Islam and the other monotheistic religions (Judaism and Christianity).

> On the matter of the application of Islamic *shari'a* on non-Muslims, we must recognize that there is a great difference between the Islamic religion that is embodied in the Qur'an and Islamic culture and civilization. There is a big difference between the two. Religion is what obliges me, and not culture or civilization. If we look at religion correctly, we find that there is no difference with any other heavenly religion. The principles and foundations are one, established by God for all people. The sources of Islamic *shari'a* are divine, represented in the Qur'an and the *sunna* [customs of the Prophet]. As for the jurisprudence of Islamic *shari'a* that human *'ulama'* undertook to interpret in their own times and that are in our hands today, I say that, in the end, it is a human effort that has no attribution of sacredness. (F. Naguib 1999, 18)

This response also points to an important distinction between the divine will and thought, and possible human corruption of that will. Such a response would find the favor of Christian and Muslim alike, because it holds up the sovereignty and ultimacy of God, clearly noting that human actions and activities are not perfect. Thus, the vice minister put forth a perspective that posited God as supreme and human forms as imperfect, indirectly recognizing that social or political systems may be flawed but that the common God of all Egyptians is perfect. In its own way, this argument buttresses the efforts to foster national unity, even if the implementation of the *shari'a* upon all citizens was a controversial topic, and one that has been divisive. (The next chapter considers how official religion in Egypt has addressed this issue of application of the *shari'a*.)

At a conference in Alexandria in early 1997, titled "Religious Enlightenment," participants included religious and governmental officials, namely the grand imam of al-Azhar, the president of the Protestant community in Egypt, and the minister of religious endowments, Mahmud Zaqzuq. In the conference, which focused on ensuring that the activities of radical groups do not distort international understandings of Islam, Zaqzuq stated, "In Egypt, there is no distinction between us as Muslims and as Christians, as long as everyone fulfills his/her responsibilities to the nation" (Halwa and Nazmi, 1997.) Zaqzuq has appeared at a number of interfaith events and has continued to put forth a similar position of unity. Another example of the government's participation at such an event was Zaqzuq's congratulatory visit to St. Mark's Cathedral in Cairo, on the occasion of Christmas 1998. In the visit, Zaqzuq and the grand imam of al-Azhar visited Pope Shenouda and expressed that "fraternity between Muslims and Christians in Egypt is an exemplary fact. Fasting [which Orthodox Christians and Muslims both undertake at different times in their calendars] brings them together in a spirit of unity, love, feeling for each other, and friendship" (Halwa 1998).

In a similar kind of celebration of the type that is undertaken each year by Christian leaders to express feeling of goodwill toward Muslims, Pope Shenouda hosted an *iftar* (the meal by which the daily fast is broken during the month of Ramadan) in honor of the Muslim celebration of Ramadan in 1997. To it, the pope invited the mufti, the grand imam of al-Azhar, the general secretary of the Arab League, the minister of religious endowments, the speakers of both houses of Parliament, and the prime minister, a few of whom spoke. Two of the speakers represented the government. Fathi Surur, speaker of the People's Assembly, said, "We come together at this time each year in love, friendship, and sincerity, Muslims and Christians, at one table. All Egyptians have lived through many periods of struggle, in wonderful national unity. During Ramadan, the Muslim can sit with the Christian at the table, and the Christian can sit with the Muslim at the table" (Bishri 1998).

In his turn, Zaqzuq said, "The Egyptian people celebrate national unity throughout the length and breadth of the country. Egyptians have faced the outsider with the symbol of the crescent and the cross in the face of aggression . . . and this spirit has continued until today" (Bishri 1998).

Throughout such public meetings, the government representative has taken a proactive stance in talking about and fostering national unity. Perhaps one might argue that it is the nature of the setting, usually an interfaith gathering, in which one would expect the government to make such remarks, but certainly the government has not shied away from participation in such forums. In fact, the government has regularly made a point of participation in such events, so that it can have the opportunity to speak about national unity.

The "Reading for All" campaign, the use of television and specifically popular serials and religious programming, and statements issued by the Ministry of Religious Endowments give a picture of the government's attempts to promote national unity through public and popular forums. Such media reach a large portion of the population through literature, television, popular position booklets, and news coverage. These are significant media in the areas of opinion formation and discussion starters among the general population. Other ministries, in particular the Ministry of Education, and other forums likewise are influential channels of information. Studies of their influence have been carried out by independent NGOs such as the Ibn Khaldun Center for Development Studies, with less positive results (see chapter 6). The Ibn Khaldun Center has examined curricula and suggested steps for improvement. The normal workings of the executive branch through its ministries demonstrate a level of functionality blind to religious belief.

Representation in Parliament

In addition to an examination of the government's public campaign to foster national unity, a look at Parliament and the extent to which Christians are found in elected bodies can be informative. It is important to look at such representation, for not all members of Parliament are directly elected by voters. A small number of seats are reserved for presidential appointment. As a scholar of parliamentary composition describes the provision,

Since the Constitution affords the president of the republic the right to appoint ten members to the People's Assembly, President Sadat and President Mubarak after him have used the provision to appoint qualified people, intelligentsia and learned people. The practice of ensuring equitable representation of women and Christians has been respected in order to recover a balance in representation of these two groups in the People's Assembly. ('Abd Allah 1998, 149)

In a Parliament of 444 seats, a small number of those are reserved for the president to make appointment he feels are necessary and in the interest of the country. It is therefore worth examining how the president has used this stipulation to address the question of balance between Muslim and Christian representation. It is important to point out that Copts historically have rejected a legal requirement to ensure balanced (i.e., proportional) representation in Parliament through designated quotas of seats, for the simple reason that Christians have not felt that they are a distinct part of the overall Egyptian population.

The table below summarizes the Coptic representation in the People's Assembly from 1984 to 2005.

While the number of Copts in Parliament steadily diminished over the period of these six elections, with the exception of 2000, when NDP

Table.

Coptic Representation in the People's Assembly, 1984–2005

Year	Copts in Parliament	Number elected	Number appointed
1984	11	6	5
1987	10	6	4
1990	7	1	6
1995	6	0	6
2000	7	3	4
2005	6	1	5

Source: 1984–95 figures from 'Abd Allah (1998, 131); 2000 figures from Egypt Human Rights Report (2001); 2005 figures from United Nations Development Programme (n.d.).

leadership actively campaigned for the Christian candidate over an Is-lamist opponent (according to Harb), the decrease in the number of Copts elected has happened at a much faster rate. In other words, while voters have been less likely to vote for Christian candidates, presidential appoint-ments have maintained a Christian presence in the People's Assembly. This pattern has continued to the present. One might therefore argue that the president has been very careful to ensure a Christian presence in Par-liament and has used his office to keep that number up.

It is interesting to note that an overwhelming majority, but not all, of presidentially appointed Christians have been members of the National Democratic Party—the governing party and that of the president—and none has been a member of the Wafd Party, traditionally the strongest opposition party and the party that has attracted a number of Christians over the years. In 1984, of the five appointed, four were members of the NDP and one was a member of the opposition Tagammu' Party ('Abd Allah 1998, 137); in 1987, three were from the NDP and the fourth was independent (138); in 1990, all except one, an independent, were from the NDP (140); and in 1995, all were from the NDP (142).

The lack of Coptic representation has been a source of debate and con-sternation. Some Christians have argued that, because the path to success in parliamentary politics is ultimately blocked, Christians have been less and less encouraged to follow that path, preferring to concentrate in areas where they are able to advance. In this sense, the argument goes, Christians are keen to pursue possible opportunities and, being wise enough to identify areas where advancement is more sure, are less willing to engage in parlia-mentary politics. This approach, however, does not bode well for the future of Christians in government for, if success is not easy, then no struggle to change the status quo would result. With no struggle, nothing will change. On the other hand, sectarian politics may not be the approach to take; par-ticipation in secular politics may be a more helpful channel (see chapter 5).

Conclusions

Throughout the Mubarak years, the government has clearly attempted to portray religion in a positive light, and to do that with regard to both Christianity and Islam. The administration, through various channels, has made a pronounced effort to maintain, and indeed strengthen, national unity, despite several divisive incidents, including two tragic episodes in the village of al-Kusheh in Upper Egypt (see chapter 7). Nonetheless, the Mubarak government has devoted significant energy to the national unity campaign and to highlighting the Egyptian school of identity in fostering a common narrative.

Sectarian conflict has continued to exist, both in rural and urban settings, yet the government has attempted to crack down on militant movements by making random and mass arrests in districts suspected of having high militant concentrations. According to one report, "Since 1992, 920 people have been killed in political violence, mostly Egyptian Christians, Government officials and police personnel, but also scores of Islamic militants. The Government campaign to crush the terrorism put an estimated 26,000 armed militants in jail, dozens of whom have been sentenced to death" (Y. Ibrahim 1996, A13).

Sectarian conflict, then, has continued to be a serious problem in Egypt during the Mubarak administration. Constitutionally, the definition of Egypt as an Islamic country has not changed, and the *shari'a* remains the principal basis for law. Socially, the Mubarak administration has been more open to Christian institutions than Sadat: there has not been tension between the state and the church. Christians have also benefited from the government's fight against extreme Islam. In his assessment of the first ten years of Mubarak's presidency with regard to interfaith social relations, Anwar Muhammad writes,

> We are moving in the direction of improvement for a number of reasons, among them a welcoming by the president so that he is open to the majority and the minority, and the opening of lines of direct communication with both of them to the same degree. President Mubarak has confirmed this since the beginning of his term. . . . Among the distinguishing aspects of the Mubarak era, also, has been an increase in the spirit of tolerance the source of which is the allowance of more freedoms than in any previous time. (Muhammad 1993, 30)

One might say that religious freedom has continued to be respected, even in the midst of emergency laws that have been used to continue to arrest those suspected of involvement in radical movements, among other purposes. As the reform process shows some signs of hope, and calls become more vocal for the revocation of the emergency laws, there is great concern among some, perhaps many, Christians that such an action would endanger their social place. Without the protection from Islamists the emergency laws provide, they argue, their future would be bleak. This is part of the reason some Christians are not enthusiastic about the possibility of political reform as proposed by Mubarak. There can be no question, though, that the Mubarak government has exerted extensive efforts to maintain and foster national unity between Egypt's Muslims and Christians.

4

Institutional Religion and the Pursuit of National Unity

> Lo! those who believe (in that which is revealed unto
> thee, Muhammad), and those who are Jews, and
> Christians, and Sabeans—whoever believeth in Allah
> and the Last Day and doeth right—surely their reward is
> with their Lord, and there shall no fear come upon them
> neither shall they grieve.
>
> Qur'an 2:62

Having looked at the Mubarak administration's rhetoric and approach to relations between Christians and Muslims in Egypt, it is appropriate to move from the government's position and role toward sectors more closely associated with civil society. To move from government and enter the realm of official religion requires the qualification that the shift is, in some respects, gradual, and in others, a marked leap.

Religious leadership, as Scott Appleby (2000, 55) claims, has an important role in addressing tension and potential conflict: "Hierarchs, sages, theologians, moralists, jurists, rabbis, mullahs, and priests, each in their own realm of authority, guide an ongoing, organic interpretive process: they correlate the contemporary experiences of the community with the hallowed symbols and stories of religious tradition."

Beyond that, as David Smock (2002, 7) asserts, "High-level religious leaders can be convened to speak collectively as advocates for peace. The focus is joint action on behalf of peace. This can be particularly effective where religious divisions are among the sources of societal division and conflict."

Those most visibly placed to offer this guidance are the selected leadership of the respective communities. This chapter examines the attitudes and activities that have contributed to interaction and cooperation among the institutions of religion in Egypt, specifically the Islamic institutions of Dar al-Ifta' and al-Azhar and the three principal Christian churches (Coptic Orthodox, Coptic Evangelical, and, to a lesser extent, Coptic Catholic).

Al-Azhar and Dar al-Ifta'

This particular sector of society may be appropriately termed Egypt's "official" religion. In many minds, there is only a fine line, if any at all, between the Islamic institutions of Dar al-Ifta' and al-Azhar and the government itself. When the current head of al-Azhar (the *shaikh al-Azhar*) was named, an article in the semiofficial newspaper *al-Ahram* read, "President Hosni Mubarak yesterday issued an official decree appointing Dr. Muhammad Sayyid Tantawi Shaikh al-Azhar" (*al-Ahram* 1996). This quote points to serious questions about the independence of the institution. Indeed, both al-Azhar and Dar al-Ifta' may be considered governmental institutions.

The twentieth-century roots of the connection between the government and al-Azhar are as recent as the period following the Free Officers' revolution of 1952. During Nasir's presidency, religion as an opposing ideology to the government was completely disallowed, leading to the imprisonment of a number of Muslim Brothers, including its founder, Hassan al-Banna. The role that al-Azhar played as a symbol of Islamic learning and tradition made its desired relationship to the revolutionary power nonadversarial. The government hoped that al-Azhar would become a firm supporter of the Free Officers' movement and used the pretext of the diminishing success of Azhari graduates in finding jobs to "absorb . . . the religious hierarchy into the revolutionary system by bringing to an end the semi-independent position of al-Azhar itself" (Crecelius 1966, 36). A major reform of al-Azhar, including the introduction of a full-scale university that could compete with the other national universities, took place in June 1961, with the National Assembly's "new law [that] totally integrates the religious system of education with the government system. In a word, al-Azhar has been 'nationalized'" (Crecelius 1966, 44). The legislation established the Supreme Council of al-Azhar, with the *shaikh al-Azhar* as chairman but with a limited role; the Muslim Research Academy; the Muslim Culture and Missions Department; al-Azhar University; and al-Azhar Institutes. *Shaikh al-Azhar*, while playing less of an administrative role at al-Azhar, exerts influence "derived from his personal reputation as a pious leader or 'knower' of Islam" (Crecelius 1966, 45). This final expression of the *shaikh*'s legitimacy with respect to his religious role is essential to the continued role of leadership he plays throughout Egypt and the Muslim world.

A similar debate runs with relation to Dar al-Ifta', established in 1895 and charged with issuing *fatawa*, or binding interpretations on Islamic law (which can also be issued by al-Azhar and certain committees within the Ministry of Religious Endowments). The main point of contention as to whether Dar al-Ifta' is a religious institution or a political one is the fact that it has an affiliation with the Ministry of Justice. The *mufti*, or head of the institution, is, like *shaikh al-Azhar*, appointed by the president of the republic (Khattab 2000, 68). The 1961 reforms were indeed important, and, as Zeghal (1999, 375) asserts, they "granted the ulema a 'profession' whose function was to confer religious legitimacy on the regime's political decisions and policy implementations, and whose returns were government salaries and civil-servant status."

While the *'ulama'* became government employees, the fact remains, however, that there have been cases of tension between the government and these religious authorities, and in most cases as a result of the presence of the Islamic movements of the late twentieth century. This tension frequently has been characterized by rifts within Azhari ranks, exemplifying the fact that al-Azhar's government status does not result in monolithic opinion among leadership. For example, Zeghal writes,

> While Mubarak's regime clearly associated al-Azhar with its anti-Islamic campaign, some ulema refused to participate in this enterprise. While al-Azhar was officially supporting the regime in its campaigns against violent political Islam, . . . other ulema explicitly withdrew from the bulk of al-Azhar's political tendencies. . . . [L]esser official shaykhs . . . were from the periphery of al-Azhar: educated in

the Azharite institution, they did not have important positions as civil servants, but specialized in preaching. . . . Even though they never lost their Azharite status and identity, the public never perceived them as supporting the official ulema at the top of al-Azhar's administration. Therefore, in the mid-1980s, a periphery set itself apart from the center of the Azharite institutions.

The periphery is much more diversified politically. Peripheral ulema usually belong to Islamic associations that specialize in the *da'wa* [and] . . . generally show affinities with the ideology of the Muslim Brothers, but they are scattered throughout the structure of the religious institutions and are not sociologically homogeneous. (Zeghal 1999, 385–86)

Among those Azharis who have publicly expressed opinions in contradiction with the official government policy are *shaikh al-Azhar* 'Abd al-Halim Mahmud, who in the 1970s called for the transformation of the legal system at a time when Sadat was not supportive of the idea; Shaykhs Kishk, Mahallawi, and Salah Abu Isma'il, who did not participate in a government campaign to engage in dialogue at the local level with Islamist youth; Shaikh 'Atiyya Saqr, who demanded the implementation by Parliament of the *shari'a* in 1984; and, perhaps most notably, Shaikh 'Umar 'Abd ar-Rahman, who has been accused and sentenced for inspiring *al-jama'a al-islamiyya* (Islamic groups; Zeghal 1999, 383, 386, 389). These persons are all Azharis, and to varying degrees they represent the institution's official stances. If Zeghal's argument is accepted, then even if they have moved to the periphery, their public association with al-Azhar has not been broken. Al-Azhar, therefore, can be said to carry the official government line while some of its "representatives" are in disagreement with the government, or are even closely affiliated with a very extreme brand of Islam. Great diversity thus exists.

Even as criticism of the positions of the institutions of religion is launched from the inside, so is it launched from without, from the Muslim community in Egypt. Criticism can come from many directions, including more extreme elements. This criticism is not an expression of anticlerical sentiment; rather, it is a criticism of the positions the official religious institutions take because they are so closely associated with the government. Criticism therefore is of the government indirectly (or directly, as some would argue) and of the institutions for abandoning orthodox religion in capitulation to the state, its needs, and its interests. As Mohammed Abu-Nimr puts it,

> Official religious leadership is being used as a tool to maintain the status quo and prevent political and social change. In many cases, the mainstream religious leadership is called upon by the political elite to intervene on behalf of the regime to rally the masses and establish support for certain policies . One of the consequences of this alliance has been the emergence of radical Islamist political groups who utilize religion to call for rebellion against political oppression and poverty. (Abu-Nimr 2003, 114)

Such an alliance, and such a response, can be demonstrated in Egypt today.

Despite the very close connection between the government, al-Azhar, and Dar al-Ifta', the latter are perhaps the best representations of authentic institutionalized Islam at the highest level in Egypt, since their leadership is made up of religious professionals rather than career government employees. This ensures to a great extent that the institutions represent religion, even if they are arms of the government. It is in this regard that a distinction can be made between al-Azhar and Dar al-Ifta', on the one hand, and the Ministry of Religious Endowments on the other. Even though they are inherently linked, the ministry is a clear part of the governmental structure, with the minister a member of the president's cabinet.

Al-Azhar and Dar al-Ifta' have disagreed over certain issues more publicly than the tightly defined modes of expression permissible within the government, rendering contrary opinions on a variety of matters ranging from the propriety of organ donation in Islam, the definition of *riba* (concerning usury or interest in lending and banking) in modern-day practice, and female genital mutilation to the permissibility of visiting Jerusalem (Khattab 2000, 68). Such open debates can take place between and within the two institutions—and be witnessed by the public—in a way that other parts of the governmental structure would be unlikely to tolerate. Dissension within these institutions certainly exists. The leaders of al-Azhar in particular have taken positions not always moderate or in line with those of the government. Beyond that, and even when such leadership is in place, the institution itself has been marked by intramural ideological struggle.

For all of these reasons, this discussion treats al-Azhar and Dar al-Ifta' as official religious institutions, as opposed to official governmental institutions, recognizing that such a clear distinction is problematic, for reasons already elaborated.

Christian Leadership

On the Christian side of the equation, there is likely to be less criticism of the characterization of the institutions of the Coptic Orthodox Church and its pope, the Coptic Catholic Church and its patriarch, and the community of the Egyptian Protestant churches and their president as the segments of official religion. None of these institutions is influenced directly by government appointment or intervention. The tension and even conflict between the Coptic Orthodox Church and the government is well documented (see the discussion of the rift between President Sadat and Pope Shenouda III in chapter 3). The Catholic Church is virtually independent as well. With respect to the Protestant churches, the president of the community of the sixteen denominations recognized by the government is the elected representative of those denominations; he voices their concerns at the levels of national and local government, and in society at large.

The most important forum for the relationship between the Coptic Orthodox Church and the state has long been the Lay Council (*al-Majlis al-Milli*). The council was founded in 1872, and Khedive Ismail took responsibility for its leadership in 1874. Its by-laws state that it is responsible for the supervision of internal church matters, of property, schools, and monasteries, and of accounts. They also stipulate that the personal status of Egypt's Christians is to be handled by the Coptic Personal Status Court (S. Ibrahim 1996a, 14). Tension between the council and the Pope has marked the history of the relationship, and it can be demonstrated that the patriarchs have used the council for their benefit and ignored, or even dissolved, the council when they have perceived it as less useful. Generally speaking, the church has remained virtually independent from the state. All churches, though, remain subject to the Ottoman Hamayouni Decree (see chapter 3), which characterizes the nature of the church, its members, and its properties with respect to national legislation.

Relations between Christians and the state—and between Christians and the society at large—are highly complex, historically as well as currently. In different periods of Egyptian history, the state has represented a particular religion. In Byzantine times, the ruling class was Greek Orthodox; in later Islamic times, the regime variously represented Islam in an official capacity, related to official Islam closely, or adhered to it. In virtually all cases, Egyptian Christians have been outside the ruling strata. One factor in the tense relationship between Sadat and Pope Shenouda was the issue of a Christian state within a state. A second factor has been the presence of a well-organized expatriate community and the role its members have played in lobbying the governments in their various new homes (e.g., the United States, the United Kingdom, and Australia) to keep the issue of Egypt's treatment of resident Christians in the forefront of foreign policy initiatives. A third factor is a disproportionate emphasis on sectarianism when reporting stories of conflict in Egypt. Such reporting, both inside and outside of Egypt, reduces problems of differing levels of complexity to a simple formula and can damage Christian-Muslim relations within Egypt. Finally, the associations in the minds of some Muslims first between Egypt's Christians and Western, mostly Christian countries and their policies, and second, between Egyptian Christians and the activities of Christian missionaries working openly to convert Egyptians to Christianity, have been damaging for Egyptian Christians. All of these factors make the public engagement of the Christian and Muslim leadership in Egypt all the more important. (Of course, critics of al-Azhar and Dar al-Ifta' as government agencies incorporate these problematic factors in their critique of the government as dependent on outside forces and beholden to them.)

Consideration of these factors enhances understanding of the nature of relations among the official religious institutions. Through their involvement and representation, the leaders play a crucial role, and their words and actions indicate a spirit of respect and cooperation between Islamic and Christian institutions in Egypt. Beginning with the Islamic institutions and focusing primarily on the person of Muhammad Sayyid Tantawi—who served as mufti of Egypt from 1986 to 1996 and as grand imam, or *shaikh,* of al-Azhar since then—this chapter examines the stated positions of such leadership with regard to the Other. Examining the Christian institutions in turn, the chapter focuses mainly on the Coptic Orthodox Church—the largest of the three church families—and its pope and patriarch, Shenouda III. However, it also looks at the Protestant churches, treated as a group under Samuel Habib (who served as president of the Protestant community from 1980 until he died in 1997), and at the Coptic Catholic Church and one of its seven diocesan bishops, Yuhanna Qolta. Of course, it is difficult to treat each one separately, since their frequent cooperation and expression of positions on common occasions mean that there necessarily is overlap and intermingling.

Official Relationships from an Islamic Viewpoint

It is easy to find examples of Egyptian Muslim religious officials who have, since the 1990s, expressed fraternal feelings with Egypt's non-Muslims. One of the most prominent and outspoken figures in the attempt to foster better relations with Christians has been Muhammad Sayyid Tantawi, who served as grand mufti of Egypt for the important ten-year period starting in the mid-1980s (1986) when sectarian tension and conflict began to re-emerge on the social scene in Egypt, after four years of relative calm at the beginning of Mubarak's presidency. Severe repression of religious movements by the regime meant that the threat had not dissipated (Zeghal 1999, 385). Through harsh measures imposed during early days of the Mubarak administration, the government attempted to ensure that religion and religious strife would not be the source of serious problems.

Muhammad Sayyid Tantawi was named grand imam of al-Azhar when Shaikh Jad al-Haq 'Ali Jad al-Haq died in 1996, a man with whom Tantawi had often sparred publicly on religious matters and who had been appointed by Mubarak in March 1982 as someone who would be supportive of the regime (Zeghal 1999, 385). Born in 1928 in the governorate of Suhaj, Tantawi is a graduate of al-Azhar and served as an instructor and professor in *kuliyat usul ad-din,* the equivalent of a seminary; he has written books on various topics, including *Israel in the Holy Qur'an and Sunna.*

Perhaps his appointment as mufti was intentionally strategic in this regard, as a moderate Islamic voice who would perhaps offset more vocal voices of Islam who also enjoyed degrees of legitimacy in Egypt, Shaikh Jad al-Haq and the popular shaikh Muhammad Mitwalli ash-Sha'arawi. The latter was especially popular because of his daily television "class" in which he interpreted the Qur'an for a group of students among whom he sat, and for the larger national television audience. Sha'arawi was known for his stricter interpretation of the Qur'an, and with respect to the treatment of non-Muslims. While he spoke of equality in rights and responsibilities, he qualified that equality by his outspoken support of the imperative that Copts pay the *jizya,* a kind of tax paid by non-Muslims in the Muslim community to retain their protected status as *ahl adh-dhimma* (Muhammad 1993, 92–93). This kind of ordering of status was an interpretation and implementation of the *shari'a* that had contributed to sectarian strife in Egypt over the course of centuries. One researcher of the relationship between Christians and Muslims in Egypt confirms this analysis of the implementation of the *shari'a,* exemplified by the imposition of the *jizya:*

> In the case under discussion, only a rigorous distinction between the Shari'ah and Islamic law can contribute to [universalist, egalitarian aspirations]; for it is only a Shari'ah systematically stripped, as a result of historical and functional analysis, of all discriminatory references contained in the classic law which was developed with the express aim of assuring the spiritual and political supremacy of the Muslim community, which could serve to bring about the two-fold aim of cultural authenticity and national unity. (Kramer 1998, 44)

Kramer's statement is a bold call by a non-Muslim and a non-Egyptian, but the basic idea has been espoused and expressed clearly by Tantawi. For example, in a case over divorce within the Christian community, where one of the spouses changed affiliation from one church to another in order to divorce, proposed legislation held that changing one's denominational or ecclesial familial affiliation would invoke the application of the *shari'a*. Tantawi and al-Azhar refused to apply the *shari'a* to Copts (U. Salama 1997, 72).

On a separate occasion in 2000, a revision of the personal status laws in Egypt was the primary topic of discussion, not only in Parliament but also in the newspapers and among the people. When asked whether the personal status laws that were being considered and debated in Parliament would be applicable to Christians, Tantawi explained that the project was meant to combine more than five hundred single laws into a single law with about seventy sections. The revision, or consolidation, of these laws was to be based on *shari'a*, which would be consistent with the Egyptian Constitution (which states that Egyptian law is to have the *shari'a* as a source). He went on to express his opinion that the effort to unify all the fragments of law was worthy, and it was particularly important as it would result in giving women rights they previously had not enjoyed (such as the right to divorce without their husband's permission, and the right to travel without first gaining approval from their father, brother, or husband). Tantawi went on to say that passing the personal status law did not mean that the *shari'a* would be applied in the cases of non-Muslims; rather, personal status would continue to be determined juridically by the faith affiliation of the parties involved in a case (Tantawi 2000).

These cases demonstrate a regard for the rights of Christians that supercedes a strict legalistic interpretation of *shari'a*. Despite criticism, Tantawi has remained steadfast in his call for good relations between Egypt's Muslims and Christians, and among all people generally. In a public lecture on human rights in Islam, Tantawi seized the opportunity to expound upon that position: "God has endowed mankind with many rights, the most important being the right to life and the right to live honorably and in security. . . . According to Islam, every human being, regardless of creed, is entitled to this right as long as they have not committed any crime" (*AUC Today* 1998, 14).

In terms of a religious basis for interfaith dialogue, Tantawi sees that dialogue is based upon common *fada'il* (virtues), such as assisting the poor and rescuing the oppressed. Islam shares these virtues with other faiths, including Christianity, and they provide a sound basis for mutual understanding and action (Tantawi 2000). Tantawi has backed up that position during his consecutive tenures at Dar al-Ifta' and al-Azhar. As grand mufti, he was the first Muslim clergyman to speak publicly in an Evangelical (Protestant) church in the history of the Evangelical (Presbyterian) Church of Egypt. The opportunity came at a public meeting in November 1992, hosted by the Evangelical Church of Heliopolis in Cairo, at which Tantawi and Samuel Habib joined the pastor of the church and a Muslim attorney to speak on the topic, "Religious Thought and Social Advancement." The forum was designed as an opportunity to "redraft national thought, knowledge, and art, everything that has value for humanity and for human dignity" (M. Naguib 1994, 92–93). Tantawi was the first to speak and was well received. While diverging from the main topic of the meeting, the mufti concentrated heavily upon the roots of good relations between Christianity and Islam: "We all know that all of the heavenly religions call for building and not destruction; for coming closer together and not separation; for fraternity and not rebellion; for love and not hatred. All of the heavenly religions call for these things. They call for humanity to live with open hearts, clean hearts. . . . The heavenly religions were revealed for the sake of cooperation, and not to fight" (Tantawi 1994, 9–10).

In his remarks, Tantawi stated that there are three groups of non-Muslims: "those who are at war with us; those who do not live with us in a single nation, but who live in Europe, Africa, or America, and thus do not bother us and we do not bother them; and those non-Muslims who have their beliefs and who live with us in the same nation" (Tantawi 1994, 13).

It is the third category that was of particular concern for Tantawi, in terms of citizenship. He stated,

> In regard to citizenship, we are all equal. There is no preference for the Muslim over the Christian, and there is no preference of the Christian over the Muslim. We all have the same rights and responsibilities. We all must carry out our responsibilities before claiming our rights. . . . There is no difference between one and the other. . . . It is on this basis that we meet all together. We do not know hypocrisy, lies, or hatred. (Tantawi 1994, 14)

The spirit of dialogue around national themes continued the next year when Tantawi again participated in a public symposium, again at an

Evangelical church, this time in the center of Cairo, the Qasr ad-Dubara Evangelical Church. The topic was "Religious Thought and Social Participation," and the symposium brought together several Christian and Muslim clergy and thinkers. Tantawi again had the opportunity to speak first. He outlined the "true" Islamic perspective on participation by saying that religion leads humanity to work for a dignified life for all, giving life importance. Religion penetrates hearts and leads people to worship God, so that they recognize and aim for the joy of the afterlife in everything they do. Religion thus contributes to the attainment of right and justice.

> All goodness that Egypt enjoys is enjoyed by all of us: peace and security. All who carry Egyptian citizenship are equal, be they Muslim or Christian, equal in rights and responsibilities. The heavenly religions all call for fairness, in word, in deed, in judgment, and in witness. Fairness with those we love and those we do not love. Those who understand religion correctly reject oppression and fight its sources. They stand on the side of right and justice, on the side of all those who raise up the cause of our nation. (Tantawi 1995, 11–14)

This strand of the national cause—that is, unity among its religious communities—runs through much of what Tantawi said and did as mufti.

In addition to appearing with Christian leaders at public symposia such as this, Tantawi has been the honored guest at several *iftar* celebrations hosted by Christian leaders during the months of Ramadan, during his tenure as mufti and now as grand imam of al-Azhar. A further important expression of religious unity that marked his term as mufti was a trip to the United States, where he and Habib received honorary doctorates in peacemaking at Westminster College in New Wilmington, Pennsylvania. The honorary doctorates in themselves were an expression of "the peace that brings Christian and Muslim together" (S. Habib 1995b, 4), and the honorees received letters of appreciation from the governor and the state legislature of Pennsylvania. During the visit, the mufti and Habib had the opportunity to meet a number of Christian and Muslim leaders in the United States, as well as the vice president. The purpose of the trip, according to Tantawi, was "to state clearly the spirit of love, harmony, and peace that has linked Muslims and Christians in Egypt since long ago, and to correct the blurred picture of Islam that has resulted from the actions of some lost groups who have resorted to terrorism, something no religion supports" (*al-Akbar* 1995).

During the visit, the mufti repeatedly made reference to the idea that "Muslims and Christians are bound by honest fraternity, sincere love, and cooperation for the sake of our religion and for the sake of our country" (*al-Akhbar* 1995). The trip was certainly a statement of Christian-Muslim cooperation, as well as recognition of the work of two leaders for the sake of their faiths and their countries. One of the questions raised in the article about the trip was "What now, after the mufti and Rev. Samuel Habib speak one language in America?" (Ragab 1995). Components of the answer can be found in the role that Tantawi has played since 1996 as grand imam of al-Azhar.

Almost from the start of his tenure as grand imam, Tantawi has stressed the importance of dialogue and good relations between Egypt's Christians and Muslims, as he continues to participate actively with Christian leaders, including Pope Shenouda. Early 1997 marked the controversy between official religion and the Muslim Brotherhood. Specifically, debate emerged over the assessment of the *jizya* with respect to Copts. It was in that context that Grand Imam Tantawi and Grand Mufti Nasr Farid Wasil stated that the *jizya* was not to be assessed. As Tantawi put it, "They have the same rights and responsibilities that we have. Copts pay the same [state] taxes that Muslims pay, and serve in the army just as Muslims serve" (Rashid 1997). Grand Mufti Wasil felt that those who called for the *jizya* to be assessed only desired there to be a *fitna*, or sectarian crisis, between Muslims and Christians, and, in his words, "*Fitna* is worse than murder" (Rashid 1997). Here was an example of the two major Islamic authorities in Egypt coming together in support of national unity. Some question remains as to whether their opinions were spurred by the administration's desire to reduce sectarian conflict, or by legitimate *ijtihad al-maraja'* (interpretation of the sources of law). In the case of Tantawi, the opinion is eminently consistent with his previously stated positions.

Tantawi's interfaith activities continue, and his participation in events hosted by the Evangelical church has not decreased since the death of Habib in October 1997, a clear iteration that, while their personal relationship and friendship was important and may have made his entry into the Protestant community more comfortable, it was not the principal reason for Tantawi's commitment to such occasions. In Port Said, in December 1997, Tantawi participated in an interreligious forum in which Pope Shenouda also participated, arranged by the Coptic Evangelical Organization for Social Services, which Habib founded. In that forum, Tantawi stated, "Difference in religious belief does not give birth to fear, but to cooperation. The matter is not the difference between religious beliefs, but in the difference in mindsets. Reasonable people establish fraternal relations between themselves despite differences in religious beliefs. Foolish people are the ones who irrationally categorize humanity on the basis of religious fanaticism" (Halwa and Musa 1997).

As grand imam of al-Azhar, his relationship with the Coptic Orthodox Church has deepened. The strength of the relationship was manifested at a very sensitive time when a group of German tourists was killed in Luxor in 1997 by an Islamic group. In response to that tragedy, the grand imam and the pope held a joint seminar on the religious position with regard to terrorism. Here, the two religious officials lined up to criticize those who commit such "crimes" as being outside of religion, and to say that they are not religious groups but rather simply criminals (Yunis 1997). This kind of statement played well in the national press, as it reinforced the administration's position, supported by prominent leaders of religious communities in Egypt. The seminar was highlighted on the first page of the semiofficial newspaper *al-Ahram*.

Al-Azhar and International Interreligious Relations

One activity in which al-Azhar has been involved that goes beyond national unity, or issues of particularly Egyptian Christian-Muslim relations, is its relationship with the Vatican. It seems natural that, in the realm of official religion, these two institutions engage in dialogue, as they represent the authority of the Roman Catholic Church and a quite legitimate historical authority in Islam. Negotiations between the Vatican and al-Azhar resulted in the formation of a Christian-Muslim committee to fight religious fanaticism and terrorism. The committee was hailed as the first of its kind in history (*ash-Sharq* 1998). The committee and the negotiations that led up to its formation were the outcome of a recommendation from a conference held at the Sorbonne in 1994, at which al-Azhar and the Vatican were represented. The recommendation named "the necessity of increased cooperation among all parties in order to maintain peace, defend moral and human values, and deepen the dialogue between religions" (Tantawi 1997). The next step was the establishment of a permanent liaison committee on dialogue, which stated its purposes as follows: (1) to clarify the meaning of dialogue; (2) to discuss issues of common importance; and (3) to increase awareness between Christians and Muslims through exchange of information and publications (Tantawi 1997).

The outcome of the process has been discussion on various themes, including that of religious fanaticism. A further example is a dialogue on human rights, the rights and obligations of citizenship, cooperation between Christian and Islamic institutions in the provision of humanitarian services, and the protection of people from the dangers of violent conflict (al-'Adas 2000, 38). The relationship between al-Azhar and Christianity, then, has extended beyond official Christian leadership in Egypt to the world at large, an indication of the seriousness with which al-Azhar has considered relations with Christians. Not only are good relations consistent with the Mubarak administration's priority, but they are also expressed in terms of the essence of Islam and its responsibility to foster better relations with non-Muslims.

Coptic Catholics

In contrast to the immense following of the Roman Catholic Church throughout the world, the Coptic Catholic Church in Egypt (an Eastern-rite Catholic church with its own patriarch) is the smallest of the three ecclesial families in Egypt. Despite the fact that the Jesuits were among the first missionaries in Egypt, coming in the fifteenth century, and that there is still a Jesuit presence, the church's parishioners are estimated between 200,000 and 500,000. In the area of relations with Muslims, Bishop Yuhanna Qolta has been significantly visible, even though he does not have the status of the patriarch, Stephanous II Ghattas. Bishop Qolta speaks with the authority of the Catholic Church, however, and has participated in interfaith dialogue seminars and symposia. He has expressed some controversial thoughts. His analysis of the situation of Christianity in Egypt with respect to Islam is astute.

In Bishop Qolta's view, social relations in Egypt have suffered because of several factors, including the kind of oppression to which all members of society have been subject, notably the presence and activities of extremist Islam; the authority that religious leaders carry and the deference that people demonstrate toward them; and the system of the state bureaucracy. Within the Christian community, these factors have inhibited the ability of believers to discover the true nature of their faith. Bishop Qolta has expressed that the minority Christian population feels oppression (which is faith-neutral) and frustration. As a result, Christians blame the dominant Muslim community for their inability to advance socially or fully express their own selves. This blame, in turn, inhibits the possibility of sincere, open, and positive relations and causes rifts or crises not only with Muslims but among Christian denominations that only grow. In Bishop Qolta's view, Egypt's Christian denominations and families are so eager to find fault with one another's theology or religious practice that there is little opportunity for positive and productive cooperation, a state of affairs that endangers the future of Christianity in Egypt. For the Christian presence to remain viable in Egypt in all its manifestations, he argues, this lack of Christian unity must somehow be rectified. Because of disunity or lack of fraternity among Christians, Christian-Muslim projects and initiatives have had a better chance of succeeding, because they put people in a position of less challenge or vulnerability with respect to those with whom they cooperate or work (Qolta 2000).

Qolta was able to advocate a conciliatory approach during the September 2006 crisis caused by Pope Benedict XVI's comments regarding the prophet Muhammad. Pope Benedict cited a fourteenth-century statement by Byzantine emperor Manuel II Palaeologos, who wrote that the prophet Muhammed brought "things only evil and inhuman." Many Muslims interpreted the remarks as particularly critical of the Prophet and Islam. Bishop Qolta, who might be expected to offer some sort of explicatory defense of the pope, stated immediately, "Pope Benedict has not dealt enough with Muslims all through his life and does not have enough knowledge about Islam and Muslims. . . . The pontiff's words have surprised the Catholics in Egypt and the whole East, as a point of fact." Qolta went on to offer a warning that such rhetoric would incite Muslims against Christians (Fathy 2006). Such an approach indicates Qolta's context of living with Muslims, his effort to seek better relations, and his understanding of how such remarks might impact Christian-Muslim relations in Egypt, and indeed beyond. His remarks, available to all on the Internet, may have helped to reduce tensions in Egypt.

Coptic Orthodox

The largest church in Egypt is the Coptic Orthodox Church. Pope Shenouda III is its current pope and patriarch, and his relationship with President Mubarak has been significantly better than it was with Sadat, who, near the end of Sadat's presidency and life, imposed upon Shenouda a kind of house arrest. There is little question that Pope Shenouda not only has served as the leader of his religious community but also has played an important political role. Some of his writings assert that politics and religion not only complement each other but cannot be separate. For example, he writes that "on the one hand, we cannot say that there is no religion in politics, unless politics is atheistic. Politicians should be people of faith. . . . There are matters from which the clergy cannot exclude themselves, unless religion is considered merely worship, that it does not have a stake in all of social intercourse" (R. Habib 1990, 54–55).

Pope Shenouda has naturally played a very visible role in national affairs, particularly with regard to religious matters. There is criticism of such official religious leaders putting on a face of unity when come together to express a view or react to incidents—such as the joint reaction of Tantawi and Pope Shenouda to the massacre at Luxor. Criticisms include claims that these kinds of joint appearances attempt to mask an underlying problem in Egyptian society with nice pronouncements and photo opportunities; that nonsectarian explanations of conflict deflect from the question of religion, which apparently plays at least some role; that such official religious representatives live a lifestyle removed from that of the people, and therefore they cannot understand the travails of those experiencing conflict; and that the very nature of their positions (including their relationships with the government) requires visible signs of reconciliation and forgiveness. Even so, there can be no question that such appearances and statements do carry weight with those who hear them, at least to generate discussion and to show unity of purpose from a religious point of view.

In an effort to examine more closely the views of Pope Shenouda and thus the official positions of the Coptic Orthodox Church with respect to Islam, religious cooperation, and religious strife in Egypt, the pope's public positions are informative. Acknowledging the religious awakening in Egypt over the past few decades, Pope Shenouda has expressed that he is not worried about increased religiosity among Egypt's Muslims. In fact,

> I feel comforted by it, because Christians feel at ease when they interact with pious Muslims who know the essence of their faith. Religion protects people from wrongdoing, deviation, or evil. Instead, I worry about the violence that appears for social reasons, occasionally motivated by external forces, that attempt to put on a religious appearance and name it Islam. I know very well that Islam is as far as far is from oppression and terrorism. (al-Banna 1998, 137)

Pope Shenouda therefore has presented a publicly conciliatory and favorable opinion of Islam, expressed in an article he wrote, "The Qur'an and Christianity" (quoted in al-Banna 1998, 372–80), in which he showed a positive perspective of Christianity in Islam.

Continuing on the idea of crime and violence in the name of Islam by *al-jama'at islamiyya*, Pope Shenouda addresses that idea again, with particular reference to the people involved:

> I do not call them "Islamic groups" but "extremist groups." Those who killed Dr. Rifa'at al-Mahgoub [Speaker of the parliament, killed in autumn 1994] transgressed the Muslim character. Extremism is aggressive against everyone, and the extremists have no religion because no religion obliges killing or violence. No religion calls for violations of the sanctity of holy places. We are sure that the perpetrators of these crimes are professional criminals and murderers.
>
> Terrorism is a danger for all of society. The Church does not have a position different from that of Egyptian society, which condemns all

faces of terrorism. As for unity among Egyptians, we are not afraid for it; we are not afraid for Egypt's unity at all. Egypt is protected in God's providence. . . . Egypt and the Egyptians are in God's care from all evil until the end of time. (quoted in al-Banna 1998, 137)

With that distinction and position enunciated, the pope has also expressed his own reaction to the semantics of the times with respect to the relationship between Christians and Muslims. He rejects the term *fitna*, stating that

Egypt does not have a sectarian problem. Muslims and Christians share a long history, with many points of meeting along the way. Nationalist feelings are such that you cannot distinguish between the Copt and the Muslim. We all must deepen our points of encounter, and not offer an opportunity to those who attempt to rattle those feelings. . . . All the events that have taken place do not affect the fact of Egypt, even if they have been serious. In our view, they do not express the view of the people as a whole. . . . Sectarianism does not have a place in Egypt and it never will. . . . Division is not in anyone's interest. We must remember that the divine intention in creation was unity. God created the whole world from one family, Adam and Eve, and after the flood, God again created the world from one family. We are all children of Adam (one father) and of Noah (again one father). God wanted the world to be of one mind and one heart, but we make distinctions. . . . In Egypt, we try to live in love. (quoted in al-Banna 1998, 139–40)

In attempting to live out this love, and in the long relationships that have existed between Christians and Muslims in Egypt (again to cite Pope Shenouda's own words),

[as Christians], we must always act with love. For example, when the tradition began of inviting [Muslims] to the *iftar* celebration at dusk during Ramadan, the idea spread to all corners of Cairo, Alexandria, and other provinces, throughout the month of Ramadan. People sit together in a spirit of love, exchanging understandings, mixing together, living together. This has taken place for a long time.

A Christian travels and leaves the key to his apartment, or his family, in the care of his Muslim neighbor, or vice versa. Egyptians have always lived this way. (quoted in al-Banna 1998, 137–38)

Continuing the tradition of hosting the Ramadan *iftar*, Pope Shenouda hosts such events each year. For example, in February 1998, the pope hosted an *iftar* bringing together the grand imam of al-Azhar, the grand mufti, the prime minister, and the speakers of both houses of Parliament. The mix of religion and state was evident, not only in those who were invited but also in the title of the event, *"Iftar al-wihda al-wataniyya"* (National Unity *iftar)."* The speakers shared their thoughts on the fraternity that exists between Christians and Muslims, and the event received media coverage.

Pope Shenouda commonly expresses such positions. Even his idealistic vision of national unity would be challenged (see chapter 3), though, and he would issue a statement in the wake of a particularly tragic incident that would be unusually critical (see chapter 7). Generally speaking, though, Pope Shenouda has been eager to come across publicly as a man who reaches out to the Muslim community with sincerity, holding up principles of his religion to support national unity. In the case of Pope Benedict XVI's remarks in September 2006, Pope Shenouda stated, "Christianity and Christ's teachings instruct us not to hurt others, either in their convictions or their ideas, or any of their symbols—religious symbols . . . any remarks which offend Islam and Muslims are against the teachings of Christ" (*Khaleej Times Online* 2006). Such remarks aim to preserve national unity and offer an alternative position on Islam. Pope Shenouda wished to make clear that the Roman Catholic pope is not the only voice of Christianity, and he recognized that Pope Benedict's remarks were polemical even if not intended as such and could have a very damaging impact on the relationships with Muslims in Egypt that Pope Shenouda had attempted to build.

In terms of teaching parishioners about the principles and encouraging them in the quest for better relations, such an effort is taking place through the Coptic Orthodox Youth Bishopric and its Bishop Musa. The Church has developed a curriculum for youth leaders on relations with the Other, including people of the other gender and people of another faith. In a 2000 interview with the author, Bishop Musa explained that, in teaching about relations with Muslims, the crucial issue is addressed so that Christians do not withdraw from society but rather participate in it as they ought. He went on to say that the Youth Bishopric is very active in attempting to foster good relations with Muslims and even has several joint programs throughout the year. The Church hopes that, through these curricula and their distribution to churches throughout the country, young Orthodox Christians will grow up with the idea that religious differences should not contribute to a breakdown within society.

Coptic Protestants

As president of the Protestant community in Egypt, the Rev. Samuel Habib continually expressed one idea—that religious differences should not contribute to societal breakdown—and worked hard to disseminate it through various circles. His efforts, while pioneering in their content, seem to sustain the belief that interaction with Muslims is critical in the expression of religion.[1] Habib served as head of the Protestant community in Egypt from March 26, 1980, when he was elected to replace the late Rev. Elias Maqqar (Virtue 1996, 102), until his death in October 1997. In this capacity, he was the head of the Protestant Council, representing sixteen approved denominations, the largest of which is the Evangelical (Presbyterian) Church of Egypt, of which Habib was an ordained minister. The position is also recognized by the government as the post through which the Protestant churches communicate with it, and vice versa.

Habib was another leader in an official capacity who did not escape criticism for being too conciliatory with regard to the Muslim community. He worked tirelessly throughout his life, both as a minister and eventually president of the Protestant community, and as founder and general director of the Coptic Evangelical Organization for Social Services (CEOSS), to foster a better basis for Christian-Muslim encounter and relations. He and Tantawi were honored jointly by Westminster College in the United

---

1. For a summary history of such interaction, see the insightful chapter "al-Wihda al-wataniyya" in Salama (1993, 449–60).

States for their combined efforts in peacemaking. With regard to his view on Christian-Muslim relations in Egypt, he felt that

> there are levels to the relationship. It is natural, if we were to speak about the extremist Islamists, or the Islamic terrorist groups that use violence and aggression, and that use weapons and such against society, against Christians, or against the government, or the police, that it is difficult for us to talk about dialogue, for they are secretive in the first place. We can enter into dialogue with other groups, be they Muslim or Christian, who are part of society. However, what is unfortunate is that the groups that use violence are very distant from the regular life of society. To engage them in dialogue or in a useful relationship with greater society is an extremely difficult task. . . . If we look, however, at the larger segments of Christians and Muslims, we find that Christians and Muslims work together in organizations and companies and in the government. They are in fine shape, and you see that Christians and Muslims live together, and that families are in good relationships, meeting and visiting each other, and there is no distinction made based upon religion. (*Tariq at-tahaddi* 1999, 253–54)

Habib never denied that there are some people who do make distinctions between people based upon religion, and he gave the example of a Muslim supervisor who did not choose to employ a Christian for that very reason. Habib's efforts were geared toward eliminating such prejudice.

Habib participated in a number of public seminars and symposia in which religious, political, and intellectual figures were invited to share their views on various topics; many of the forums were (and continue to be) arranged by CEOSS. The opportunity for such prominent religious leaders to come together and express their views allowed Habib to share his vision for Egypt and its people of two faiths. In his introduction to the transcript of the speeches given at the forum on "Religious Thought and the Advancement of Society" in November 1992, Habib enumerated the three goals of the meeting as follows:

> The first goal was, through dialogue on the topic "Societal Advancement," to link the Islamic perspective and Christian perspective, by

which there would be mutual acceptance. The second goal was to hold a meeting attended by Muslims and Christians together in a church, so that all in attendance would feel that the church is a natural place, in the service of the nation and its advancement. The third goal was to express the Egyptian reality, that Christian and Muslim participate together in one task, and do so in all places of production, for the sake of Egypt. (S. Habib 1994b, 5)

The idea that a church is a place of work, and not merely a place for worship, was stated more explicitly in Habib's introduction to the transcription of another forum which brought together Habib, 'Ali Mahjub, the minister of religious endowments, and Ahmad Kamal Abu al-Majd, a Muslim scholar, around the topic "Religious Thought and Citizenship" in January 1994. In that introduction, Habib reiterated the common social experience that Christians and Muslims share in Egypt, and he went on to address the role of the church:

> When the church has been a place for worship, the church has concerned itself with the lives of its faithful, and has supported them in forming their beliefs and behavior, through religious values. The church also has a national role. The church is not intended to be removed from society but is obligated to contribute to the general good, either through its ideas or through its national and social works. The church therefore has invited [participation] in such forums, expressions of national unity. . . . I thought to hold these forums in a church because the church in Egypt embraces the Egyptian citizen, and works for the sake of the nation. (S. Habib 1994b, 5–6)

In opening the church for dialogue and announcing the social role of the church, he was attempting to break down a barrier symbolized in religion, and demonstrate that religion could, and should, be a basis for good works.

Such efforts for the dialogue of religious and intellectual exchange continued, and Habib was tireless in hosting and speaking at these forums. He felt that "in dialogue sessions, thoughts and investigations are presented in the form of research, analysis, and study. Dialogue sessions in all cases are distinguished, for in them, a variety of opinions and ideas are presented, and the differences in opinions are marked by mutual respect by all" (S. Habib 1997, 7).

Likewise, he expressed his thoughts at a conference entitled "Religious Thought and Participation":

> We hold this conference on the way to building Muslim-Christian relations and to deepen our roots in Egyptian society. It is through these encounters that we give weight to the reasonable people of our society, both Christians and Muslims. We also give value and weight to the moderates for, despite the differences in our religious understandings and beliefs, we are careful to build bridges and deepen our relationships, in order to ensure just peace in our country, for the sake of Egypt. (S. Habib 1995a, 17)

Some would criticize his emphasis on dialogue and esoteric discussion as not having practical applications, since the approach appears to be more academic or even homiletical through the format of lectures on topics that may not be of interest to the grass roots. Others would point to the positive steps made in bringing people together to consider various points of view on topics that have intellectual and cultural value, even if not immediately pragmatic. They would also point to the grassroots social role that CEOSS has played for the past half century, with such dialogue forums as one aspect of its approach.

Habib was a very thoughtful and charismatic man who gained the respect of the Protestant community, as well as other religious communities. His death on October 6, 1997, was a significant loss for Egypt, and for those who were sincerely committed and engaged in dialogue. His efforts continue, though, through the office of the president of the Protestant community, as well as through CEOSS.

Conclusions

Through an examination of official religion, this chapter has shown how some key representatives of official religion have expressed their desire to engage in interfaith relations. It is not surprising that the institutions of religion in Egypt have been so supportive and engaged, but the question remains, to what extent these efforts have been able to offset the effects of more extremist and exclusivist manifestations of religion. The efforts of official religion have been well received by the government, clearly because of its own interest in maintaining national unity. One may continue to ask which came first: the government's program of supporting national unity, or the religious institutions' explicit and visible efforts to demonstrate unity. The matter is further complicated by the fact that there is not necessarily a clear line of distinction between the government and Dar al-Ifta' or al-Azhar. One could also wonder to what extent the Christian leaders are under the sway of the government. The questions are not moot, but their answers may not be as significant as some authors have made them out to be. The institutions and personalities of official religion do enjoy degrees of legitimacy in the eyes of the citizens, and that is what matters in the end.

There are obvious questions raised by focusing on official religion. One is the impact such statements and discourse from above have on the general public—the "trickle-down" effect. As Appleby puts it,

> The unique dynamism of lived religion—its distinctive patterns of interaction not only with secular, nationalist, ethnic, and other elements of political or personal identity but also with its own sacred past—means, among other things, that religious behavior cannot be confidently predicted merely on the basis of an individual's or group's affiliation with a specific religious tradition, especially if that tradition is conceptualized in the abstract. (Appleby 2000, 56)

Not all Egyptian Muslims, therefore, can be expected to act according to the official leadership; similarly, neither can all Egyptian Christians.

In today's Egypt, for example, because of the concern over disruptive rhetoric, mosques have to have a governmental seal of approval, as do their preachers. Nonetheless, the messages and sermons cannot be completely controlled, so there is a chance for stirrings of sectarian strife. In the case of churches, priests and pastors have greater freedom to preach, as there is no requirement of government approval, except that it is illegal to proselytize. (A reality faced by preachers that often contributes to anti-Islamic sentiment is loud broadcasts from the mosque during church services.)

There is a range of opinions among Christians about the purpose of interfaith dialogue, from those who believe that it must lead to conversion to those who understand it to be a way to better understanding and cooperation. Among both Muslim and Christian communities, therefore, there are disagreements about the approach and the aim of interaction and relationship. Even so, "if religions are to play a significant peacebuilding role in the twenty-first century, their leaders must give priority to establishing and supporting ecumenical and interreligious dialogues and cooperative ventures designed to prevent or transform conflicts that are based on religious or cultural disputes" (Appleby 2000, 245).

It is certainly possible, and especially desirable in the Egyptian context, to include social and even political issues and disputes in the set of agenda items for dialogue.

Because of the different approaches within each community, people align in different ways outside their religious community. Such alternative alignments cause disagreements among people within each community to the extent that faith may be doubted and people called apostate. One realm of alternative alignments is the political party, where the place of religion and interfaith cooperation has different implications.

5

Political Parties and Toleration

Ideology, Elections, and Religion

The first years of the twenty-first century are a time when political reform and allowance of new political parties are foremost in the Egyptian political system. In such a context, the ideas of cooperation and reconciliation between and within political affiliations are crucial. Sectarian strife would not help to advance the cause of reform, and establishment of new political parties along sectarian lines would only exacerbate tensions. This chapter examines the important groundwork that has been laid for sectarian cooperation within political alignments.

The unifying context of the 1919 revolution, particularly as it emphasized Egyptian nationalism over sectarian divisions, meant that Christians and Muslims worked together to overcome the dominance of the British and were less concerned about one's dominance over the other. The fact that the Wafd was the national majority party and that Makram 'Ebeid, a prominent Copt and strong nationalist, had a leadership role—he served as secretary-general of the party for a period of fifteen years (El-Feki 1993, 41–42)—demonstrated the extent to which national unity prevailed. El-Feki observed that the Wafd was "the only party to have had two Coptic ministers in all their cabinets" (26). "Bourgeois Copts were heavily represented [in the regime] during the thirties, through their massive participation in the Wafd party" (Kepel 1986, 157). Thus, the Wafd made a serious commitment not only to tolerate religious pluralism in Egypt and within its own party ranks, but also to support and encourage it, indeed to preach it.

Cooperation has a significant place in the history of political party composition in Egypt in the twentieth century. There are also examples of more exclusivist movements that have attempted to act as political parties and have sometimes been successful. Perhaps the most prominent case is the Muslim Brotherhood, formed in 1928 not as a political party but rather as a movement. The Brotherhood has attempted to function as a political party in more recent times, either attempting to operate as a party on its own or through alliances with legal parties, or with its candidates running as independents. It has also sought a role as an approved party in the context of a reforming political system.

For the 1984 elections, when religious parties were declared illegal, the Muslim Brotherhood entered into an alliance with the Egyptian Labor Party (Hizb al-'Aml) and the Free Liberal Party (Hizb al-Ahrar). The alliance used as its campaign slogan *"al-Islam huwwa al-hall"* (Islam is the solution; Hendriks 1987, 26–27). In the most recent election cycle, November–December 2005, the Brotherhood made its most significant advance yet, winning nearly one-fifth of the parliamentary seats with its candidates running as independents, and the slogan has become well known and widespread.

The political map of the last two and one-half decades demonstrates the spectrum of party platforms with respect to cooperation and toleration, particularly with regard to Muslim-Christian relations. That map may be enhanced by looking at election results, to gain a perspective on the feeling of the general voting public. It is important to emphasize that conclusions about public support can only be made based on the numbers of registered voters and outcomes at the time of a particular election, a number estimated to be very low. In fact, in the 1995 parliamentary elections, the Independent Commission for Electoral Review reports, "Turnout was inconsistent in this election. Some voting areas were empty in Cairo while rural area stations were more crowded" (Independent Commission 1995, 8). This chapter also examines Hizb al-Wasat, or the Center Party, which has not been legalized but was proposed as a party and later became part of the nongovernmental sector. It has received press coverage and has been known as a party. The intriguing characteristic of this party is the idea of tolerance and cooperation it puts forth. Hizb al-Wasat's ideas may not be particularly startling in themselves, but they are interesting in the context of the party's leadership, which is composed of former Muslim Brothers as well as recognized Christians. Other parties, that is, the Wafd and the Muslim Brotherhood and its allies, are well known for their stances—positive or negative—on toleration and inclusion. This chapter thus focuses on a movement that is less well known.

A Map of Egypt's Political Parties

Since the Free Officers' Revolution of 1952, a dominant single party, the official government party, has characterized the Egyptian political scene. There have been other officially recognized parties since 1977, when President Sadat dissolved the Arab Socialist Union (ASU) and its three component platforms, marking the political spectrum from left to right. In order to institutionalize the idea of a multiparty democracy, three new parties were created. The National Democratic Party was the center strand of the former ASU and has remained the premier party in Egypt. The leftist wing of the former ASU became the National Progressive Unionist Party (Hizb at-Tagammu'), and the right wing became the Free Liberal Party (Hizb al-Ahrar). Thus, "official" opposition political parties were legalized (Post 1987, 18).

The National Democratic Party

The single official party was set up primarily to mobilize the people around the regime. While the name of the state party has changed over the years—the National Rally Party, then the National Union Party, then the Arab Socialist Union, and since 1978 the National Democratic Party (NDP), the party of the president that controls the legislative branch—the purpose has been the same. Domination in elections and control by the president have been the norm. This domination is exemplified by the fact that many government officials at senior levels as well as governors and other public officials are members of the NDP. This party has the clear advantage of being the official state party, thus giving it access to significant financial resources as well as social capital. Another advantage is that it has direct access to the media, since most of the television and radio stations are government controlled. As a result, its influence on the viewing and listening public is not insignificant. This party's positions are indistinguishable from the official policies of the government, including those on pluralism in Egyptian society and national unity. The correlation between the government and the NDP extends to the idea of toleration and the official positions of the government on Christian-Muslim relations, as discussed in chapter 3. The fact that almost all of the Christians serving in Parliament over the past twenty-five years have come from the NDP demonstrates this assertion.

Hizb al-Ahrar and Tagammu'

The two opposition parties that were legalized by Sadat and remained strong into Mubarak's presidency were the Free Liberal Party (Hizb al-Ahrar) and Tagammu'. The former is a right-wing party favoring the continuation of Sadat's policy of *infitah,* or economic opening, including the privatization of many of the sectors controlled by the government. It also has opposed the continuation of subsidies on food and rent. Although it did not emphasize this during the campaign, its platform for the 1984 elections called for the application of *shari'a* (Post 1987, 19). It can be surmised from its position on the *shari'a* that Ahrar would not allow full participation of the Coptic Christian minority in Egypt. The party's platform for the 1995 parliamentary elections did not mention *shari'a* but did state that "*Hizb al-Ahrar* supports Arab unity and the necessity to strive for it" (Egyptian National Committee 1995, 151).

The idea of support for Arab unity can be interpreted in more than one way, as the discussion of the Arab school of identity showed. Over the course of two decades, a shift from a strict adherence to Islam to a more inclusive platform can be detected. Of course, such a conclusion depends on how "Arab unity" might be defined by the party leadership. If it means Arab unity in the sense that Michel 'Aflaq and the founders of the Ba'ath Party intended it, then it would necessarily mean inclusion for all, including Muslims and Christians alike. If, on the other hand, Arabness is defined in terms of Islam, then it is more restrictive and exclusive.

From the left, Tagammu' (the National Progressive Unionist Party) was the other party Sadat made legal in 1977. While it is described as a leftist party, the Tagammu' Party does not define itself as Marxist, even though a Marxist wing is important in the unity the party brings together, as are its Nasirist wing and the many prominent intellectuals who have associated with the party (Hendriks 1987, 29). Among those intellectuals was Muhammed Sid-Ahmed, a prominent journalist and member of the party's secretariat until his death in 2006. In an interview early in the Mubarak presidency, the program of the Tagammu' Party was described in light of religion and in the context of urban migration from rural areas where Islamic fundamentalism found fertilization: "The *Tagammu'* [has made a] decision to relate openly to the masses who express their problems through religion and religious institutions. That's our idea, to break through to the public, to enter debates with them, to try to isolate the more retrograde elements, to expose them to another way of thinking which is not opposed to the religious approach, but does represent an alternative" (Sid-Ahmed 1982, 22).

This more secular approach was reflected in the shift that the party made between the 1984 and 1987 elections. In 1984, all opposition parties included some reference to the *shari'a*; by 1987, the Tagammu' had renounced such a position (Hendriks 1987, 28), consistent with its nonsectarian outlook.

Much contemporary sectarian tension in Egypt has been attributed to Sadat's peace treaty with Israel. Feeling that the sectarian strife is not healthy, Sid-Ahmed criticized the former president and the mood in Egypt after the peace was signed: "Things are looked upon in a false perspective here. Sadat, with his partial peace, has actually fostered contradiction between peace with Israel and social peace in Egypt. He's made out of this issue of peace with Israel such an identity question in Egypt that you can't reconcile both. His attempt has not been a step forward, but a real step backwards in terms of comprehensive peace" (Sid-Ahmed 1982, 22).

By the time of the 1995 elections, the Tagammu' platform still attempted to reconcile the religious tension, but in a characteristically secular way. Its platform stated that, in addition to other political and constitutional reforms, the Tagammu' called for placing "conditions to accomplish the democratic political reforms: respect for the civil rights of the Egyptian citizen, *equality between all Egyptians with regard to all rights*, [and] a guarantee of the basic rights of each Egyptian" (Egyptian National Committee 1995, 141; emphasis added).

The Wafd and New Wafd

It is important to identify the New Wafd as one of the most powerful and influential of the opposition parties in Egypt. The roots of the New Wafd Party are found in the nationalist Independence Party of the early twentieth century. With the Free Officers' coup and the banning of all parties, the Wafd went by the wayside, although it could not simply disappear. When Sadat made opposition parties legal in the late 1970s, the New Wafd Party organized and petitioned for legal status in 1978, which it was denied at first. Because of the Wafd's known wide base of support, the government attempted to prevent its return. In February 1984, however, two leaders of the new party, Ibrahim Farag and Fuad Serag ad-Din, went to court and won legal rights for the party to engage in political activity (Vatikiotis 1991, 441). The first decade of Mubarak's presidency was marked by deference to the courts and their legal interpretation. In this case, and in others, Mubarak was commended for letting the judicial ruling stand.

The New Wafd was traditionally secular but with strong Coptic support. The 1984 elections, though, marked a change for the New Wafd. It entered into an alliance with the Muslim Brotherhood, which cost the party votes among Copts, who in turn seemed to vote in favor of the NDP (Vatikiotis 1991, 441). The New Wafd went so far as to call for the implementation of the *shari'a*, but so did many of the opposition parties in 1984. Even though the Brotherhood was still not a legal party, Mubarak tolerated the alliance, "apparently in recognition of the relative conservatism of the Brothers and the fact that their participation added legitimacy to the process" (Post 1987, 19). By the 1987 elections, the Wafd participated on its own, as it had dominated the Brotherhood in 1984 and knew that it had suffered to some extent from a loss of the Christian vote. It had also lost support from prominent secular intellectuals, such as Farag Fuda, who left the party in 1984 over the alliance with the Brotherhood. In 1987, the Wafd returned to its secular roots and used its historic slogan, "Religion for God; the homeland is for all" (Hendriks 1987, 28). The Wafd had reestablished itself as a strong opposition party. The only party not to enter into an electoral alliance with another, it was also the only party to demonstrate that it could garner the minimum 8 percent of the national vote required to have representation in Parliament (Post 1987, 22). With such encouragement, the Wafd remained among the strongest of the opposition parties. Even with the rigged elections (S. Ibrahim 1996d, 4), the Wafd and the Tagammu' each managed to win 5 seats in Parliament, the best showing of any of the opposition parties ('Abd Allah 1998, 55).

Hizb al-'Aml al-Ishtiraki

A particularly interesting party that has emerged as one of the primary opposition parties in Egypt in the last twenty years is Hizb al-'Aml al-Ishtiraki (the Socialist Labor Party [SLP]). The party has reflected ideas of nationalism in an Islamic context, without explicitly calling itself Islamic. Even though in 1989 there was a desire among the leadership to name the party the Islamic Socialist Party, such a name would have disqualified the party from legal existence because Egyptian law prohibits the existence of religious parties (Singer 1990, 32–33). Sadat had originally encouraged the party to form in 1978, presumably "as a 'loyal opposition' to compete with the Wafd and the Tagammu'." During his crackdown on religious groups, Sadat arrested the party's leadership and outlawed the party. It was reinstated in 1982 when it offered its support for Mubarak (*Middle East Report* 1987, 20). Its first major initiative was in the 1987 elections, when it organized an alliance of opposition parties to oppose the National Democratic Party. Its initiative carried the name of the SLP and included Hizb al-Ahrar and the Muslim Brotherhood. Because of its religious character and because the Wafd already had determined that it was strong enough to participate in elections on its own merit, the Wafd declined the offer to participate in the alliance. The alliance was quite successful, winning 17 percent of the vote for a total of 56 seats (out of 400 elected seats). Of the 448 total seats in Parliament, the alliance held 60, distributed as follows: the Muslim Brothers held 38, the SLP itself held 16, and Hizb al-Ahrar held 6 (Post 1987, 17). Jamal As'ad, a distinguished Christian, headed the SLP election list in Assiut, in Upper Egypt (Singer 1990, 35–36). The distribution clearly indicates that the religious nature of the party was the primary attraction among voters and that the popularity of the Muslim Brotherhood, legal or not as a party, was still very high.

Despite the emphasis of the Islamic roots and program of the Labor Party, the leadership has attempted to maintain a strong sense of nationalism. In order to do so, its president, Ibrahim Shukri, has expounded upon the appeal the party might have for Egyptian Christians. Shukri's religious rhetoric was particularly divisive during the fifth party conference in 1989. During the conference, Shukri emphasized that "a religious citizen is what the party aspires for." He went on to say in a speech,

> A good Copt who prays and fasts, is good to his people and neighbors, and does not commit adultery is close to our hearts. At the same time, Islam in this country is not merely a written belief. It has become a system of living for all those who are living on this land. In the past, Islamic civilization in Egypt was established by both the Muslims and Copts. Thus the civilization in the future would still be established by both Muslims and Copts alike with God's will. (Singer 1990, 35)

This idea had penetrated parts of the party membership, as indicated by a statement of a Cairene member: "Our party's ideology depends on its contact with the culture of the Egyptian citizen. It takes into consideration the value system of the Egyptians. Being a traditional society, it has certain characteristics, the first of which is religion; whether Islam or Christianity" (Singer 1990, 72).

The party member seemed to contradict himself when he also stated, "I stand with my full power in the Islamic faction of the party and I do not approve of, nor allow, the secular tendencies that want to remove Islam from society" (Singer 1990, 38). This statement indicates the essence of the division of the party in 1989: those who emphasized religion, and those who emphasized a much more secular kind of socialism.

Further, despite his soothing words about the possibility for the inclusion of Copts, Jamal As'ad spoke against Shukri during the conference. A socialist and vice president of the party, the prominent Copt was welcomed when he took the podium with cheers of "*Allahu akbar*" and "Long live national unity!" He went on to criticize Shukri as "contradicting the law of parties and the constitution," blaming Shukri for the religious character the party had acquired that rejected the secularists, i.e., the socialist wing of the party (Singer 1990, 48).

As a result of the schism that was unfolding in the party's conference between those who favored a secular socialist party platform and those who supported an Islamist agenda, a number of decisions were taken by those socialists who felt that they had been betrayed by the Islamist wing. These decisions were intended for application by the party as a whole but were not subsequently applied. They included a formal split within the party, recognizing an independent socialist faction separate from the Islamic faction, the removal of Shukri as party president, and a repeal of all decisions taken by the Islamists (Singer 1990, 49–50).

At the outset, people had been attracted to the SLP for the charisma of its leader, for the services it was able to provide, and for the blending of socialism and Islam in its ideology, which called for political freedom, an end to corruption in the government, social justice, and pan-Arabism. The fifth party conference marked the end of the party's moderate image and outlook. What became clear was that political Islam, manifested in a rather extreme form, was a prevalent current within the party, which, Singer prophetically writes, "might hurt the SLP in the future" (1990, 127–28). By ensuring NDP victory in the 1991 elections and sealing the electoral failure and fate of the SLP, the government clearly signaled that it would not tolerate opposition—specifically Islamic opposition—to the regime. Nonetheless, the SLP, with its Islamist slant, was a visible and important player in the 1991 and 1995 elections.

By 1995 the religious character of the party was explicit. The party had added an explicitly religious and Islamist tone to many of the items in its platform. In particular, it called for "political reforms dependent upon *shari'a* meaning writing a new constitution protecting the rights of the citizens . . . establishing equality between Muslim and Christian citizens in terms of civil and political rights." At the same time, it called for an end to the "current despotism that the Executive powers are practicing" and an implementation of "all the principles of *shari'a* law, holding accountable any person or body that deviates from them" (Egyptian National Committee 1995, 137).

The party leadership, despite its marked shift away from secularism and toward Islamism, attempted to reconcile the issue of religious equality with the centrality of Islam in the SLP's ideology and revised platform.

Despite the rhetoric, however, the general population recognized the party as closely linked to the more conservative Islamic groups, as did the government. Even with the opening of the 1995 elections to fourteen parties, harassment and violence marked the elections. The "violence and bloodshed [was] unprecedented in the parliamentary life of Egypt [with] nearly 40 casualties . . . [and] almost 400 injuries" (Independent Commission 1996, 6). Many of these complaints came "from the Ikhwan [Muslim Brotherhood] and Islamists stating that they were subjected to mistreatment and outright violence by the authorities" (Independent Commission 1996, 7). The rigging of the elections was presumably to exclude the Islamists from the Parliament, and indeed not a single member from Hizb al-'Aml was elected to Parliament ('Abd Allah 1998, 55).

Parliamentary Election Results, 1984–2005

Comparing the results of the first two parliamentary elections during Mubarak's presidency, a significant number of votes went to candidates affiliated with parties aligned with Islamic groups, most notably the Muslim Brotherhood. In 1984, the New Wafd Party got 61 seats in Parliament through the elections, whereas Hizb al-'Aml got a mere 4 ('Abd Allah 1998, 41–43). In the next election, in 1987, Hizb al-'Aml got 60 seats, whereas the Wafd Party got 35 and no other opposition party received any seats (Post 1987, 17).

The first impression would be that, in these two election years, the Muslim Brotherhood was the compelling reason for the overwhelming success of the party with which it was aligned. There is at least some degree of truth in that conclusion, but the conclusions of the Wafd Party leadership after the 1984 elections, that it was strong enough to compete on its own merit, cannot be dismissed. Of the seats the Wafd won in 1984, only 8 were to be held by the Muslim Brotherhood (Post 1987, 22), meaning that the overwhelming majority of the seats won by the Wafd actually went to Wafd Party members. In 1987, the Wafd, running on its own, gained a formidable number of seats, but it is also important to point out that the other opposition party to be named on the ballot, the SLP, was engaged in an alliance with other parties and groups, including the Muslim Brotherhood. The number of seats allotted to each part of the SLP's alliance was fewer than the number of seats the Wafd received. "On this basis, the [Wafd] party has protested Ibrahim Shukri's self-appointment as opposition spokesman in parliament" (Post 1987, 22). As head of the SLP but not legitimately head of the alliance, the Wafd argued, Shukri had no authority or basis on which to name himself opposition spokesman, a role Wafd leadership felt it had earned by virtue of the election results.

The next round of parliamentary elections, in 1990, were literally insignificant for the opposition, in terms of results, as there were only 6 seats won by any opposition party: 5 by Hizb at-Tagammu' and 1 by the Nasirist Party ('Abd Allah 1998, 53). The main reason for the poor showing was that the principal opposition parties, including the Wafd, boycotted the 1990 election because of the continuing state of emergency declared by the administration. They feared that the state of emergency would allow the government to interfere in the elections as it saw fit.

The state of emergency that prevailed in 1990 affected the way the 1995 elections were conducted and opposed. For the opposition parties, 5 seats each went to the Wafd Party and Hizb at-Tagammu', and 1 each to Hizb al-Ahrar and the Nasirist Party ('Abd Allah 1998, 55). It was in this context that a new party was proposed, Hizb al-Wasat (Centrist Party).

In October and November 2000, another round of elections took place in a three-round process supervised by the judiciary—a first in Egyptian elections. Preliminary reports claimed that the elections "have been free to date [after two rounds] of the large scale ballot-tampering which characterized earlier polls" (Langohr 2000). In this election, despite running as independents, the Muslim Brotherhood won 17 seats, "despite a huge campaign of harassment by police designed to keep Islamists out of parliament—the only blemish on what has been hailed in Egypt as an unprecedented clean vote" (Hammond 2001, 31). The Wafd won only 7 seats, including one in al-Wayli district in Cairo, despite the NDP candidate who "distributed leaflets exhorting voters not to vote for a Christian" (Hammond 2001, 31, 80).

The 2005 parliamentary elections took place under the shadow of proposed reform in the political system in Egypt, with the first contested presidential elections taking place in the same year. Spanning three rounds in November and December of 2005, the elections were marked by a crackdown by officials on the third round, when it was apparent that the Muslim Brotherhood had already made significant gains by running candidates as independents in the first two rounds. The NDP, or official government party, seemed to remain in firm control, winning 311 of the 454 seats (444 are elected and 10 are appointed by the president). However, the balance of the results informs a different picture: Muslim Brothers won 88 seats as independents, nearly 20 percent of the total. Opposition candidates won significantly more seats in the 2005 elections than in 2000. Other party tallies included unaffiliated independents with 22 seats; the Wafd, 6; Tagammu' and Karama, 2 each; and al-Ghad, 1; twelve races were postponed (*Arab Reform Bulletin* 2005). In terms of the Christian candidates, only Yusif Butros Ghali, the minister of finance, was elected, and 5 were appointed among the 10 the president may appoint, for a total of 6 in the current parliament (United Nations Development Programme n.d.).

The significant decline in elected Christians between 2000 and 2005 (from 3 to 1) can be analyzed in two ways. In the 2000 elections, the relatively high number of Christians elected can partly be attributed to an active NDP campaign in support of them (as members of the party). In 2005, only two Christian candidates ran, both on the NDP ticket, and one withdrew before the election actually took place. There was, therefore, less encouragement by the party to include Christian candidates. The one who did run was not only a cabinet minister but was also from a prominent and well-respected family in Egypt's political class. Not only was the NDP less assertive regarding Christian candidacy, but perhaps also the electorate was less enthusiastic about supporting the NDP, as indicated by the election results. Alternatively, the electorate may truly have made a significant change in supporting Islamist candidates and was therefore less eager (or less able, based on demographics) to support a Christian. In any case, the one Christian who did run was successful, and the number of Christians in Parliament remained stable at 6. The clear emergence of the Muslim Brotherhood as a viable factor is significant.

The Culture of Political Platforms

Several parties have attempted to use the theme of nationalism as a rallying point, in both the late twentieth century and the earlier era of Egyptian history, notably as Egypt was attempting to throw off British colonial control. Nationalism was a pervasive theme during the twenty years on either side of the turn of the last century. Egyptian politics at that time might rightly be characterized in terms of nationalism. More recently, in the era of the republic, as more and more parties were allowed on the political scene, some parties tended to look at Egypt's party history and observe that the theme of nationalism not only had been successful in mobilizing support, it was also a natural theme that was sure to stir passionate feelings in Egyptians, young and old.

The second—and, one might conclude, opposite—tendency in Egyptian politics in the late twentieth century was a religious fervor that had been building since the Arab defeat in 1967. Religious identity was perhaps more divisive in the late twentieth century than it had been in the early part of the century and impacted the strategic approach of Egypt's political parties.

The traditionally nationalistic Wafd Party of old, when offered the chance, reorganized and sought success in elections. It saw the general support for the Islamist political ideology as sufficient reason to enter into an alliance with the Muslim Brotherhood in 1984. It also recognized its own strength after the election results were in. The alliance of parties, including the SLP and the Muslim Brotherhood, as well as at-Tagammu' and al-Ahrar in 1987, was evidence to the same recognition.

The struggle within the SLP at its 1989 party convention between the socialist faction (which some would call the secular wing) and the Islamic faction brought to light the struggle existing not only within the SLP but within Egyptian society as a whole. Many consider the success of the Islamist factions in politics to be the motivating factor for the government to call for emergency rules and to put a ban on total political participation, disallowing those who are clear about their ties to religious activists. Such an action not only has motivated some opposition parties to boycott elections but also has exacerbated the friction between religious activists and the authorities.

The deeper issue, analogous to that of the SLP in 1989, has been the struggle to reconcile nationalism and religious trends. How can the authenticity of religion, particularly within an Islamic society, be reconciled with a desire to assert rights for all, particularly those who do not confess the same beliefs as the majority faith community and culture? Is faith a matter of private or public expression? To what extent does, or should, religion demand and be allowed expression in the political realm? Attempts have been made—some successful and others quashed—to assert religion through political parties. It is thus in this context, and with this aim, that the founding leadership of the proposed centrist Hizb al-Wasat sought to popularize the term *middlers* as an alternative expression of reconciliation, referring to the "middle way" it espoused.

Hizb al-Wasat

Hizb al-Wasat's first official appearance on the Egyptian political scene occurred in January 1996, when the necessary papers were submitted to the parliamentary committee on political parties for application to become a political party. In the group's documents, as submitted for approval, was a list of the founders, which included thirty-six individuals representing liberal professions from the nine Egyptian provinces of Cairo, Giza, Manufia, Port Said, Buhaira, Minia, Assiut, Aswan, and Fayoum, and thirty-eight individuals representing the commercial and agricultural sectors of all of the same provinces save Assiut. The man named to be the single official representative of the founders was Abou Elela Mady (Abu al-'Alaa Madi Abu al-'Alaa; Hizb al-Wasat 1996, 118–24). An engineer by training, Abou Elela is known to be one of the most prominent of his generation (he was forty-four years old in 2006) in the Syndicate of Engineers, particularly because of his association with the Muslim Brotherhood. It can be surmised that the syndicate was closely watched because Abou Elela was a member of the board of directors. He also worked among the leadership of a coordination committee of the syndicates to draft a new national charter, a document that was eventually signed by a number of political party representatives (*al-Majalla* 1996, 28). His own leadership in the proposed party, combined with the participation of a number of other notable members of the Muslim Brotherhood, prompted strong speculation that Hizb al-Wasat was simply a cover for the outlawed Muslim Brotherhood. Nonetheless, Abou Elela Mady denounced this speculation and denied any relationship to the Muslim Brotherhood (Harbi 1996, 12). In fact, according to Gilles Kepel,

> [Hizb al-Wasat's] program was based on civil liberties, human rights, national unity, and so on and thus departed from the ideology of the Brothers in subscribing, without ambiguity, to Western principles of democracy. In this it found itself in opposition not only to the Brothers, for whom an Islamic state applying the sharia was the only political system of any value, but also to the government, whose repressive practices were directly targeted by Al Wasat's insistence on civil liberties. The initiative was rejected out of hand by the [Muslim Brotherhood's] Supreme Guide [Mustafa Mashur], who viewed it as a threat to his authority; and it was disapproved by the government, which in early 1996 still had to consolidate its position and thus was unable to accept any project for rallying middle classes that might compete with its own social vision and methods. (Kepel 2002, 296–97)

The question of membership was one that plagued the proposed party throughout the time period of the political party committee's consideration of its application. The tie to the Muslim Brotherhood was always the matter at the forefront, beginning at the top with Abou Elela himself. Throughout the month of January 1996, the Egyptian and international Arabic media covered closely the "surprise" of the party's application and Abou Elela Mady's leadership role in it, as well as the ongoing public debate as to the party's ties. Denials abounded, particularly by Abou Elela Mady, when he would characteristically respond that "the new party is a kind of partisan container expressive of the founders who enunciated their will by establishing it, in order to iterate their views and opinions on national issues." He also was quick to point out that among the number of founders was a prominent Christian, Rafiq Habib, son of the then president of the Protestant community in Egypt, the late Rev. Samuel Habib (*al-Hayat* 1996). Kepel asserts that those members of the Muslim Brotherhood involved in the formation of the party felt that including Habib was a "testimony . . . to their open-mindedness" (2002, 372). Such analysis might be accurate if Habib were an inactive, token Christian. He was, however, one of the important founders and ideologues of the movement.

Certainly, there was more to say than the denial that the party was related to the Muslim Brotherhood. In his leadership position, Abou Elela was repeatedly asked about that relationship, and was pleased to be offered the opportunity to expound upon the party's program.

In an interview with *al-Wasat* magazine (an Arabic weekly news magazine similar in style to *Time* or *Newsweek,* bearing a common name with the proposed party but no other relationship), Abou Elela shared that the party rejects terrorism, defining it as the "use of hatred and violence to impose an opinion or to achieve political, economic, or social agendas." The party proposed "absolute freedom in the context of the Constitution and the undertaking of frank national dialogue among all currents" to put an end to terrorism. The party also gave priority to the population and housing crisis in Egypt. It was critical of the peace process and negotiations because "peace must be comprehensive and just, without one party dominating another, or one lacking in rights" (Harbi 1996, 12–14). The papers of the proposed party include sections on contemporary Egyptian problems such as unemployment, squatter communities and housing, corruption, health and the environment, and public transportation. It also dedicates chapters to freedom and rights, national unity, terrorism, the family and women, NGO participation, development and the economy, education, tools for the formation of public opinion (culture, media, and the arts), and international relations and national security (Hizb al-Wasat 1996, 22).

While the Muslim Brotherhood has a program that addresses a number of the same issues and problems, any direct connection cannot be proven. In addition to the denial of any such connection by Abou Elela, the most prominent Muslim Brother in the party's leadership, two other important denials must be taken into consideration. First, the denial by Ma'mun al-Hudaybi, the official spokesman of the Muslim Brotherhood, was covered in several of the papers. When asked about Hizb al-Wasat and Abou Elela's involvement as a prominent Muslim Brother, al-Hudaybi replied,

This party does not represent the Brotherhood, but we cannot constrain a person's movement if he wishes to form a party. We know that it has a number of Muslim Brothers, as well as a number of Christian brothers. The party is moving according to some of the Muslim Brotherhood's principles. . . . If this party was a Muslim Brotherhood party, Brotherhood leaders from the Office of Guidance would have been among its leaders, but it does not represent us. (*Al-Wasat* 1996, 15–16)

Of course, it would not be in the interest of the party or the Muslim Brotherhood to acknowledge publicly any relationship, since the party had not been approved for legal status. With the continuing ban on parties with religious affiliation, any such affirmation would destroy the party's chances for approval and would prematurely destroy the Muslim Brotherhood's opportunity for a link.

A third source of denial that there was any relationship was Rafiq Habib, a researcher on current issues in Egyptian political and social matters, who has a particular interest in the role of the church in society. One of the founding members of the party, Habib wrote the introduction to the documents submitted to the committee on parties. Needless to say, his prominent role in the formation of the party was a statement in itself, as Habib is Christian. Even though some of the press felt that Habib's participation was a "cover for the Muslim Brotherhood's party" (I. Khalil 1996, 8), Habib denied extensively any relationship between the party and the Muslim Brotherhood. In an interview with the major Arabic daily *al-Hayat*, published in London, he reiterated this position, saying that the party program was in complete accordance with his own thoughts and that the party "represents a national vision in accordance with the cultural context in which Egypt exists" (Salah 1996, 5). Because of his own participation and enthusiasm for the party (in addition to his analysis of the church and society in previous books and articles), Habib was accused by Pope Shenouda of being "an insurgent Protestant" and by Rifa'at as-Sa'id of having converted to Islam (Ramih 1997, 93).

In a candid interview describing the split the party caused between the party and the Muslim Brotherhood, Habib explained that the membership of some Muslim Brothers caused problems within the Muslim Brotherhood, which did not approve of the new party because it was against the procedure and constitution of the Brotherhood to allow its members be a part of, or help to establish, another party. As a result of this conflict, some of the Brothers also involved in al-Wasat left the party, and others left the Muslim Brotherhood (R. Habib 2000b).

The party's platform is also informative in what it states about citizenship, national unity, and the Christian element. The chapter in the platform document on national unity offers a fairly clear picture of the party's stated ideal on Christian and Muslim participation in the national life of the country.

> The participation of the Christian brothers in the defense of the soil of this secure country, i.e., one nation, Muslim and Christian citizens, affords them full rights of citizenship, civil, political, and legal rights. Each citizen also has equal and complete responsibilities, granted by the Constitution and propagated in the law.
>
> We do not affirm the calls of the secularists who strive for the separation of religion from life. The experiment of the last forty years has shown, with the events of communal disharmony, that the nourishment of national unity with the support of religion is an important matter. Each Muslim and each Christian ought to feel his nationalism and his nation's unity. . . . Religion is the strongest source of moral obligation. (Hizb al-Wasat 1996, 31)

It is clear that the party was attempting to walk a fine line between being Islamic and being inclusive. That effort is particularly evident in its call for the implementation of *shari'a*, where it notes that in a pluralistic country, the *shari'a* ought not be imposed on a non-Muslims (Hizb al-Wasat 1996, 32). Habib describes the *shari'a* as "the underpinning of our nation *(umma)*. It is not a religious stand against other religions but the point of origin of our law" (quoted in Hammond 1996, 14).

Indeed, it was the attempt to bridge the gaps others had created, to be a "middle," that led the party to call itself *al-Wasat*, the center of many things, according to Habib: "a middle civilization, neither East nor West . . . an economic system neither capitalist nor communist; a society glorifying neither Westernization nor *takfir*, the demonization of what doesn't conform; and—a novelty in Egypt—a party of young people, the middle generation" (quoted in Hammond 1996, 14).

The appeal for a Christian, according to Habib, of a party such as al-Wasat that adheres to Islamic religious ideology is not in the religion itself but in its civilization it has dictated:

> In a sense, all Christians are living in a state of exile *(uzla)*, and so coming closer to political Islam is difficult for all to go through. You face trouble whichever direction you come from, Protestant or Orthodox Copt. The Christian community doesn't understand yet that there is a civilization of Islam which we all share. When Copts hear the word "Islamist" they fear, and I think the media is responsible. The state media is causing civil-religious strife *(fitna)* in order to push the Christian community to be fearful of anything Islamic. (quoted in Hammond 1996, 14)

Recognition of the central importance, and undeniability, of the society and culture in which both Christians and Muslims live in Egypt was important for Habib, and he thought it would be important for others as well. In fact, there was one other Copt on the list of founders, and it was expected that many Christians would join the party if it became legalized, despite the controversy surrounding its Islamic character.

When the party's application was rejected in late 1996, the founders launched an appeal because they felt that everything was in good order and that there was nothing in the papers to justify the party's rejection (R. Habib 2000b). In the meantime, expecting the appeal process to last a while, the founders joined with Nasirists and secularists in mid-1997 to apply for a license to publish a newspaper, called *al-Mustaqbil* (*The Future*; Huwaidi 1997, 10). The reasons stated for the project were to "fill a void in the press which [according to Habib] 'lack a cultural scheme to define the founding principles of the nation'" and to make a renaissance happen "by creativity and renovation" (Huwaidi 1997, 11). The newspaper project was eventually rejected as well, as the government decided that no party or political newspapers could be established within Egypt, and the proposal was seen as closely tied to the Wasat movement and other parties (R. Habib 2000b).

When the appeal for Hizb al-Wasat was rejected in May 1999, the organizers submitted papers for the consideration of a second party, Hizb al-Wasat al-Misri, within forty-eight hours, hoping to cause a stir and to ensure the continuation of the party's ideology in the public sphere. In the end, the successor party was also rejected, on September 5, 1999. This rejection coincided with the passage of a law that prohibited the creation of any new parties (R. Habib 2000b).

In January 2000, the founders determined to continue the project of al-Wasat in the form of an NGO called Misr: For Culture and Dialogue. Expectations were high that the organization would be approved, since the law concerning NGOs was more permissive than it had been and the committee had had a limited time to decide one way or the other on the application. Any objection must be clearly stated. The papers were submitted on February 9, 2000, and Misr was registered on April 10 after the legal period of sixty days (R. Habib 2000a). The founders had great hope that the success of the organization would exceed any success the proposed party might have enjoyed, since an NGO may legally engage in a far greater range of activities than the limited political objectives open to a political party.

The NGO expressed its intention to work in the areas of politics, economics, religion, and society and aimed to present a particular vision and certain values to the society. It naturally included both Christians and Muslims (although at the time of its founding Habib was the only Christian on the board of directors), and its board included cultural liberal leaders who focused on cultural specificity and who encouraged the al-Wasat project (R. Habib 2000a). Its basic ideology, then, was the advancement of a middle road, based on Arab-Islamic civilization. This trend, consistent with the entire al-Wasat project, is in contrast to the Islamic movements that focus on a religious vision and also have social, political, and religious activities. It is also in contrast with the so-called nationalistic movements, which primarily focus on the interest of the nation. Arab-Islamic civilization and values, according to the ideologues of the al-Wasat movement, can embrace society as a whole, accepting that Islam is both the prevailing religion and a cultural movement. It is interested in the advancement of certain values that are common to all citizens of the community, Christian and Muslim alike (R. Habib 2000a).

In the end, the participation of Abou Elela was a warning light to the Egyptian government with respect to the proposed Hizb al-Wasat. Even though he resigned from the Muslim Brotherhood, he was still associated with the movement and its ideas, as were others on the list of founders. The close association that was made to the popular slogan "*al-Islam huwwa al-hall*" (Islam is the solution) was not denied by Abou Elela. He even affirmed that the party's documents were a translation of that idea into program ('Ali 1996). Nonetheless, in a 2005 interview, Abou Elela made clear that he agreed with the government's ban on religious parties. As the proposed party made a third attempt to secure licensing as a political party in 2006, only 7 percent of the founding members were from the Muslim Brotherhood (Hamzawi 2005), a significant decrease from the first two attempts. The group still seeks licensure, but Rafiq Habib has since withdrawn from the project.

Conclusions

From this discussion of the map of political parties in Egypt since the 1984 election campaign, it can be seen that the religious element not only re-emerged but became central in the mindset of the parties' leadership, in the platforms they proposed, and in their popular appeal. The role the Islamic activists played in the election process of 1984 and 1987 certainly influenced how they were regarded in the 1990 and 1995 rounds and the way in which those elections actually took place. By 2000, when there were calls for fairer elections, the government responded, allowing a large number of independent candidates to run. In 2005, the Muslim Brotherhood made a very significant advance in the parliamentary elections, gaining hold of nearly one-fifth of the seats despite interference by the government in the third round. The government's "campaign against the Muslim Brotherhood and continued restrictions on the formation of political parties demonstrate that Egypt is still a long way from truly free and fair elections" (Langohr 2000).

The result was that the voting public expressed its support for Islamic politicians, who won the largest number of seats of any opposition, even though it was accomplished independently. The leadership of the Wafd, the traditional nationalist party and the party that usually has had the greatest appeal for the Christian segment of society, had predicted that "in a reasonably fair vote, [it] should win at least 100 seats" (Hammond 2001,

80). The 2000 and 2005 elections, then, were both great disappointments for the Wafd and a startling development for Christians, who saw the Islamist trend become the dominant opposition.

The fact is that the Islamic element has come to play a major role in Egyptian election politics. Among parties associated with the Islamic activists, there are at least some strong factions that support equal relations and participation with Christians. The SLP faced an internal crisis that reflected the struggle of the wider Egyptian context between socialism (or secularism) and religion, particularly Islam. Christian participation in the leadership of the party demonstrated the SLP's unwillingness to give in to the religious faction within the party and affirmed its commitment to values of equality.

Al-Wasat provides an example of an organizaton that attempts to be inclusive and faithful to its cultural context: it has striven to be clear that it has no relationship with the Muslim Brotherhood and that it is a project for all Egyptians—Muslims and Christians, men and women—even though there is a strong Islamic influence on this proposed party and NGO project. It perhaps represents an alternative for those citizens who take pride in their Arab-Islamic societal and cultural environment but to some extent feel outside because of their religious community membership. The fact that al-Wasat has been rejected as a political party but remains committed to exerting some influence on the ideas and culture of contemporary Egypt as an NGO while maintaining its efforts to participate legally as a party, perhaps also represents an alternative method for improved tolerance, increased knowledge of the Other, and more positive interaction for the betterment of society.

In light of Mubarak's announcement and the ensuing approval of the referendum to amend the Constitution and allow for a reformed process of elections, the role of Islamists, including the Muslim Brotherhood, must be taken seriously. In May 2005, the Muslim Brotherhood joined the Kifaya movement to boycott the referendum, claiming that the ruling government would retain too much control of the process of reform. Given the popularity of the Muslim Brotherhood and the results of the 2005 elections, there is growing concern among Christians—and Muslims—that allowing for free elections, an approach that would not differentiate among Islamic groups and movements, would bring the Islamists to power. Are the emergency laws that have been in effect since Mubarak became president in 1981 a safeguard against increased influence by the perceived extreme elements, or are they a hindrance to democratic reform and freedoms, or both? Some Christians prefer the maintenance of the emergency laws so that their status is protected.

The possibility for an Islamist government raises many questions, including what the future would be for the process of reform and democratization, and what the place of non-Muslims in society and politics would be. The model of Turkey may be helpful but cannot be assumed. In a recent conversation, a Christian argued that no specifically Islamist party should be allowed to participate in the political process. She explained that she has no specific animosity toward Islam or Muslims but rather fears that, if an Islamic party were approved, then some Christians would want to form a Coptic party. In such a scenario, sectarian conflict would only increase. Efforts to reduce conflict and manage the potential for a crisis are facing new challenges in the efforts to reform the political system, and the next few years will be especially informative, assuming the reform process moves beyond the failed attempt in 2005.

6

The Special Role of
Nongovernmental Organizations
in a Culture of Pluralism

The case of al-Wasat is a good example of how the opportunities for a party with a religious tendency are extremely limited. The Egyptian government has drawn clear battle lines with respect to Islamic extremists, making significant attempts to control the role that religion can play in politics and other forums of public opinion. The government has imposed less on the nongovernmental organizations (NGOs), perhaps more accurately called private voluntary organizations (PVOs), than it has on the political parties. For this reason the al-Wasat project determined that, in order to achieve greater levels of participation socially, it should make a concerted effort to form as a legal NGO while continuing to seek licensure as a party.

The Mubarak administration perhaps realized by the mid-1980s, when Islamic activism was reemerging within Egyptian society, that it would be wise to shift its own posture "from indiscriminate confrontation to selective accommodation" (Bianchi 1989, 93). This kind of policy direction made it possible for religious activists to exert influence in the associational sector of Egyptian society. For al-Wasat's founders, the opening was clear; it transformed its structure to begin to implement its program in a way that was neither inconsistent with nor antagonistic toward the law or the administration. In mid-1999, a much stricter law was passed regarding the formation of NGOs. In an editorial, Hasan El Sawaf summarized the law, stating that it "prevents NGOs from any political activity . . . [even though] establishing a political party is controlled by even stricter laws, rendering such a task all but impossible." In the same editorial, he commented, "The new law governing the guidelines within which NGOs are allowed to operate reeks of totalitarianism" (El Sawaf 1999, 4).

The Misr: For Culture and Dialogue project fits nicely into the realm of voluntary associations that have been defined as "areas which foster individual autonomy and provide experience in the exercise of social and political rights and responsibilities" and include "trade unions, professional syndicates, voluntary societies and clubs, pressure groups, and political parties" (Zubaida 1992, 4). While this definition encompasses a wide range of organizations, it describes "areas" where the government ideally would not have a hand. In Egypt's case, if pressure groups (which exist in scant numbers and are closely watched) and political parties (which are under tight governmental control) are excluded, most of these groups could accurately be grouped together as voluntary associations.

Nonetheless, trade unions, chambers of commerce, and professional syndicates do exist and are significant indicators of trends in Egypt. In 1999, twenty-four professional syndicates had a total membership of more than three million people, equivalent to one-fifth of the labor force. Members

> under the age of forty, that is, some 60 percent of the membership of the syndicates, have increasingly voted for anti-government candidates [in national elections], most of whom are Muslim Brothers (MB). By 1993, six of the seven biggest and most important [syndicates] were controlled by Islamists—the Bar Association, Engineers, Doctors, Pharmacists, Dentists, and Commerce syndicates. The Teachers' syndicate became the only major syndicate not totally under Islamist control. (S. Ibrahim 1996b, 166)

A case that demonstrates the extent to which the Islamic activists have penetrated the syndicates is the Pharmacists' Association. Coptic Christians, who are represented in the pharmaceutical profession disproportionately, have historically dominated this syndicate. "But by the end of the 1980s, the MB had managed to dislodge them from the syndicate board and even the post of chair" (S. Ibrahim 1996c, 59). The government, however, managed to reduce Islamist control of the syndicates by passing a law requiring that a quorum be present at elections or, in the lack of one, the government would appoint judicial administrators (Kepel 2002, 292–93).

Religious NGOs

Organizations that have a religious thrust or which have focused upon religion in Egypt as a matter of study are of particular interest. The participation of religious PVOs and NGOs has led to a certain level of influence in society. Two editions of a report on the state of religion in Egypt and their specific focus on religious associations in Egypt help inform this influence. Specific cases are also informative, and two NGOs offer interesting insight on the role the private voluntary sector can play. The first is the Ibn Khaldun Center for Development Studies, a nonreligious NGO that worked in the area of research, particularly on matters of religion in society and the place of minorities, until it was closed in 2000, and then continued when it reopened in 2003. An illustration of positive efforts by an NGO to foster better relations between Egypt's Christians and Muslims is the Coptic Evangelical Organization for Social Services (CEOSS), which is considered one of Egypt's largest and most successful NGOs working in the area of community development and is widely recognized as a leader in this area in the Middle East and Africa.

Egypt, Civil Society, and NGOs

At the end of the 1990s in Egypt, there were upward of twenty-seven thousand civil society organizations, more than fourteen thousand of which are registered with the Ministry of Social Affairs (S. Ibrahim et al. 1999, 18). Approximately three-fourths of these organizations operate in one field of development, such as social assistance, elder care, community development, culture, or literary activities. About one-fourth of the registered organizations are located in Cairo (al-Sayyid 1993, 231).

Al-Sayyid refers to the mosque- and church-based associations as "neo-traditional" and notes that they "have continued to be centers of social and political activities, often beyond the control of the government" (al-Sayyid 1993, 233). These are not new settings for such activity, since they date back to the times of the pharaohs and were the sites for revolts against Napoleon. "Those who carry out educational, medical, social, and political activities in mosques and churches are not traditional clergymen, shaykhs, or priests, but young professionals who received their education in the country's Western-type universities and who are alienated for a variety of reasons from the country's social and political system" (al-Sayyid 1993, 233).

This description offers a clue to at least two aspects of religious associations. First, the kinds of services they offer are services that usually would be expected from the government. In spite of the government's promise based upon the socialist principles of the Nasirist revolution, it has been lacking in its ability to deliver. The demand that has been expressed by society has found supply in the form of religious associations.

This ability to provide for the needs of the people was no more evident than immediately following the terribly frightening and destructive earthquake of October 1992. "During the October 1992 earthquake, within hours, Islamist-controlled PVOs and syndicates managed to outdo the government in relief efforts" (S. Ibrahim 1996b, 167). Embarrassed at a time of crisis and in front of international media, the government legislated that all aid would come through it, but its weakness was clear, and the strength of the Islamic associations had become quite apparent and had appeal.

The second insight this description provides is the kind of person who offers the services. It is not the religious professional but rather a person trained in the field of the service provided. In the case of medicine and medical care offered by mosque- or church-related associations, for example, not only was medical care available at affordable prices through such associations but also opportunities for the employment of younger physicians that were "superior to [positions] offered by the ministry [of health, which provides more than 75 percent of practicing physicians with positions], as well as a reinforcement of their religio-political commitments" (Zubaida 1992, 8). A two-sided demand is thus supplied by such associations, making them doubly appealing.

In 1995, in an ongoing effort to report on religion in Egypt, al-Ahram Centre for Political and Strategic Studies introduced its first report, *al-Hala ad-diniyya fi Misr* (The State of Religion in Egypt). It purported to raise Christian and Muslim awareness of each other's beliefs, institutions, and modern expression. Two editions were published within a four-year period, one in 1995 and the second in 1998.

In the 1995 edition, the chapter on Islamic associations begins with their history in contemporary Egypt, dating back to 1878. Such Islamic associations were established in response to the missionary efforts of foreign churches in the second half of the nineteenth century. The text then goes on to chronicle the development of Islamic associations and their participation in political, economic, and social facets of community development. The second part of the study examines the geographic distribution of Islamic associations, demonstrating that the plurality is in Cairo (al-Ahram Centre 1995, 233–35, 243). It then goes on to take the case study of *al-Jama'iyya ash-Shara'iyya li'Ta'awun al-'Amilin bi'l-Kitab wa's-Sunna* (The Group of Islamic Law for the Right Practice of the Sacred Texts), an association that has been active since the early part of the twentieth century and was influenced by the struggles between the Muslim Brotherhood and Jamal 'abd an-Nasir. The study characterizes this case as a "moderate model of religious associations" (al-Ahram Centre 1995, 237–41).

The next chapter is dedicated to Christian associations, tracing their history back to 1881, when Butros Ghali formed Jama'iyyat al-Misa'ai al-Khairiyya al-Qibtiyya. The movement developed as a result of Protestant missionaries. The report traces history as it does for the Islamic groups, and also places associations in their geographic context. It then includes examples of Protestant, Orthodox, and Catholic organizations working in community development to assert a balance among the denominations and families. It starts with the Coptic Evangelical Organization for Social Services and then describes the work of the Coptic Orthodox Bishopric for Public, Ecumenical, and Social Services (BLESS) and the Catholic Church's Caritas. Finally, it outlines a case study of one of the best-known examples of Christian community service, garbage collection, in Mansh'at Nasr in Cairo (al-Ahram Centre 1995, 247–72).

Among the important conclusions of this section of the report was that religious associations represented a "significant percentage of the total number of civil associations in the country, with Islamic and Coptic associations accounting for 34% and 9% respectively" (al-Ahram Centre 1997, 23). This statistic not only confirms that religious associations play an important role in Egyptian society, but it also begs the question whether the work they are doing is parallel and overlapping or complementary and cooperative. The answer to this question is especially important in thinking about efforts at this level to foster better relations between the two communities.

The 1998 report includes only a single chapter on religious associations. The introduction to the chapter offers the beginning of a response to the question above: "Religious associations—Islamic and Christian—have aspired, since their establishment in the last century, to support values of religious tolerance and varieties of schools, in addition to their cultural and political roles in the struggle against occupation and in raising up the value of national loyalty" (al-Ahram Centre 1998, 309).

The 1998 report goes on to point out the following with relation to religious associations in Egyptian history: Muslim and Christian associations have competed in a positive way since they appeared on the scene; Christian associations have focused upon areas where there has been a heavier concentration of Christians; and there are more religious associations in Cairo than in other provinces (al-Ahram Centre 1998, 309). It then examines cooperation between Christians and Muslims in terms of the associational map of 1996, an analysis of the relationship between religious communities' presence and the establishment of religious associations, and finally a comparative case study of the Young Men's Muslim Association and the Young Men's Christian Association (al-Ahram Centre 1998, 309–10).

These reports, available to the Egyptian general public, attempt to offer a comprehensive study of the role religion has played in society. They are very helpful to the reader, especially in their stated task of educating Egyptians about their compatriots' various faith traditions. One of the projects of the Ibn Khaldun Center for Development Studies was its study on education, which concluded that the Egyptian school system does not offer sufficient curricula on the variety of religious expression found in the country. As a result of a detailed study of various curricula in Egyptian schools, such as Arabic language, religion, history, and civics, a report was drafted, "Egyptian Education and Tolerance" (*al-Mujtama' al-madani* 1999, 7). The report contended that there is an imbalance in the emphasis on Islam in the national curriculum in comparison to Christianity, which is hardly mentioned. Appearing prior to this report, the two editions of *The*

State of Religion in Egypt attempted to address this imbalance, even though the report was not intended to be adopted as part of school curriculum. It did, however, focus on the population more broadly.

The Ibn Khaldun Center for Development Studies

The Ibn Khaldun Center closed in 2000, then reopened in 2003. It has been in the midst of controversy for much of its existence; from its start in 1988, the subjects it has chosen to put on its very public agenda have been controversial. They include the rights of minorities, voters' rights and registration, religious education, and freedom of the press, among other topics. During its operational period (and arguably for what it represented while closed), the center was not only part of civil society but its main focus was on the very concept of civil society, especially as it is manifest in the Arab world. The founders chose not to register the center as a civil association with the Ministry of Social Affairs but rather as a professional firm, subject to taxation, despite its not-for-profit status. The reason is that its founders recognized that the former type of registration "grants government officials large administrative authorities, which enable them to interfere in the affairs of the associations" (Ibn Khaldun Center 1990, 5). From its conception, the center's visionaries felt the center needed to maintain its independence in order to retain integrity in the work it would do. Saad Eddin Ibrahim is the director and chairman of the board of trustees of the center.

The center's overarching theme, inherent in every program it implements, is civil society and democratization in the Arab world. Programs of particular relevance to this discussion are the Ethnic, Religious, and Racial Minorities in the Arab World project, the Religious Movements program, and the State of Education in Egypt project. The first of these projects, Ethnic, Religious, and Racial Minorities, was an ongoing project that became a central focus. It was conceived based on the fact that minorities in some countries are not well integrated and the recognition that there is a need for "models and mechanisms for identifying and protecting minority rights and privileges" (Ibn Khaldun Center 1990, 16–17). Work in this area has included publication of a seminal work entitled *al-Millal wa'l-nihal wa'l-a'raq: Humum al-aqaliyyat fi'l-watan al-'arabi* (Ethnic, Religious, and Racial Minorities in the Arab World), annual reports under the same title, books focusing on various minorities, and reports in the Arabic and English versions of the center's regular magazine, *Civil Society*. The conference on the Middle East's minorities that this program convened drew considerable attention (see chapter 7).

The center's treatment of minorities has been controversial and even explosive at times in Egypt, since it includes Copts among those it classifies as a minority. Many Christians and Muslims argue that the Christians of Egypt are not a minority because they are part of the national fabric and are virtually indistinguishable from Muslims in terms of language, skin color and features, and ethnicity; others point to the numeric and demographic differences, as well as limits on their social mobility, as sufficient criteria to name the Copts as a minority. In the annual report for 1993, the center points to sectarian violence and a lack of opportunity for professional advancement as two of the significant ways Copts experience discrimination. The report recommends political reform in conjunction with efforts to bring more moderate Muslims in contact with Christians so that sectarian tension ends (S. Ibrahim 1993b, 46–48).

Seeing that the problem of sectarian strife was not a short-term problem, and because of the work of the Religious Movements program, which has been active in researching Islamic activism and in rehabilitating former Islamic militants (Ibn Khaldun Center 1990, 17–18), and because of the lack of research on public education in Egypt, the center initiated a research project in 1998 focusing on the extremely important area of the formation of young Egyptians. As Walzer (1997, 74–75) points out, "It is commonly and rightly said that the point of multiculturalism is to teach children about each other's culture, to bring pluralism of the immigrant society [in this case, another indigenous group] into its classrooms [in order to] recognize them . . . and to lead them to understand and admire their own diversity."

Starting with the observation that students "go through six to twelve years of formal schooling without learning anything about the religion or culture of Copts" (Ibn Khaldun Center 1990, 25), the center aimed to see where the deficiencies and imbalances were most pronounced and then to work on a revised curriculum to "contribute to a proper, sympathetic, tolerant, egalitarian attitude formation; and hence, the reduction of inter-religious tension" (Ibn Khaldun Center 1990, 25). A draft of the study, which was carried out by a number of experts in religion, history, Arabic literature, and film making, both Muslims and Christians, was distributed to more than one hundred authorities, including the shaikh of al-Azhar and the minister of education, and to some members of the press before its distribution to a wider audience. A public media attack was made on the project's editor, Ahmad Subhi Mansur, and on the Ibn Khaldun Center that they were infidels for suggesting their findings (*al-Mujtama' al-madani* 1999, 7). Even so, the center published a suggested outline for a curriculum for secondary school students to study Christianity.

The curriculum begins with a discussion entitled "Acceptance of the Other," defining the human condition as essentially social and elaborating on who the Other is and the Other as a manifestation of God's love. The section on how to accept the Other who is "different" includes the themes of respect for differences, active dialogue to find common ground, and openness and love for others. The final section of the first part of the curriculum deals with the blessings of accepting the Other, including serving others, learning the virtues of the Other, and preserving the harmony of society. These topics are presented with an eye to understanding basic tenets of Christianity in a way that is understandable and appealing. The curriculum goes on to introduce Christian thinking with regard to violence and to demonstrate Christian participation in society (Fawzi n.d.). Each of these sections aims to portray Christianity in a positive way so that some stereotypes are broken down and new perceptions may be formed, but also to focus on heritage and values that are recognizably held commonly by Christianity and Islam.

The Ibn Khaldun Center has been an example of Christian-Muslim cooperation. In several of its programs, it has attempted to overcome sectarian tensions through creative means for the betterment of Egyptian society. There can be no doubt that the ideas and agendas it has put on the table will continue to have impact, although while in prison in 2002 Ibrahim did not have plans to reopen the Center (Hammond 2002, 37). The center's efforts in themselves caused tensions, not so much between Christians and Muslims but rather between the center, the state, and more radical Muslims, the very triangle of relations among civil society, state, and political Islam to which the center dedicates much study.

On June 30, 2000, the center's director, Saad Eddin Ibrahim, was arrested, along with twenty-six colleagues from the center. In the catalogue of charges against Ibrahim, the following were reported: "defaming Egypt's reputation by publishing rights reports on sectarian tensions between Christians and Muslims; intending to monitor Egyptian parliamentary elections; forging voting documents; and illegally receiving funding from the European Commission" (Hammond 2002, 36).

At his May 21, 2001, trial, Ibrahim's lawyers were sure that he would be acquitted, but, in fact, he was sentenced in what was largely considered to be a message to civil society in Egypt "to stifle freedom of expression and to intimidate the whole Egyptian human rights movement into silence" (Halawi 2002). Related, but at a more personal level, Ibrahim's "guilty verdict . . . was widely regarded as politically motivated against someone who had severely embarrassed the government and President Hosni Mubarak himself with his vocal public campaigns for more civil rights" (Hammond 2002, 37).

Clearly, the arrest of Ibrahim and the closing of the center had to do with many factors. Two of the charges are immediately germane to this study but are not necessarily more central to Ibrahim's conviction than any of the other charges.

The charge of defamation was rooted in Ibrahim's work on tension and violence between Muslims and Christians in Egypt and on election rights and procedures during the 1995 election. The latter of these aspects was clearly political; the former, too, was political, but it is highly ironic that while in prison, the "Islamists gave him a warm welcome. Ibrahim spoke of a 'special rapport' with the Islamist prisoners" (Hammond 2002, 37), presumably incarcerated for attempting to advance their agenda of replacing the secular government with an Islamic one, an agenda that, if successful, would likely have negative effects on the Christian community. It is thus an agenda that Ibrahim would have studied in the context of tension and violence between Christians and Muslims, and of which he has been critical.

The charge of illegal receipt of funding from abroad came as a result of a quarter-million-dollar grant the center had received from the European Union to work on voter registration and education. Ironically, "in response to the [latter charge], the EU issued statements confirming they were satisfied with the way Ibrahim had made use of their money and repeatedly praised his activity in the field of human rights" (Halawi 2002). The legal basis for the conviction on this charge, however, was grounded in the 1992 law requiring NGOs and charities to gain government approval before they could accept grants from abroad. This decree was instituted in the wake of the October 1992 earthquake and Islamic groups' provision of assistance to victims; normally, the decree would not apply to organizations like the Ibn Khaldun Center, which is registered as a professional firm (Weaver 2001, 49). The irony, according to Mohamad El-Sayed Said, deputy director for al-Ahram's Centre for Political and Strategic Studies, is that

> the legal system itself is intrinsically contradictory, and so vague that people are suddenly accused of a "crime" they had been committing for years under the eyes of various law enforcement agencies. Not only did the prosecution fail to define the crime adequately; worse still, the behaviour suddenly defined as criminal is exactly what people are urged to do according to the open door policy . . . initiated . . . after all . . . [by] the government. (Said 2001)

Ibrahim was released on December 3, 2002, when Egypt's Court of Cassation, its highest appeals court, rendered null the seven-year sentence, which Ibrahim was serving for a second time (MacFarquhar 2002) after having been released on February 7, 2002 and granted a retrial. The retrial resulted in a sentence on July 29, 2002, of seven years with hard labor. After nearly nine months, Egypt's Court of Cassation overturned the guilty verdict in an acquittal by the country's highest court that could not be contested by the government (Sachs 2003). The second conviction has deeper meaning for the question of state and civil society in Egypt.

> Throughout Ibrahim's trial and retrial, the rhetoric of state security prosecutors and prosecution witnesses revealed a dominant state jealous of its prerogatives and unwilling to conceptualize politics as

anything other than a zero-sum game. Prosecutors insisted on the right to prosecute despite the EC's signed affidavits absolving Ibrahim of the embezzlement charge, the right of the state to monitor and intrude upon the activities of NGOs, the right of the state to be free of "defamation" and the right of the state alone to decide what is best for society, with minimal input from representatives of society itself. (El-Ghobashy 2002)

Ibrahim, in an effort to push for reform of the political system, announced his candidacy for president in the presidential elections of 2005, the first proposed to allow a multicandidate ballot. The election resulted in Mubarak's reelection by an overwhelming margin.

The Ibn Khaldun Center reopened on June 30, 2003, and resumed its activities of chronicling and participating in Egyptian civil society, including monitoring of elections and the process of democratization, studies of sects and minorities, and work on gender and human development. It represents a forum for research and study on several aspects of social study, including Christian-Muslim relations in Egypt.

The Coptic Evangelical Organization for Social Services

The Coptic Evangelical Organization for Social Services (CEOSS) is principally a community development organization actively engaged from the grass roots to the intellectual level in improving the common lot of Christian and Muslim Egyptians. It is difficult to separate CEOSS from its founder and general director, the late Rev. Samuel Habib, who has already been presented as president of the Protestant Community of Egypt. It is in the work of CEOSS that Habib's theology and philosophy are implemented. Indeed, during the time when Habib served contemporaneously as CEOSS's general director and as president of the Protestant community, there was often an inherent confusion as to which hat he wore, but the two were complementary for him, even if overlapping. The dual role was perhaps what enabled Habib to develop ideas and to test them out in practice.

Habib established what would become CEOSS in 1952 when he was ordained to a special ministry of teaching literacy in an Upper Egyptian village. The rural village, Herz, is located near the city of Minia and is populated almost entirely by Christians. Working with an American Presbyterian missionary, Davida Finney, and another Protestant Egyptian pastor, the Rev. Menis Abdel-Nour, the project was underway. The program was initially designed to teach literacy to people so that they could read the Bible. This idea was consistent with the "Protestant Reformation" that had taken place in Egypt less than a century before, resulting in the translation of the Bible into Arabic. Such a project, then, aimed to enable people to have access to the Christian scriptures.

As the popularity of the program grew, and more people and villages became aware of what was being accomplished, not only did programs expand but the number of staff needed to implement the programs of literacy, leadership training, home economics, agriculture, and income-generating projects also increased. Habib saw these various areas of service as ways to address integrated problems in the communities in which he was working. When the Ministry of Social Affairs established a registry of associations in the early 1960s, CEOSS registered, recognizing that it would be easier to move in the communities in which it was invited to work if it was officially registered (*Tariq at-tahaddi* 1999, 117).

The registration of CEOSS with the government had two important ramifications for CEOSS. First, it had to assume the place of an NGO and thus could no longer be a part of the Evangelical (Presbyterian) Church of Egypt. While ties have remained, they have been less direct or formal. In the case of Habib's dual role in the 1980s and 1990s, the link became highly personalized. The second ramification was that CEOSS, in applying for registration, announced that it wanted to serve both Christians and Muslims. By approving the registration, the government gave CEOSS the chance to do so. Until today, CEOSS has been deliberate and very clear that it does not aim to serve Christians alone, but rather any Egyptian regardless of religious background.

CEOSS's work has expanded over its half-century of operation to communities from the Nile Delta in the north to Minia and beyond in the south. CEOSS's philosophy of community development is that a community must first invite CEOSS to enter; it does not impose itself or its programs on any community that does not express a desire for cooperation.

By the late 1980s and early 1990s, CEOSS was receiving many more invitations than it could possibly accept due to its staff and resource limitations. These communities ranged in composition from almost entirely Christian, to an even balance of Christians and Muslims, to almost entirely Muslim. Once a community formally invites CEOSS and the invitation for cooperation looks promising (according to criteria determined by CEOSS), a meeting is arranged between CEOSS development staff and members of the community leadership to determine ways that cooperation can be fostered, and what programs the community feels would be helpful for its needs. In the early years of the twenty-first century, CEOSS shifted its focus to one of enabling local communities and local community-based organizations to undertake community development on their own, with CEOSS as a facilitator or catalyst, thus giving a more central role to communities themselves.

Empowerment of the poorest of the poor is basic to CEOSS's philosophy, derived from its theology of service to those parts of the society that are most in need. According to Habib, "The organization works with people in the lower levels of society and helps them to attain their correct position within the larger community" (Rizk 1996, 23). It is with such people, and through the programs of the organization, that communities of Egypt begin to move toward a level of self-reliance, as the principles of democracy become the norm.

Through the "fundamental strategy of turning the helpless person into a decision maker in his/her community," impoverished people and communities begin to assume greater and greater responsibility for their current, and future, conditions. By assisting the communities to establish relations with local NGOs and government agencies, self-reliance is reinforced (Rizk 1996, 23). CEOSS does not work in "charity" but rather in solidarity and partnership with the communities, because the communities are expected to participate fully in the decision-making processes, as well as to make a financial contribution to the projects that are implemented so that a sense of ownership exists and so that a sense of commitment to a project is fostered.

CEOSS works with Christians and Muslims blindly—that is, it does not distinguish between people of different faiths. In fact, in many of the communities in which CEOSS works, the population has a Muslim major-ity. Habib elucidates the basis for this nondiscriminatory policy:

> CEOSS calls for enlightened religious thought, which holds firm to sincere faith in God, on the one hand, and which calls for an enlight-ened understanding of religion, on the other. CEOSS thus calls for the respect and acceptance of the "other" in spite of diversity and difference. To that end, CEOSS's concern for humanity is based upon the idea that divine law exists for the sake of humanity, and not the inverse. CEOSS is aware of the importance of its own role in building an adequate and just society. CEOSS works with people to attain a dignified life, just as it works to nourish and empower them so that they become able to make the future, and as it works with society to attain its unity. This [and other aspects] makes up CEOSS's policy. It puts these principles into practice in its own administration and in-ternal functioning, as it strives for them in the communities in which CEOSS works. (S. Habib 1995c, 5)

A great deal of money is represented in CEOSS. It is an organization with an annual development budget in excess of a million dollars, some of which comes from contributions from agencies and churches abroad. When asked about the mission of CEOSS, whether it is truly engaged in development for the sake of human dignity or if its ulterior motive is the conversion of Muslims to Christianity, Habib would typically respond by saying that a great deal of money is spent by Christians and Muslims to convert each other. If 2 percent of each community actually converts, that leaves 98 per-cent of each steadfast in their faith tradition. Only a small percentage, then, is the result of so much time, effort, and money. If all of these energies and resources were spent on making the society a better place in which to live, including improving relations between the faith communities, wouldn't Christians and Muslims all be better off? (S. Habib ca. 1993)

If this is the theory, how well is the idea put into practice? Two fac-ets of CEOSS's work in bridging the religious gap in Egypt are especially relevant. The first is the area of community development, and the second is its program of dialogue that involves leading Christian and Muslim thinkers.

CEOSS's process is one of working within a community. Religious tolerance is an important part of CEOSS's guiding principles. The examples of how the principle is made tangible in the field of community development are many. One program that CEOSS has concentrated on integrating into its work with communities is the family planning program. Its focus on family planning began in May 1965 when it published a series of articles over the next few years in its own publication, *Risalat an-nur* (Letter of Light), a magazine that, since its inception, has been designed to bring social concerns to those who have completed certain levels of the literacy program. The first article that appeared in the magazine was called "The Problem of Rabbits." Additionally, Habib was the first to publish a book in Egypt from a Christian perspective on family planning when, in 1969, he wrote on the population problem worldwide and in Egypt, the reasons for its aggravation, the problems that result from population increase, what is meant by family planning, the different perspectives of the church with regard to family planning, male and female fertility, and some family planning methods.

Hoping to help rural families understand family planning and convince them of its importance for the family practically and economically, CEOSS initiated a program in 1974 to help families learn to limit the number of children they would have by teaching birth control methods and caring for a pregnant mother through birth. In order to reach many people, it was important to seek the support of local clergy, Christian and Muslim, so that the people who are to benefit from the program understand that their religion does not oppose the ideas (Naguib and Zaghlul 1989, 22).

Over the course of thirty years, between 1964 and 1995, the number of communities with which CEOSS worked in the area of family planning increased from thirty-six at the outset to eighty. The number of women who practiced family planning in those communities rose from 10,547 to 55,013 (S. Habib 1995c, 31). Because of its leadership role in this area, CEOSS was on the local planning committee for the International Conference on Population and Development, held in Cairo in September 1994. Because CEOSS is committed to participating in the national development process, and because it is respected as having been successful in family planning, CEOSS has cooperated with the National Population Council.

As a social organization rooted in the Christian faith, CEOSS has recognized the importance of religion and the role it plays in communities. It can attribute a significant portion of its success to its work with local religious leadership. CEOSS knows that if religious leadership support CEOSS's ideas and work, then the community will be more likely to accept it. In the area of family planning as in other areas of its work, CEOSS has organized meetings bringing together Christian and Muslim clergy, particularly from the communities in which the programs are being carried out, but it also invites nationally recognized religious figures to make them more acutely aware of the population problem, its dangers, and the role religious institutions can play in facing it (S. Habib 1995c, 30).

In 1994, three important sessions were held involving prominent religious leaders to discuss the issue of population, and to share perspectives from Islam and Christianity. The first brought together the minister of religious endowments; the chairman of the National Population Council, Dr. Maher Mahran; Pope Shenouda III; and Habib. The second brought back Mahran, and centered around the question, "After the International Conference on Population and Development, What Now?" The third brought such speakers as the vice minister of religious endowments, 'Abd ar-Rashid Salem, Habib, and the general secretary of the National Population Council, Mahmud 'abd ar-Rahman (S. Habib 1995c, 30).

The forums for dialogue that CEOSS and other organizations convene resemble academic settings, and the presentations even can become homiletical. The efficacy of this type of forum is debatable since they may not have the same kind of impact on the grass roots that other kinds of projects do. They do garner media coverage, and the topics covered are aimed at the intellectually curious and can be a point of departure for discussion at many levels of society. CEOSS's primary work, community development, has a direct and tangible impact in Egyptian communities—both majority Christian and majority Muslim. Those activities, complemented by the public forums and publishing, form the bulk of CEOSS's work and arguably have the greatest impact on Christian-Muslim relations at the grassroots level, both at the level of relationships between CEOSS field workers and the host community's (mostly Muslim) leaders, and between Christians and Muslims in the communities themselves.

An example from a different level of society, a grassroots community from which CEOSS received an invitation to work, illustrates the point. Members of the community committee of al-Hikr, a squatter community a few kilometers north of Ramsis Square (a main square and the location of the Cairo train station), related this anecdote in 1994. The community itself is overwhelmingly Muslim, about 95 percent of the population. The community had been denied any kind of government service because of its squatter nature.

When CEOSS first received an invitation to work in this community, it agreed to accept after meeting with the local committee that had formed to discuss the community's needs. When CEOSS staff started to move into the facility made ready for them (CEOSS staff, all Egyptian, live in the community in which they work several days of the week in order to better become familiar with the community and its people, to understand the community dynamics, and to demonstrate their full solidarity with the community), some local Islamic leaders expressed their opposition. One *shaikh* in particular even went so far as to preach on the next Friday against the involvement of Christians who he felt were only interested in the community so that they could convert its Muslims. CEOSS staff members met with the angry *shaikh* and other religious leaders in the community, along with the community committee that had issued the initial invitation, and the result of the meeting was an agreement that CEOSS would work for a trial period, implementing one program. A decision would then be made as to whether the work would continue. During the trial period, those who had opposed CEOSS's involvement saw that the staff were not interested in converting the community but rather were truly anxious to cooperate to improve the lot of the people of al-Hikr. The *shaikh* became so convinced of this that he preached a Friday sermon calling on all to support CEOSS's involvement. Such a story brings to life the role that religious leaders can play in shaping local opinion, and the philosophy of inclusivity and acceptance that is one of CEOSS's guiding principles.

The work of CEOSS depends upon religious cooperation and sharing. By hosting a series of celebrations of the *iftar*, CEOSS shares intimately with Muslims during their celebration of one of the most blessed times of the Islamic calendar. Each year, CEOSS hosts such celebrations, even though Ramadan and the *iftar* have no sacred meaning for Christians. The common celebration is not only an acknowledgement of the religious life of the Other, but it is also an acceptance and sharing of it.

In three *iftar* celebrations during Ramadan 1414 (according to the Islamic *hijra* calendar, or February 1995 according to the Gregorian calendar), CEOSS hosted the mufti of Egypt, the Ministry of Religious Endowments' representatives in Alexandria and Minia, the vice president of the High Council for Islamic Affairs, and other notable guests. Such *iftars* are opportunities for expressions of positive social relations. In the Cairo *iftar*, Muhammad Sayyid Tantawi, the then mufti of Egypt, said,

> The Holy Qur'an states that God created all people from one father and one mother and we, praise God, have lived in Egypt for about fourteen centuries as loving brothers . . . together on one land, under the shade of one heaven, breathing the same air, in neighboring homes and fields, working in the same factories and offices, using the same utilities. We live together in honor, trust, and human fraternity for the sake of holding up truth, progress, and advancement of our country. (N. Salama 1995, 6)

The host, the Rev. Habib, shared the following: "During this holy month, we all sense our one humanity that pushes us to goodness and to serve others. We have lived, and continue to live, as one family, Muslims and Christians, enjoying together the partnership that links us, whatever our differences, for we are all part of this single nation, Egypt, from which we are, and for which we live" (N. Salama 1995, 8–9).

These are examples of the rhetoric expressed by both the invited and the host at such occasions. Such celebrations of *iftar* are usually considered by all to be happy and bridging occasions.

CEOSS has also worked very hard to foster good relations among regional and national religious figures in other, more academic yet public, settings. Chapter 4 treats official religion and discusses examples of forums and topics where dialogue at top levels has taken place. CEOSS's Muntada (Forum) program works to engage leaders in such dialogue. The result of the component of CEOSS's former Studies and Dialogue program, the Muntada today continues in the same tradition. According to CEOSS's

Web site (www.ceoss.org.eg), the program, established in 1992, "brings together Christians and Muslims, clergy and lay people, intellectuals and individuals from the entire array of society for the sake of promoting mutual understandings on contemporary issues in religion, culture and civil society . . . [which has resulted in] a move from coexistence to cooperation."

On several occasions religious leaders have had the opportunity to discuss and debate such contemporary topics as "Religious Thought and Social Progress" (Nov. 1992), in which Habib, Tantawi, and Muhammad Salim al-'Awa participated, marking the first time an Egyptian mufti had spoken in a Protestant church in Egypt; "Religious Thought and Citizenship" (Feb. 1994); "Religious Thought and Social Participation" (1995); "The Mission of Religion in the Information Age" (Nov. 1995); "The Church and Economic and Social Transformation" (June 1996); "The Egyptian and the Challenges of the Next Century" (Aug. 1996); "Arab Protestants and Zionism" (Dec. 1997); "The Right to Differ and Be Different" (Mar. 1999); "Religious Thought and the Future of Values at the Threshold of the Next Century" (May 1999); and "Religion and Human Rights: An Historical and Social Comparative Study" (1999).

Although the topics may read like a list of esoteric subjects, the debates brought together religious leaders from different parts of the Muslim and Christian spectra to discuss their perceptions of the matters at hand. If the subjects themselves were not the main focus, then it was the ecumenical and interfaith encounter, indeed collegial dialogue, that was the primary focus of the occasions. Where there is not always agreement, there is respect. Such events are covered widely in the Egyptian media, so that evidence is documented of cooperation at the highest levels of thought and institutional religion.

CEOSS has worked for more than fifty years in the field and continues its work under the directorship of Nabil S. Abadir, who was elected by the board of directors to become general secretary after Rev. Habib passed away in October 1997. Over the course of its history, it has been an important participant in efforts to foster better relations between Christians and Muslims in Egypt. It is a significant example of a civil society organization that has dedicated much of its resources to that end, either directly or indirectly.

Conclusions

This chapter focuses on NGOs that have attempted to foster better relations between Christians and Muslims, even in a context of conflict and distance. This sector has reached from the very top of Egyptian society to the very grass roots to improve the sensibilities of Egyptians with regard to their compatriots of other faiths, and indeed the Other more generally. Smock (2002, 9) describes the importance of the NGO community by stating, "Faith-based nongovernmental organizations (NGOs) and other religious organizations very effectively contribute to peace through conducting training on conflict resolution, mediating between parties in conflict, engaging in conflict prevention, promoting nonviolent methodologies, organizing postconflict reconciliation, and devising other approaches to conflict resolution as part of their relief and development programs."

Whether through the design of a more inclusive educational curriculum, community development activities, interfaith celebrations of religious occasions and holidays, or forums of discussion and debate, there are many hopeful examples of cooperation among Egypt's Christians and Muslims. NGOs, both religious and secular, play an important role in providing many kinds of services to the people, including services that the government cannot or does not provide. Such service provision gives NGOs a special kind of access to convey a social message. NGOs that have an inclusive and accepting ideology can serve society by helping to reduce sectarian tension at a grassroots level and can therefore compete in good works. Such works contribute to the management of conflict and, possibly, the elimination of animus.

7

Incidents of Tension

Rhetoric of Cooperation in a Context of Fitna

During the Mubarak presidency, there have been many opportunities for cooperation between Muslims and Christians in Egypt. Chapters 3–6 examined the depth of cooperation at several levels of Egyptian polity and society. A significant test of any actor's tolerance and acceptance of the Other comes when a specific incident or event brings underlying tensions to the fore. This chapter examines three events that took place between 1994 and 2000, when militant radical Islam was perhaps at its strongest, but during which the cooperation explored in previous chapters permeated various levels of Egyptian society. These events have been selected for examination not only because of their inherent significance but because they illustrate themes often invoked in discussions of the relationship between Egypt's Muslims and Christians. By drawing the specific events together, the level of tolerance and acceptance that ensued in their wake can be demonstrated, as well as the kind of rhetoric that is not uncommon in the larger discourse.

The three cases chosen for discussion here are (1) a proposal to include the Copts on the agenda of a 1994 conference, "The United Nations Declaration on the Rights of Minorities and People of the Arab World and the Middle East"; (2) the reaction and debate in Egypt over legislation proposed in the United States in the mid- to late 1990s to monitor religious persecution around the world; and (3) the violent clashes that took place in the village of al-Kusheh, in the Suhaj province of Upper Egypt during the first week of 2000. Each of these events brings into focus at least one important aspect of the debate on Muslim-Christian relations in Egypt. In the case of the conference on minorities, the issue was whether Egypt's

Christians qualified as a minority on the same basis as other minorities in the Middle East, that is, because of difference in language, culture, ethnicity, or some other factor. In the case of the U.S. legislation to monitor persecution, the issue was Western, and particularly American, patronage of Christians and other religious minorities in other parts of the world, specifically the Muslim world. In the case of the clashes at al-Kusheh, the issue was partly the governmental role and partly the nature of the roots of such clashes: is religion the primary motivation for conflict, or do such clashes result from social, economic, or other tensions. This chapter's quest is not to provide a definitive conclusion to the larger issues that will surely persist and be debated, but to examine the responses from various actors to get a sense of Muslim-Christian relations and efforts to reduce levels of potential conflict in the midst of heightened tensions.

Should Copts Be Included among Minorities in the Arab World?

In May 1994, the Ibn Khaldun Center for Developmental Studies co-sponsored with the London-based Minority Rights Group a conference entitled, "The UN Declaration on the Rights of Minorities and People of the Arab Nations." The Ibn Khaldun Center has concentrated on issues of minorities as one of its primary themes, consistent with its dedication to the idea of civil society. In its final statement, the conference reported that its goal was "to familiarize specialists and the general Arab public on the content of the 'United Nations Declaration on Individuals Belonging to National, Ethnic, Religious, or Linguistic Minorities'" (Ibn Khaldun Center 1994). Perhaps this manner of expressing the goal, that is, focusing on the content of the declaration without indicating judgment of its intention, was intended to offset much of the debate that surrounded the conference. The controversy around the conference led to the relocation of the conference from its intended venue of Cairo to Limassol, Cyprus, a place less accessible to disruptive activity and considered neutral and European. The source of the controversy was in the title originally proposed for the conference—"Conference on the International Declaration on the Rights of Minorities (al-uqulliyyat) in the Arab World and the Middle East"—and the inclusion of the Copts on the conference agenda "next to the Kurds of Iraq, the Berbers of the Arab Maghreb, the Druze in Israel, and the Armenians in Lebanon" (ad-Dahabi 1998, 70–71). Later, after controversy erupted, the conference organizers changed the name of the conference so that the conference would not be derailed. The revised title was "Conference on the International Declaration on the Rights of Minorities, Confessional Groups, and Peoples [al-uqulliyyat wa't-tawa'if wa'sh-shu'ub] of the Arab World and the Middle East" (U. Salama 1994, 16). When the prominent writer Muhammad Hassanain Haikal published a response to the idea of Coptic inclusion in the Egyptian daily al-Ahram, under the title "The Copts of Egypt Are Not a Minority, But a Part of the Human and Civilizational Bloc of the Egyptian People," the debate began. In that article, Haikal wrote,

> The Copts of Egypt are not a minority among the minorities of the Arab world and the Middle East, not in the ethnic sense like the Kurds in Iraq or the Berbers in the Arab Maghreb, not in a confessional sense like the Druze or Armenians in Israel or Lebanon, and not in a religious sense alone. That is the secret of Egyptian particularity over the course of the human experiment in this country, just as it is the secret of the unity and holding together of the civilizational body of the Egyptian people. . . . Perhaps that is what Lord Cromer meant when, upon leaving Egypt, he said, "I did not find any difference between a Muslim and a Copt in Egypt except that one of them prays in a mosque and the other prays in a church." (quoted in ad-Dahabi 1998, 71)

Following the publication of that article, many words were printed about the issue, and a debate followed in the print media in an attempt to provide insight and a degree of resolution to the matter.

Of course, simply based upon the criteria of religious belief and numbers, Christians in Egypt are a minority in the midst of the Muslim numerical majority. The weekly magazine Rose El Yossef contributed to the discussion by publishing the discrepancy between official government statistics, which said that in 1976 there were 2.28 million Copts, and in 1994 between 3.36 and 3.8 million Christians. The pronouncements of the Church, on the other hand, reported 4 million Copts in 1976 and 8 million Christians in 1994, also pointing out that, even among Copts, there are different estimates (U. Salama 1994, 15, 17). The Ibn Khaldun Center's director, Saad Eddin Ibrahim, wrote to Pope Shenouda, patriarch of the Coptic Orthodox Church, to "clarify the stance of the Ibn Khaldun Center and the conference with respect to the Copts, saying that he does not consider them a minority but a part of the fabric of the nation . . . and that the intention was to discuss the concerns of the Copts." The pope not only remained steadfast in his refusal to accept the inclusion of the Copts on the agenda of the conference but also in his position that he "likes neither that the Copts think of themselves as minority nor that anyone would call them a minority" (U. Salama 1994, 16). Clearly, the official position of the Coptic Orthodox Church was to assert unity among religious groups and to state unequivocally that all Egyptians are part and parcel of the nation, without the need for differentiation. This stance is certainly consistent with the stance of Copts who rejected the proposal for the 1923 constitution that called for the allotment of a number of seats in the Egyptian Parliament to Christians based on the mere fact of their Christianity (S. Ibrahim 1996a, 12).

A number of high-placed Orthodox Christians who were invited to participate in the conference did not attend, including William Sulaiman Qalada, a prominent historian of the Copts; Samir Morcos, director of the Coptic Center for Social Studies; and Yunan Labib Rizk. If Copts are ethnically, linguistically, and sociologically the same as Egypt's Muslims, then, according to Samir Morcos, "Religion is all that remains—a minor distinction when you consider that Copts took part in all political struggles. The concept of 'minority' serves to polarize because it sets a dynamic of a minority against a majority" (al-Gawhary 1996, 21). Considering the context of an upsurge in activity among radical Islamists in the first part of the 1990s in Egypt, Morcos's desire to preserve national unity resonated when he stated, "In times of crisis you are made to feel your Coptic identity but at the same time your best protection is to emphasize your 100 percent undivided Egyptian-ness" (22).

A number of recommendations came about as a result of the attention the conference gave to the possibility of discrimination between Christians and Muslims in Egypt, including the removal of religion as a listing on the national identity card, revision of laws requiring presidential approval for church repair and construction, discussion about national educational curriculum, and consideration of official holidays in consultation with the Christian calendar of holy days. It is important that some Christians felt that Muslims ought to speak out on some of these issues, a strategy that would give the issues at hand a different weight (al-Gawhary 1996, 22).

It is also significant that some Muslims who were invited to participate also refused, rejecting the idea of Copts as minority in Egypt. Among them were Muhammad Salim al-'Awa, a prominent lawyer, a founding member of the proposed al-Wasat Party, a participant in the "Misr: For Culture and Dialogue" NGO project, and a member of the Arab Group for Muslim-Christian Dialogue, a regional institution made up of journalists, intellectuals, and clergy who deal through dialogue with issues and ideas relevant to people of both faiths throughout the region. The prominent Muslim historian of Egyptian politics and Coptic participation therein, Mustafa El-Feki, also was invited to participate and in fact did attend the conference but requested not to participate in the special session on Coptic concerns so that he could attend other concurrent sessions. (Indeed, El-Feki participated in the workshop on Lebanon [Salama 1994, 16].) These reactions demonstrate the commitment of official religion, as represented by the Coptic Church, as well as that of others involved intellectually in preserving the unity of the country, to national unity. Some other reactions to the conference and the issue at hand also shed some light.

As a follow-up to the conference on minorities, an intellectual workshop was held in Cairo in November 1994 at the Ibn Khaldun Center. It is significant that a Muslim thinker presented a paper entitled "Anxieties of Copts." In his paper, Essam El Din Hassan affirmed that "freedom of opinion and expression must be granted and religious fanaticism must be eradicated by education which promotes political, cultural and religious plurality in Egyptian society" (Hassan 1995, 14).

The point of view of the government was made clear by the president himself when Mubarak spoke to the preparatory committee of the national dialogue committe. In that meeting on May 29, 1994, Mubarak stated,

> Our society does not know any distinctions based on ethnicity or religion, confession or class; in our society, the groups of the population have been united since the dawn of history; all of the currents and

> ideological schools melted in our society's pot in which the Egyptian
> social fabric is held together. There is no room for sectarianism, nor is
> there space for intolerance or class divisions. (ad-Dahabi 1998, 74)

Such a strong reaction from the president indicates the official position.
The timing of the speech was important, too, because it came within two
weeks of the end of the conference. With respect to other official documentation of the government's position, the Reading for All campaign is
a series that is published and subsidized by the government (see chapter
3). The presentation of the matter of Copts and minority status by Edwar
Ghali ad-Dahabi in his book *The Egyptian Model for National Unity* reinforces the position of a single nation without differences. An entire chapter
is dedicated to the minority status question, and a major section of that
chapter treats the conference on minority rights. The first few sentences of
the chapter are a clear expression of that stance:

> What angers Copts the most and what hurts their feelings is talking
> about or treating them as a minority or sect. What always makes them
> feel good is treating them in their capacity as an inseparable part of
> the entire fabric of Egyptian society. . . . This goes back to what they
> have known since the Arab-Islamic conquests, which saved them
> from the persecution of the Christian Roman Empire, that religious
> difference does not detract from the unity of blood and fate among all
> the children of Egypt. (ad-Dahabi 1998, 65)

The official government position was quite clear: unity must not be broken
by the attempt of an organization with international ties to reintroduce a
potentially divisive theme, even in the context of resurgent Islam and the
effects it might have on the religious communities in Egypt.

In considering the response of political intellectuals, Muhammad
Salim al-'Awa refused to take part in the conference, despite an invitation. The secretary-general of the Tagammu' Party, Rifa'at as-Sa'id, was
interviewed in 1998 about pluralism in Egyptian politics and the role of
Christians. In that interview, he was asked specifically about the desig-
nation of Copts as a minority in the conference on minority rights. He
responded:

In mathematical terms, one can say that the Copts are a minority. However in political terms the meaning is altered. In fact if the minority surrendered to the majority in thought and practice, it no longer has a cause to fight for. Similarly, if the Copts surrender to the majority, their cause will not be a sensitive one. Joining a party is facultative, but joining a country is obligatory. Those who like it stay, and those who do not, can leave. As long as joining a country is obligatory there will never be a differentiation between a minority and a majority. It was a fault from the part of the Conference on Minorities to think that the Copts are a minority, because there is a difference between religious and ethnic minorities. Ethnic minorities have the right to self determination (i.e., the Kurds). The matter is different for religious minorities who are a part of the national entity. The fundamental problem with the UN conference on Minorities is foreign funding. "Those who pay rule." Hence it was inevitable to mix the Berbers with the Kurds and the Copts when benefiting from foreign funds. (quoted in Lebib 1998, 16)

This politician's words may have been ambiguous with respect to national unity, but he was certainly direct in his criticism of the conference. As-Sa'id's differentiation between statistical and political minority status went to the heart of the matter debated in the wake of the conference on minorities. For Christians, the issue of numerical minorities in modern-day Egyptian politics and society has long been a concern.

The final statement of the May 1994 conference addressed some of the concerns around the use of the word "minority" and offered an entire section to attempt to clarify and bring to a close the commotion caused by the conference and its inclusion of the Copts on the agenda. The fourth section of the statement, "From 'Minorities' to 'Ethnic' and 'Racial' Groups," read as follows:

In plenary and workshop sessions, participants discussed the reasons for the uproar that was aroused in Egypt and in other places over the use of the word "minority" to describe this group or that, which differs from the ethnic, religious, or national majority. Despite the fact that "minority" is a scientific and neutral sociological concept, not implying any value judgment except as negatively taken by those to whom the term was applied, the participants were motivated to recommend the use of another more acceptable term, or return to traditional terms, such as 'ethnic,' 'racial,' and 'peoples.' Because the aim of the conference and of organizations working in the area of human rights was to seek the essence of the problems and not to get stuck in semantics, the conference accepted this recommendation, and the Ibn Khaldun Center will consider it in its research and advocacy work in this way. In spite of the length of the name, and the injection of words, attention and concern is given to the subject and the content. (Ibn Khaldun Center 1994)

With that statement, a position was made clear. The effect of the conference was to be felt for a long time, however, precisely because of the semantic implications. Several levels of Egyptian society and politics rallied around this very public debate and attempted to preserve the national unity by emphasizing the equality and indistinguishable nature of Egypt's Christians and Muslims. Referring to themes that often come up in such a debate, the debate following the conference on minorities brought the sensitive issue of Christian and Muslim participation in the nation to the forefront. The fact that such issues are so sensitive and bring such passion to the debate indicates that there are feelings of inequality and that efforts have been made to keep them under the surface of the national discourse.

The issues raised by this conference brought the Christian-Muslim relationship in Egypt to the forefront. What is especially important is how the domestic debate played out. While the conference itself was an international conference (it was sponsored by a non-Middle Eastern fund), it was essentially a regional discussion, as it dealt with the peoples of several countries of the Middle East. The matter of the Copts' inclusion on the agenda became an Egyptian discussion with very little interference from or participation by outside factors. Such a debate demonstrated the ability of Egyptian civil society to deal with a potentially controversial issue in a reasoned way. This ability is central to the functioning of civil society. Even though some participants boycotted the conference, the debate was open. The conference itself made important modifications to its approach in recognition of the issues raised by the debate.

One issue is how members of each community think about members of the other community. If members of each community think of themselves simply as members of the defined community, then the debate becomes tautological, since discussion to the contrary is contradicted by the basic assumptions. If the idea of community is defined in multiple layers (religious, national, linguistic, and so on), then the debate becomes more vibrant. If one community's members think of themselves as part of the more powerful majority, then a position of privilege and control is assumed. In Islam, such a concept is described with the non-Muslim minority having a status of protection, called *dhimma*.

Equal or Second-Class Citizens—Who Decides?

"Every country has the right to legislate whatever laws it wills to apply in that country, but not to impose [those laws] on other countries" (*al-Ahram* 2000b). This quotation is a concise statement of Pope Shenouda's position with respect to the United States' proposed (and eventually passed) legislation entitled the Freedom from Religious Persecution Act. The movement in the U.S. Congress, culminating in May 1998 with passage of the named act, was intended to create an office to monitor religious persecution throughout the world and mandate the imposition of various degrees of penalties, the most serious of which are economic sanctions, against countries that participate in or allow religious persecution. Two paragraphs in particular express the intent of the law:

> The United States government is committed to the right to freedom of religion, and its policies and relations with foreign governments should be consistent with the commitment to this principle.
>
> To express United States foreign policy with respect to, and to strengthen United States advocacy on behalf of, individuals persecuted for their faith worldwide, is to authorize United States actions in response to religious persecution worldwide. (Morcos 2000, 147)

The proposal was met differently throughout the world. In Egypt, there was significant concern with regard to the implications of such a law upon Muslim-Christian relations within the country and upon Egyptian-American relations in international politics. In an article on interfaith dialogue, Tarek Mitri, a Lebanese academic who participates in the Arab Group for Muslim-Christian Dialogue (and who has served in the Lebanese cabinet) puts the difficulty quite well:

> In many places, religious plurality has a long history, marked by continuity but also by a variety of adjustments. At present, many examples suggest that living together across religious differences has to be constantly reconstructed and its model reinvented. This reconstruction and reinvention is not only a matter to be negotiated by actors in a particular local or national context. In the Christian-Muslim case, it is affected by the global power relations and the related mutual perceptions. (Mitri 1999, 79)

The reconstruction and reinvention to which Mitri refers is something that Egypt certainly knows very well; it often takes place during periods of trial or tension. The second part of Mitri's observation is more explicitly applicable in the context of the U.S. law, which upset the national negotiation of relations between Christians and Muslims in Egypt by the intrusion of global power relations. Taken to an extreme, Mitri proposes that "power relations . . . are such that many Islamists, whose forefathers were concerned with the questions of independence and progress, are worried about their survival as Muslims" (Mitri 1999, 79).

Egyptian Christians living outside Egypt, it must be noted, inadvertently supported the imbalance in preserving and reinventing relations between Christian and Muslim in Egypt caused by the Freedom from Religious Persecution Act. Rightfully concerned about the treatment of Christians in Egypt, *aqbat al-mahjar* (Copts of the diaspora) went to great lengths, particularly in the United States and England, to advocate for passage of the law. For example, the International Coptic Federation placed advertisements in major U.S. newspapers highlighting grievances regarding inequality between Christians and Muslims in Egypt (Napoli 1998, 29); the British Coptic Association reprinted the text of a former member of Parliament who spoke on the persecution of Christians in Egypt before a congressional human rights hearing on the act (*Coptic Voice* 1998,

7–9); and the American Coptic Union insisted that "acts against Egyptian Christians were not 'isolated incidents,' but occurred regularly.... [and that] officials of the Egyptian government did not give equal protection to Christians, but acted in collaboration with terrorists attacking Christians" (Early 1998).

When the act was passed by Congress, the spokesperson of the American Coptic Association issued a memorandum, titled "To God be the glory," that read, "This is a historic day in the life of persecuted people around the world. . . . Let us pray in thanksgiving to God for such a victory" (Kheir 1998). Such advocacy has been described by Christians living inside Egypt as an attack on the well-being of Egypt's Christians and is seen as very dangerous because "heavy-handed US intervention might exacerbate rather than improve the situation of the people legislation is intended to help" (Gavlak 1998). Many Christians inside Egypt who feel that they are not accorded equal rights perhaps accept this perspective, but the reaction within Egypt, upon which the remainder of this section concentrates, did not focus on the fact that there might be problems. Recognizing the problems, the Arab Organization for Human Rights issued a statement that expressed

> deep concern about allegations in the US relating to Egypt's national unity . . . [and that] the US "is not qualified to play the role of protector [since] Egyptian Copts are in no need of such protection." . . . [C]laims by "some Egyptian Copts in the Diaspora" are opposed by all Egyptians, especially their fellow Christians. "Copts [in Egypt] are the first to reject [U.S.] protection. . . . [P]roblems and negative behaviour towards Egyptian Copts" could be solved by "persistent efforts leading to the complete respect of human rights for all citizens." (N. Khalil 1998)

In Egypt, strong negative reaction came from many levels of society, and the Coptic Orthodox Church was among the first and loudest to reject such intervention. Such rejection is represented by Pope Shenouda's remarks in a statement of November 6, 1997, in which he said, "We do not accept foreign intervention in our internal affairs, which we are working to solve calmly" (*an-Nahar* 1997). Pope Shenouda also said, "We can achieve more through love and brotherhood than through pressure" (Curtiss 1998, 72).

At several other levels, Copts in Egypt expressed their rejection of American intervention. Yousef Sidhom, editor-in-chief of the Coptic weekly newspaper *Watani*, stated that "sanctions imposed upon Egypt, for which Egypt's Christian community would be blamed, would harm that minority." He went on to say that "addressing human rights would help the whole community," referring to Christians and Muslims (Curtiss 1998, 72).

Samir Morcos, who by the late 1990s was a consultant to the Coptic Center for Social Studies, which he founded and had directed, wrote a book in which the second part focused on the Copts and the American legislation. The book's title is *al-Himaya wa'l-'aqab* (Protection and Punishment) with a subtitle, "The West and the Religious Question in the Middle East"). One of the subtitles of his book is "A Particular Study of the Copts: History, Citizenship, Concerns, and the Future." Morcos lays out an argument that is quite consistent with that of the patriarchate, that relations between Muslims and Christians in Egypt are not always perfect but that these relations are something that Egyptians need to work out on their own. The introduction is written by one of the most prominent Muslim proponents of cooperation and positive relations at the social and political level, Tariq al-Bishri, and throughout the introduction and the text of the book itself, the persistent theme is self-determination and rejection of outside interference. This line of argument was put forth, with a tint of conspiracy analysis, in an article Morcos wrote from a historical perspective about the foreign intervention for the Lebanese paper *an-Nahar*. In it, he identifies five phases and strategies of foreign intervention in the Middle East: protection of religious groups during the Ottoman period, sheep stealing and destruction during the American missionary period, internationalization of Egypt during the British colonial period, disintegration and internal strife in the post-World War II period, and finally expanded intervention in the matters of the countries of the region in the post-cold-war era. He concludes, "The birth of the present is just an episode in the long chain of repeated history. It confirms that the strike against national unity is one of the goals of the West's strategy over the course of past centuries, ever since the West found its way to us" (Morcos 1997).

The official Christian point of view is thus clear: an unequivocal rejection of the American legislation and U.S. intervention in matters that are seen, at least by many Egyptians, to be internal matters particular to Egypt. It is appropriate to compare the official Christian reaction to the official Muslim reaction. In a speech given at the opening of an-Nur mosque in Rud al-Farag, in Cairo, the grand imam of al-Azhar, Muhammad Sayyid Tantawi, stated his support for preserving national unity "between Egypt's Muslims and Christians especially in the [Coptic Orthodox] Church's rejection of Western propaganda and fabrications with regard to persecution of Christian brothers in Egypt." He asserted that "these fabrications aim to shake up the security of the singular nation and the Nile, and to interfere in Egypt's national affairs" (Sulaiman 1997). This statement also indicates the sensitive place of some Muslims, especially those with official status. Since the U.S. legislation would aim to protect the status of Christians in Egypt, Muslims were not particularly able to react harshly in a public way. Tantawi's support for the Coptic Orthodox Church's position allowed the Christians, the supposed beneficiary of the legislation, to reject the "offer" in no uncertain terms and in a strong way, thus denying that persecution exists and taking the onus off Egypt's Muslims. Because of the sensitivity of the situation, representatives of Egypt's official Islam were not overly outspoken on the matter.

At the intellectual level, a statement was issued in November 1998 that included the signatures of fifty artists and authors, both Christian and Muslim. The declaration was facilitated by Jamal As'ad, a former member of Parliament and Christian member of the Labor Party. It stated,

> We affirm the Coptic Church's position with regard to Israel and the Church's rejection of American intervention in Egyptian affairs. From the outset we do not deny the presence of some disturbances and problems from which Copts suffer in Egypt, problems to which we all need to pay attention. We are the ones responsible for solving these problems in Egypt, and therefore we reject any American intervention

in the affairs of Egypt under the pretext of defending the Copts. (*Rose El Yossef* 1997)

A similar reaction was issued by the Tagammu' Party's secretary-general, Rifa'at as-Sa'id. In a statement on behalf of that party, he declared,

> The point of departure of Tagammu''s position on the matter is the basic principle of protection of Egypt, respect for the right of citizenship, and respect for the Constitution, which mandates freedom of religion, the right of all to enjoy freedom to worship, and the right of all to employment in positions without discrimination based on religion. We reject any foreign intervention and consider it a harmful attempt to ruin the relationship between Egypt's Muslims and Christians . . . [and] to play the same game that the British colonizers played previously. (Hurib 1997)

Here, Sa'id concentrates on ideas of citizenship and the legal basis for equality of religion, rather than national unity in a more poetic way. His focus on the Constitution buttresses his argument that Egypt's polity ensures equality in religion for all of its citizens.

The reaction of the government is also informative and indicative of the sensitivities of its place in the discourse. As in the case of official Islam, the Egyptian government was not in a strong position to be outspoken in accepting or rejecting the International Religious Freedom Act, for three main reasons: it would be on trial, it receives extensive financial aid from the United States, and its leaders are primarily Muslims. The government was, however, in a position to open the country to international observers and fact-finding missions, as well as to speak out, albeit in a softer tone. The government, after all, would be on the receiving end of any punitive action taken by the U.S. administration for violations of the principle of religious freedom either by the Egyptian government or other actors in Egypt.

As early as August 1997, Egypt's Ministry of Foreign Affairs took up the "fabrications of the persecution of Copts." Not only did it begin to prepare files refuting the "lies and fabrications" that had been circulating abroad with respect to cases of persecution, but the ministry also "charged its ambassadors in the United States and Europe to respond to the campaign with notarized documents and facts" (*al-Isbu'* 1997).

In statements to the press in February 1998, Mubarak's top political adviser, Usama al-Baz, expressed the hope of the Egyptian government that "the United States Congress will 'please get off our backs' about the status of Coptic Christians in Egypt" and the government's concern that the U.S. action could strain relations between the United States and Egypt (*Civil Society* 1998, 11–12). Denying any official discrimination against Copts and maintaining that the matter was a domestic affair, al-Baz stated,

> Some circles in America take the liberty of accusing Egypt of persecuting Copts. . . . First of all, it is none of their business to speak specifically on the status of the Copts in Egypt. This is up to the Egyptian people. . . . To the Congress, I would like to say, we view the [United States] as a friendly country. It is a reliable partner. We have worked together for a better Middle East. [But you] should not rush to point a finger at domestic affairs such as the treatment of Copts. Copts here are opposed to it, you can ask the pope. . . . We have no minorities here in Egypt. We have a Christian community that is on equal footing with the Islamic community. The Copts are not a minority because you cannot distinguish them. . . . Here, belonging to the state is not based on religion, but on citizen[ship]. If some people discriminate it is wrong, but it is not the policy of the state to discriminate against them. (*Civil Society* 1998, 12)

Al-Baz asserted that such legislation, and such focus on Egypt, would go far to reduce the level of trust in the U.S.-Egyptian relationship. In his words, one recognizes the many levels of problems Egypt sees with the legislation, including the potential disintegration of international relations and the difficulties that could result internally. The government also had a degree of difficulty in speaking on the matter. Unable to speak on behalf of the Christian population but knowing what the official Christian position was, it referred anyone who wanted to know more to the pope.

A further response the government could make to international attention caused by the U.S. legislation on the treatment of Copts was to receive observer delegations curious to know more. For example, from March 10 to March 15, 1998, a delegation visited Egypt from the New York City Council of Churches. The delegation met with Pope Shenouda as well as President Mubarak. The report the delegation made stated that it

> found no evidence of government-sanctioned persecution of Christians. . . . "Isolated incidents" [of discrimination] sometimes occurred in Egypt, but . . . the government was not "turning a blind eye" to offenses against Christians. . . . The delegation found that there was a disproportionately small number of Christians in parliament but . . . that many Christians seemed to be doing well financially. The delegation found no need for a "crusade" to deliver Egyptian Christians from persecution. (Early 1998)

Such a delegation had no discernible interest in supporting one position or the other but was welcomed by the government and leaders from the Christian and Muslim communities. To be sure, these official representatives had a stake in the outcome, and the visit of the delegation was short, focusing on a small sector of the population. The essential point is that the official response of the government was one of openness to the inquiry and such delegations' visits. By permitting the fact-finding delegation and even appearing to welcome it, the government indicated its official denial of the charges implied in the U.S. legislation calling for international religious freedom, which included Egypt by name in the accompanying report.

A further response worth considering is the welcome the Egyptian government gave to the United States Commission on International Religious Freedom (USCIRF) when it visited Egypt in March 2001. The commission was the monitoring group established by the International Religious Freedom Act. Officials from government and religious bodies received the commission while nongovernmental actors did not. "The delegates got a frostier reception from Egyptian human rights activists—some of whom have encouraged forthright discussion of the Coptic question—than from the Egyptian government, which flatly denies the existence of discrimination" (Langohr 2001).

From this discussion, it should be clear that the potentially divisive issue of the U.S. legislation brought together many actors from various levels of Egyptian society and politics with basically one voice: a rejection of international intervention in a problem avowedly existent and reserved for solution by Egypt's own people. Whether the problem of religious discrimination exists was not the point, and most admit that discrimination—although not to the degree of persecution—does exist. An apparent "glass ceiling" for Christians seeking to fill the higher governmental positions, the difficulty of obtaining permits for church construction and repair, and other perceived social biases support the claims of discrimination.

Most Egyptians expressed their feeling that Egyptian society is mature enough to deal with such matters fairly on its own. Should Egypt's Christians be "protected" by the United States? The answer to that question by all concerned was a resounding no, at least publicly. There is still debate over the possible positive effects the legislation may have had in Egypt, including the change that the provincial governor, rather than the president of the republic, now can sign church repair and construction permits. Many Egyptian Christians quietly hope for more protection from some source, believing that social, and in some cases violent, discrimination does take place; and further, that the government is not often their advocate in such situations. Nonetheless, the presence of the emergency laws, on the books since 1981, is considered an important safeguard against the emergence of a much stronger Islamic sociopolitical presence. In terms of the public debate and discourse of the parties examined here, however, a clear consensus was reached on two fronts. First, the various levels of the Egyptian sociopolitical landscape roundly rejected outside intervention in this debate and discussion. The recognition and assertion that Egyptians must deal with the issue is consistent with the " 'nested paradigm' of conflict transformation, whereby local actors, people already embedded, or 'nested,' in the conflicted community, collaborate in a wide range of activities and functions" to address the issue (Appleby 2000, 18). Second, there was strong agreement, as those who engaged the issue worked through it, that Egypt's national unity would withstand this challenge.

Al-Kusheh: Rural Challenge and National Response

The controversies involving the minority rights conference and U.S. legislation to protect international religious liberties were debates at the official rhetorical and intellectual level and helped to crystallize a rhetoric of national unity. A particularly violent case of tension illustrates and represents a very different dynamic. During the early part of the 1990s, the Egyptian government was engaged in a virtual war with Islamic radicals. Several examples of violent sectarian clashes and attacks motivated by "religion" can be held up. These cases are testimony to the fact that all has not been well between Christians and Muslims in Egypt, and the level of suspicion of the Other has increased with each incident.

Of particular concern have been attacks against Christians that resurfaced after a lull during the 1980s with the burning of a Coptic Orthodox church and the murder of Christians in Dairut, in the Assiut province of Upper Egypt, by Islamic radicals in January 1991 (Y. Ibrahim 1991); the killing of more than fifteen Christians, again in Dairut, in May of the same year (Y. Ibrahim 1993, 2); the murder of four Christians by axing in Tema, in October 1992, and the burning of more than sixty homes, dozens of Christian-owned shops, and a church (Y. Ibrahim 1993, 2); and the killing of twenty-one Christians in the course of one month: nine in a church in the village of Abu Qorqas, three farmers in their fields, and nine more in a village, all in Upper Egypt in February and March, 1997 (*Cyprus Weekly* 1997). In the middle of this period a prominent columnist, Fahmi Huwaidi, wrote a long column, entitled "An Apology to Every Copt," in which he stated, "In spite of the fact that I do not know those who did it, nor their motives or intentions, I do know one thing that I want to announce officially. That is that the killers were Muslims and the killed were Christians, and that the injured is all of Egypt" (Huwaidi 1997).

In the social-psychological process of intercommunal reconciliation as outlined by Fisher, an apology is an important step. Even though Huwaidi could neither speak for those who perpetrated the attack nor "eradicate the consequences of the wrongdoing" (Fisher 2001, 38), he made a sincere and very public attempt to acknowledge the wrongdoing and move toward reconciliation.

Most visible internationally were the attacks in Luxor in November 1997 of dozens of German tourists by a group suspected of having ties with *al-Jama'a al-Islamiyya;* these drew to the attention of the world the violent activities of the decade in Egypt, brought Christians and Muslims together in a prayer vigil for the victims, and led to calls for the Islamic group to end the violence (*al-Birq* 1997).

Two incidents in the village of al-Kusheh in the Suhaj province of Upper Egypt further exacerbated perceptions and fears, particularly the tragedy of the killing of more than twenty Christians on January 4, 2000, and the ensuing burning of dozens of homes and the destruction of the St. George Church in a nearby village (Schiller 2000, 6). Accounts of the incidents varied in the immediate aftermath, depending on the source.

> No one seems to really understand how what began as a routine squabble between a vendor and a customer escalated into rooftop gunbattles between Christians and Muslims in Al Kosheh and beyond on January 2. Al-Kosheh's Christians claimed they were victims of a police-backed Muslim aggression. Muslims on the other hand, argued that the crisis came to a head after a mob of Christians supported by a heavy-duty forklift raided their neighborhood and destroyed their property. (Apiku 2000, 11)

What is clear was the resulting deaths of twenty villagers, thirty-three persons injured, damage to thirty-three Christian-owned shops and two cars and forty-five Muslim-owned stores, and the arrest of twenty-two people (*Cairo Times* 2000), as well as a resultant sectarian fear, mistrust, and anger between Christians and Muslims that pervaded the country, and a ubiquitous sense of strife throughout Egypt. What was particularly alarming, not only to the Christian community but also to the large number of Muslims with a strong sense of national pride in the unity of the country's citizenry, was that all of those killed, and many of those injured, were Christians; and that those who were arrested in the crime were Muslim, some of whom were officers in the police force. The facts of the incident are important, but an examination of the reaction at several levels of Egyptian polity and society is also revealing.

It is appropriate to start, once again, at the level of official religion, with the statement of Pope Shenouda. Pope Shenouda issued a statement that reflected a change in his own, usually guarded and more positive, expression. Pope Shenouda had, in the past, issued muted statements reminding the community of faithful Coptic Christians that Egypt belongs equally to

Christian and Muslim alike and that all must work to improve relations with their neighbors, regardless of faith orientation. Even his statement in the wake of the killings at the church in Abu Qorqas in 1997 was a recounting of the story of the day, with short obituaries of each of those who were killed (*al-Kiraza* 1997)—important for the Christian community locally and nationally to read because it humanized the victims, but neutral in that its position was neither condemnatory nor blaming or critical.

Pope Shenouda's statement in the wake of the incidents in al-Kusheh was in a similar form, published as the lead article in the Coptic Orthodox Church's official magazine, *al-Kiraza*, in the Friday, January 21, 2000, issue. The headline read, "Our Martyrs in al-Kusheh." Consistent with statements the pope had made in the past is the conciliatory tone expressed with regard to the central government. "We have confidence in the authorities in Cairo. However, the problem lies among the authorities in the area where the incident occurred" (*al-Kiraza* 2000). Given the fact that the Christian community in Egypt is a minority, it is natural that the official church would not want to incite the government by appearing to put any degree of blame upon it directly. Here, the statement avoided accusing the Egyptian government of being involved in either provoking or passively permitting such an incident. It did not, however, indicate that officials were without guilt in the matter. The second part of the sentence makes this clear. Much of the rest of the article chronicles, through eyewitness accounts and statistical analysis, the heinous character of the tragedy and the role that local officials played (or failed to play) in containing the extent of the aggression.

His criticism was couched in a rhetoric of nationalist expression that is familiar by now, and included a call for justice, as well as a long list of Christians who were killed and injured in the attacks, similar to the stories in obituary form that appeared in the article on Abu Qorqas. The overall tone can be discerned from the following excerpts:

> It is painful that the reputation of Egypt, which we love from the bottom of our hearts and of which we sing in every place, is damaged in print, on the Internet, foreign news agencies, journals, and broadcasts. All of that for the sake of a village in Upper Egypt, the

village of al-Kusheh, in which the local police failed to keep the peace. The matter ended in heinous imagery described by some as a massacre, and by others as a butchery. *We all wish to solve the problem of al-Kusheh. . . .*

The first duty of security officers is to prevent a crime before it happens. If they cannot, they at least must stop it before it spreads. . . . *We trust in the leadership in Cairo, but the problem is with those responsible in the district of the incidents.*

True reconciliation—not superficial—can take place only after the blood of the victims receives justice.

May Egypt live in security and in goodness. (*Al-Kiraza* 2000; emphasis in the original)

A message is embedded within each of these excerpts. The first passage, consisting of the opening sentences of the statement, presents a message of nationalism and patriotism with the idea that the problem can be solved within Egypt. It attempts to clear Egypt's reputation abroad, especially in light of the efforts the Church made to oppose the U.S. legislation less than three years before the incident in al-Kusheh. The second passage refers to the principle of law and the role of civil officials, being clear in its condemnation of the local authorities and not the national ones. The third excerpt makes clear the Church's demand for justice in resolving the matter. The fourth is the closing sentence, invoking a blessing upon Egypt and expressing the desire for harmony and unity in peace.

The pope and the Church may have felt constrained from open criticism, fearing further disruption from heightened tensions, but the Church certainly was clear in its condemnation of the incident. It affirmed its trust in the national government, seen as the symbol of national unity, and its own patriotism. The events of al-Kusheh took place during the first week of the new year. The timing was significant for Egypt's Christians, who celebrate Christmas on January 7. The tragedy meant that a damper was placed on the annual celebration that year. The first week of 2000 was also the last week of Ramadan in the Islamic calendar. Anticipated hopes for "Y2K" were augmented by the fact that Christians and Muslims in Egypt would be celebrating important holidays within days of each other

(Christmas on January 7 and *'id al-fitr* on January 9), a very rare convergence of the solar and lunar calendars that would not happen again for another thirty-three years. The expected jubilant mood for the two holy occasions turned dour, and both occasions were less celebratory than usual. Nonetheless, in an effort to emphasize to the nation that relations were normal between Christians and Muslims, and to maintain a traditional level of contact, official representatives of the Christian and Muslim communities made customary exchanges of congratulatory visits on the occasion of these holidays. The pope, the mufti, and the grand imam of al-Azhar all participated in such exchanges, which were also an opportunity to speak about the events of the previous week.

On the occasion of *'id al-fitr*, Pope Shenouda led a delegation to visit Muhammad Sayyid Tantawi, who took the opportunity to offer some words to the church leaders, saying, "We are all brothers who meet in obedience to God, upon whom we call to gather us together, always in trusting fraternity, and to keep Egypt free of conflict . . . , and to make us a center of security, tranquility, and peace." Shaikh Tantawi also affirmed the "depth of the love that binds the two, and that binds Muslims and Christians in all corners of Egypt" (*al-Ahram* 2000a, 1).

In an interview of Shaikh Tantawi just three weeks after the events of al-Kusheh, he remarked that the pope's visit was not necessarily an act of reconciliation. He went on to say that even though reconciliation must take place, it can only happen when those who committed wrong are identified and punished for their acts. Reconciliation takes place when justice is served. Tantawi reaffirmed that, in the case of Egypt, Christians and Muslims live together on the land. Both share the same responsibilities and rights in the law, which is established blind of religion (Tantawi 2000).

It is noteworthy that the leaders of the Islamic community were not as outspoken as they might be otherwise. The obvious reason is that, similar to the case of the U.S. religious freedom legislation, Muslims were not in a position of strength to speak out about national unity and good relations, since extensive rehearsal of such themes would naturally be taken with some degree of skepticism given that the majority of the victims in al-Kusheh were Christian.

Despite perceptions that "the government's mismanagement of the last situation in Kosheh helped create an atmosphere of mistrust" and that "what happened in Al Kosheh is a reflection of the government's neglect of economic and social tensions rather than a reflection of sectarian relations in Egypt" (Elghawaby 2000), the official government position was to affirm the idea of national unity in spite of the crisis at hand. "Prime Minister ['Atef] Ebeid proposed an anti-violence drive proceeding along five tracks simultaneously: political, social, economic, security, and religious. . . . [Further,] the authorities make every effort to highlight ritualistic expressions of fraternity between the Muslim and Coptic communities" (Sid-Ahmed 2000, 8).

To diffuse the crisis, a local council changed the name of al-Kusheh to Qariyat as-Salam (Village of Peace), effective January 31, 2000 (Kassem 2000, 3).

Prime Minister 'Ebeid expounded on the matter of al-Kusheh in a printed interview, focusing on several germane areas:

> The government will not allow superseding the principle of citizenship. All Christians and Muslims are, in the face of the state, citizens. Religious affiliation does not afford more rights, privileges, or protection upon anyone. . . .
>
> Egypt is not in a religious crisis. If it so happened that individual Christian or Muslim religious leaders attempted to assert that, they would be challenged decisively. All political, economic, and social rights are conferred upon all Egyptians without discrimination or inaccessibility.
>
> The village of al-Kusheh will become again a model village—a model of positive communal relations and love, of Christian and Muslim homogeneity—a village of love. (Suraya 2000, 13)

These expressions are consistent with the government's position of equal citizenship before the law for all Egyptians, and rejection of the idea of religious crisis within the country. They also offer hope and promise for the future, that the government will somehow be able to ensure that the village in which such a tragedy had taken place only a few short weeks before would become a symbol of the Egyptian reality of Christian-Muslim harmony. The government's position was aired on Egypt's Channel 1 on January 20. Channel 1 is one of the government-run stations in Egypt. In a program called *Akhbar an-nass* (News of People), the focus was on Christian-Muslim relations in the wake of al-Kusheh. In the program, aired as a documentary, people of the village were asked if there were problems between Christians and Muslims of the village. Without exception, those interviewed responded negatively. One replied, "[Christians and Muslims] are part of the fabric of the community and there are no tensions whatsoever."

President Mubarak naturally spoke about the issue as well. In a meeting with intellectuals, he "denied any discrimination between Muslims and Copts" and attributed the incidents to "outside groups. The problem arose from a money dispute between two individuals. This dispute was exploited by seditious elements and rumor mongers" (Abou El-Magd 2000, 3). On the occasion of Police Day, Mubarak gave a speech in which he affirmed national unity. His answer to questions about the role of the police in the incident carried a bit of irony, given the major debate about the Freedom from Religious Persecution Act: "Egypt has a long history of tolerance and inter-faith coexistence, which refute claims of religious persecution. The law treats all people equally regardless of their political or religious affiliations. All people are treated as citizens living in one country. We seek to establish democracy in all aspects of life" (*Egyptian Gazette* 2000).

The reaction among political party representatives was much more mixed, more critical of the incident and the path that led to it. For example, Rifa'at as-Sa'id of the Tagammu' Party wrote that "we close our eyes in order not to see the real tragedy" (Abou El-Magd 2000, 3). Rafiq Habib, one of the Christian founders of the unlicensed al-Wasat Party, said, "We are not in crisis time. It's not a kind of systemic discrimination but Christians and Muslims are becoming more prejudiced and looking at each other differently and so the gap is widening. Emotions are boiling under the surface. . . . [I]f it is not addressed, our national unity will crumble" (Elghawaby 2000, 11).

Such an outlook recognizes the fragility of the state of religious harmony in Egypt and the need to address it, but also the idea that unity remains. Developing this idea, Muhammad Salim al-'Awa wrote,

The clash between Muslims and Christians is the larger danger that can threaten this nation . . . and open the door for its enemies to control its destiny.

The presence of differences between those who live together and trade together is natural. No one can avoid or prevent it. However, if the differences grow to result in killing about religion, identity, ethnicity, or political choice, it is a catastrophe annulling the nation and losing the spirit of community among the people. (al-'Awa 2000, 17)

Al-'Awa (2000, 17) called for the application of law to all citizens of Egypt, which would provide insurance that such an event would never happen again in Egypt.

The political parties therefore seemed to reflect the hope for the preservation of national unity, even if they were skeptical that it would be an easy task. In a telling article by the prominent columnist Fahmi Huwaidi, "An Apology Is the Beginning of the Solution," which repeats his theme of apology issued in the wake of Abu Qorqas, Huwaidi made the following assertion, affirming the difficulty that Egypt will have in managing religious strife: "The village of al-Kusheh—by virtue of its conditions, its history, its social composition and its economic circumstances—is not different from most villages of Egypt. What happened in al-Kusheh in the first days of the year could be repeated in any Egyptian village at any time" (Huwaidi 2000, 24).

There can be no doubt that al-Kusheh was a strong wake-up call for Egyptians, who had faced all of the sectarian issues presented throughout the 1980s and 1990s, from academic debates over the status of Copts as minorities to policy challenges such as the U.S. religious freedom legislation, to the presence and activities of Islamic radicals that brought Mubarak to the presidency prematurely and have been a constant presence on the ground in Egypt throughout his presidency. As all of those issues played out, the rhetoric of national unity and religious harmony in Egypt was consistently presented. When Egypt was confronted with such challenges, most of the levels of Egyptian society and polity rallied around traditional themes of unity and harmony, relying upon historical arguments and contemporary realities. National unity had always been a rallying point for Egyptian government officials, religious officials, political parties (even if to a more fragmented degree), and nongovernmental organizations. Al-Kusheh was a more difficult challenge, bringing closer to the surface fears and tensions that have existed throughout. The sheer brutality of the incident and the government's handling of it—at a time of anticipated celebration—called people's attention to a heightened state of tension.

Nonetheless, even in this new challenge, a crisis apparently of sectarian dimensions, symbols of national unity were held up. Perhaps because the actors were so accustomed to the rhetoric did it come so easily. Criticism of the rhetoric was also pronounced, though. The search for a solution continued, but the question remained: how deeply is the rhetoric taken to heart? Mohamad Sid-Ahmad wrote that demonstrations of national unity

> remain formal, occur at the upper level of society and do not extend to the grass roots level where mutual suspicion and distrust will continue to prevail as long as reasons for friction are not adequately addressed. . . .
>
> In the final analysis, the problem can only be resolved through genuine democracy; it will continue to fester as long as democracy remains formal, superficial or distorted. And even if it were possible to freeze the internal reasons of social violence, it is beyond our power to freeze the regional and global reasons. (Sid-Ahmed 2000, 8)

Conclusions

This analysis suggests that the three cases examined in this chapter, and what they represent in terms of larger issues, are intertwined and affect each other. The resolution of an internal problem depends on its isolation from external interference. In the era of globalization, internal and external have become moot terms, as they both have so much impact in the social, economic, political, and religious realms. In addition, what is most clear is that preexisting relationships can contribute to the smooth resolution of issues in times of crisis. Relations can be drawn upon to produce positive results. In times of calm, therefore, work must be done to develop relationships across sectarian lines to preserve the calm and proactively nurture better relationships, and to have established relationships in times of heightened tension. The three cases of crisis examined in this chapter all contain examples in which some actors were prepared to face the crises together—in deeds and in written words—from a constructive point of view, in efforts of reconciliation, and in attempts to move forward. Thus, governmental, official religious, political party, and NGO relationship building can and does play a role in minimizing the effects of sectarian conflict.

Each of the cases represents a different kind of potential crisis. The first, the conference on minorities, represents a regional issue with pragmatic implications for people throughout the Middle East, in each of their respective countries. It was an intellectual conference focusing on an issue that goes beyond an academic topic. The issue of majority-minority relations is one that is manifest in many ways throughout the region. The inclusion of a specific agenda item about Egypt's Christian-Muslim relations spawned great debate that raised issues latent in society. The second, the U.S. legislation, represents a case of national-international interaction, and the proper role for the international community in a matter deemed to be domestic. The fact that Egypt depends to a great extent on American assistance further complicates this matter, as does the role of emigrant Egyptian Christians and their advocacy role with their governments. In addition, the assumed association between Egyptian Christians (who are indigenous) and the "Christian" West, further augmented by the presence of Egyptian Christians in the diaspora, and the missionary connections local churches have with the worldwide ecumenical Christian family, added layers to the dynamics of the debate. Who becomes whose protector? The third case goes beyond either of these two themes and gets to a core issue for many living in Egypt: when is tension (and violence) sectarian, and does it matter if other factors are involved, if such incidents are presented as sectarian? Certainly, other factors may predominate, but if the presentation and perception of an incident is sectarian, then fears and animosity are exacerbated.

Even so, the roles of government, religious leaders, political leaders, and others in positions of opinion formation are important to ease the tensions that can and do arise in each kind of case, and if relationships are strong to begin with, the emergence of crises can draw on the relationships to work through them. Such an approach has been visible in the three cases examined in this chapter. Each actor played a role that varied depending on the circumstances, but concerted efforts generally yielded positive results for national unity, at least in the short term.

8

Conclusions on Christian-Muslim Cooperation in a Context of Conflict

In a country where there is obvious historical and contemporary sectarian tension and conflict, cooperation can exist as a modicum of interaction between the groups in tension with each other, and it can play a role in reducing the level of sectarian conflict. During President Mubarak's presidency, Egypt has experienced perhaps one of its most difficult times of sectarian conflict. During this period, there have been clear signs that political Islam has become a major actor on the sociopolitical scene. These signs have included increased visibility and agenda advancement in the professional syndicates, resulting in Islamist domination of the major syndicates' elected posts; greater attention paid by the population in general to the social services provided by religious organizations; militant activities, including attacks on tourists, government officials, and Egyptian Christians; and the considerable efforts made by the government to portray a more moderate version of Islam, combined with a concerted campaign to demonstrate public officials' religious commitment.

A symptom of these signs has been a period of heightened tension between the Christian and Muslim faith communities in Egypt, where religious identity is an important religious and social marker. In addition to the burning of Christian churches and monasteries, the rise in manifestations of political Islam has contributed significantly to questioning among the Christian community about the future of the country and the role that Christians will have in it. Much has been made of a *fitna ta'ifiyya* (sectarian conflict). Articles in daily newspapers have addressed the possibility of sectarian conflict, buttressing it by their traditional reporting and refuting it on the op-ed pages. This kind of duality in the everyday psyche of the people has only served to increase perceptions of tension between the communities.

The preceding chapters have not in any way intended to minimize the perceptions or the lived realities of people in either community, nor have they attempted to demonstrate that the situation in Egypt during Mubarak's presidency has been void of any conflict or full of peace and harmony. In fact, these chapters have attempted to demonstrate that, *in the midst of tension and actual conflict, numerous examples of cooperation can be found that not only are not anomalous but that have served an important purpose.* Indeed, it is in times of heightened tension and conflict that examples of cooperation are pronounced and especially important in the process of refuting the suggestion of *fitna*. The kinds of cooperation cited are not unique to times of heightened conflict. In fact, many of the examples of cooperation cited are long-standing practice—such as courtesy visits on the Other's holidays—not motivated by escalation in tension, but perhaps more visible at such times.

What Is Missing

This book examines the rhetoric and action of sectarian tolerance in Egypt at several levels: official government, official religion, political parties, and nongovernmental organizations. This examination does not cover the spectrum of sectors across the sociopolitical map in Egypt, but it does transcend the statist approach and looks into institutions of civil society.

Notably missing are the political Islamic groups (alternately called "radicals" or "extremists" and, more popularly, "fundamentalists" and "Islamists"). These groups are among the most active of any sociopolitical opposition, be they manifest in political parties or as action groups, legal or banned. Such groups within the category of radical political Islam are perhaps the least tolerant of the current government, Western powers, mainstream Muslims within Egypt, and non-Muslims, including Christians and other "infidels," which would also include, for them, many Muslims. These groups have not been ignored but rather have been treated here more conceptually. Their emphatic reemergence has been one of the principal reasons for the escalation in tensions in Egypt, most tangibly manifest since the mid-1970s, and thus has warranted this closer examination of intercommunal cooperation. Their inclusion in the realm of civil society may be based upon their active contributions to society through social services and to politics in the form of an alternate perspective in the state of affairs. They cannot be excluded from civil society because of their illegality alone, but their intolerance of others requires further examination and may be a basis for exclusion from the realm of civil society.

The level of interaction between faith communities at a grassroots level is more difficult to capture than that at an official or organizational level. While it may be impossible to measure, there is nonetheless strong cooperation at the level of common interaction, such as the friendships that undeniably exist between Christians and Muslims at the elementary school level, study groups at the university student level, good collegial relations in the workplace that permeate personal relations as well, and professional interaction that is motivated by commerce and not religion. If it were possible to measure ways in which the undeniable feelings of suspicion and fear, the muted expressions of discrimination, or the presence of a glass-ceiling phenomenon in the professional and political realm prevent positive individual relations, then the debate over the relationship between Christians and Muslims would take on a more real, down-to-earth dimension.

A study of relations at the grassroots level poses difficult problems. Such problems include finding a sufficiently representative sample of Christians and Muslims, urban and rural populations, and men and women; establishing requisite levels of trust for candid interviews; and developing an interview strategy that would deal sensitively with a very charged political and social issue.

Even so, individual opinions have been expressed. An example of one person's feelings on the matter is seen in the question and response of a fifty-year-old Christian woman at a Christian shrine in Cairo. Umm Badri asked a fellow visitor to the shrine, "Are you Muslim or Christian?" and without waiting for an answer, stated, "It doesn't matter. We are all descended from Adam and we are all one family" (Sachs 2001, A4). These remarks express the irrelevance of one's religion in one person's mind, but the initial question contradicts that irrelevance. By posing the question, or thinking to ask the question, she indicates that religious identity in fact does matter. Instead of attempting to weigh positive and negative individual sentiments and relationships, this research focuses on public sociopolitical actors instead.

The Interplay of Actors

The main focus of this book has been the approach of the political and religious elite to interfaith dialogue. This focus has the multiple advantages of considering the opinion makers' roles in interreligious relations; identifying the role of the government in fostering national relations and representing the people; understanding the role that religious leaders play for their communities; and evaluating the import of relationships beyond these tiers into the sociopolitical realm of political parties and NGOs.

Beyond each of these taken separately, the interplay of the various groups is crucial. If Christian leaders spoke of good relations but had no relationships with their Muslim counterparts, such a disconnect would be revealing. The interrelationships between government officials and religious officials are defined by structural rules as well as public discourse. The relationships religious leaders have established with each other are visible, whether seen as mere duty or as authentically strong. The relationships between governmental officials and religious leaders on the one side and NGOs on the other in dialogue meetings connect institutional religion and organizations with closer ties to the grass roots. Debate within and among political parties about toleration and interfaith relationships brings out the sociopolitical aspects in specific ways not otherwise addressed. All of these interactions are oriented toward the elite, but, because of their intricate nature, they involve a level of accountability to ensure that the discourse and actions remain headed in a positive direction. It would be very difficult for this web of relationships to come apart without serious implications for the country.

The web of relationships having developed as they have, the political and religious leaders act interdependently to ensure the sustainability and continuity of interfaith relations in Egypt. When a crisis arises, the sociopolitical elite rush to assert national unity and to preserve Christian-Muslim relationships at the highest levels in a public demonstration, to identify issues and leadership direction for a deescalation of the crisis. Such mutual efforts support the idea that religion can play a positive role in peacemaking. Rather than becoming a source of conflict, these relationships can play a reconciling role. Beyond the scope of preserving positive interfaith relationships, leaders can also play a positive role in working cooperatively to resolve other social issues. A common voice on issues of national import, such as population growth and family planning, literacy, or economic development, then becomes possible.

Dialogue, of course, does not always translate into the quotidian experience of the people. Dialogue as a formal exercise, involving opinion makers, clergy, and politicians who discuss topics of intellectual relevance, can seem too lofty and esoteric to affect the general populace, and such dialogue is not all-inclusive. The ways in which the topics and panel are presented through the media and NGOs, though, can have significant impact. Dialogue defined more broadly to include other kinds of interaction can have a different effect as well. Often, "dialogue" is defined as formal discussion, but it is also defined in terms of the "dialogue of life," which refers to the natural interaction of parties. According to Leonard Swidler, interreligious dialogue functions in "the practical, where we collaborate to help humanity; the depth or 'spiritual' dimension, where we attempt to experience the partner's religion or ideology; [and] the cognitive, where we seek understanding [of] truth" (Smock 2002, 6). The daily engagement of Christians and Muslims in Egypt, if considered actively, can also therefore be a form of positive dialogue.

Rereading the Theoretical

In terms of citizenship and toleration, as 'Ashmawi points out, the liberal tradition's idea of citizenship is not at all incompatible either with states that are nonliberal or with ideas promulgated in Islam. 'Ashmawi is very intent on proving that ideas of liberalism are consistent with what Islam says about roles for Muslims and non-Muslims. His article "Copts Are Not Ahl adh-Dhimma" (1995) shows, however, that the debate goes on and that not all are of the same opinion. The mere appearance of his article is proof positive of that, as the article could not have appeared in an intellectual vacuum.

Hanna's discussion of tolerance is a proposal for what is required in Egypt if it is to continue to be a leader in the Arab world. Tolerance has both a political and a social component. In McClure's framework, political tolerance has not been exhibited because there is no case of violation of the letter of the law. Social tolerance, however, is more in keeping with Hanna's description and provides a framework within which to understand the cases outlined here.

A liberal idea of the citizen exists in Egypt at both the intellectual and legal levels. The citizen as actor is consistent with the implication that the citizen has a role that can be juxtaposed to the state, as expressed by Habermas's model.

In Parsons' conceptualization, "citizenship in the modern sense signifies equal conditions of membership in the societal community rather than in the state" (quoted in Appleby 2000, 128). This important distinction recalls a central theme of this project: tolerance and acceptance. Do all Egyptians share "equal conditions of membership in the societal community," an equality that is socially rather than politically mandated, and thus an equality that is accorded by members of society upon other members? In terms of social and legal citizenship, the debate must remain open. Legally, according to the Egyptian constitution, Islam is the religion of the state. Nonetheless, government officials from the top down assert that Christians enjoy the same rights as Muslims, and bear the same responsibilities. In terms of government rhetoric, this equality is borne out. Legally and in practice, all Egyptians have rights of ownership, rights to travel, to secure an education, to gain services, and so on. Even so, religion is listed on the national identification card. Such identification, however, does not deny the formal relationship between the individual and the state, and the basic equality of rights.

Equality in social citizenship is more difficult to establish, as a positive relationship among citizens depends upon a level of toleration. The institutions of government, official religion, political parties, and NGOs examined here help to advance a more equal social citizenship, but there are other forces at work both at the institutional and individual levels, forces that include mutual suspicion as well as more tangible factors. Omission of an analysis of individual one-on-one interaction means that the question of citizenship cannot be answered at every specific level here. Even so, social citizenship is indeed afforded Egypt's Muslims by an important portion of Egypt's Christians, and vice versa.

Social citizenship has much to do with toleration. What has been demonstrated is that the institutions considered here indeed strive, not only in their words but also in their works, to increase the level of toleration. In doing so, they attempt to push the Egyptian society at least as far as "openness to others," and perhaps as far as "enthusiastic endorsement of difference," on Walzer's continuum. It has even been shown that many venture beyond this continuum to assert "enthusiastic endorsement of sameness," that there is in fact no difference between Christian and Muslim in Egypt. To extend to this point is to shift the paradigm beyond toleration and to make the issue one of common identity, where the goal is unity and citizenship, not difference.

Identity

Various perspectives on identity within Egypt can be categorized into five "schools," Egyptian (Pharaonic), Mediterranean, African, Arab, and Islamic. The Egyptian school is problematic because it does not fully accept Egypt's Muslims as inheritors of the long history of Egypt's civilization. Even so, many proponents of national unity put forth that heritage, perhaps as an attempt to transcend (or mask) the divisions that exist within contemporary society with a unifying past. The Mediterranean identity school as a point of reference is also problematic because it looks toward Europe to the exclusion of the heart of the Islamic world. Islam as a school of identity plays an important role, clearly more so among those who propose Egypt as an Islamic state than those who tend to be more inclusive, but even those Christians who strive for inclusion and who focus on national unity recognize the Islamic nature of society. Catholic bishop Yuhanna Qolta explained that the great need among Christians if they are to remain a vital entity in Egypt is accepting the predominant cultural context. He was forthright in his acknowledgment that Egypt's environment is Islamic and that much of the Christian community is influenced by that prevailing culture (Qolta 2000). The African school is deficient in its focus on the continent at the expense of important Christian and Islamic influences that originated in the Middle East, but one might argue that by looking to physical situation as well as human contact and traffic, as opposed to some aspects of religious or cultural impact, greater tolerance is possible.

If these four schools do not adequately describe the source of identification among those who promote unity and advocate tolerance, then perhaps the perspective of the Arab identity school is the most fitting. Those who promote the Arab character of Egypt recognize the Islamic influence, while at the same time they do not exclude non-Muslims and in fact affirm the legitimacy of their place. This school has a history throughout the course of the twentieth century of participation and leadership by Arab Christians. However, this school focuses on the Arab nation rather than any single nationalism. It speaks of Arab unity, but not specifically of any particular nation's unity.

To resolve this difficulty of identity, it is appropriate to draw on elements of each of these schools in promoting national unity and tolerance in Egypt—recognition of the country's ancient history and its claim on today's Egyptians, whether Christian or Muslim, the Arab and Islamic influence on the country's modern history and culture, and African geography and connections.

At the governmental level, there is a clear tie to the revolutionary ideas of the Free Officers and thus to Arab nationalism. However, throughout the course of the revolutionary period (1952–present), different emphases have been made. Increasingly, Egyptian historic identity has been highlighted, as has the Islamic identity, if in a moderate form. At the level of official religion, Muslim leaders naturally identify with Egypt's Islamic past, and Christian leaders highlight the longer history, even while recognizing Islamic identity and the importance it holds for others. Some Christian leaders emphasize the Christian history of Egypt, even though it does not conform nicely to one of the schools. From both Christian and Muslim perspectives in official religion, a high level of tolerance is exhibited toward the Other, the Other's outlook, and the Other's right to enjoy citizenship rights and responsibilities.

At the level of political parties, the Labor Party and Hizb al-Wasat are discussed in chapter 5. The Labor Party, because of its alliance with the

Muslim Brotherhood, has expressed a strong affinity with Egypt's Islamic identity, but not without recognition of Egypt's Arabness. This party to some extent inherited the mantle of Makram 'Ebeid's nationalism in the early part of the twentieth century. That is, Egypt is Islamic, but Christians participate in that Islamic polity. It is the mixture of labor ideas and political Islam within this party that makes it so colorful, and one that is clearly not homogeneous in its thinking. With regard to the rejected Hizb al-Wasat, again, an Islamic culture is present in the overriding ideology. The Christians who participated in the project recognized, affirmed, and campaigned for that idea. The idea that Islam is a culture with values that all can share and that these values ought to be laid out in a political framework is a clear indication of the affinity the Middle Party and its founders felt with Islam. The fact that both parties studied here have a religious bent is significant, as it was emphasized that parties with such a tendency can (and in fact do) tolerate people of other religions, as long as the basic ideology of the party is upheld.

Finally, in the realm of NGOs, it would only be fair to say that the NGOs identified have attempted to participate in Egypt's political and social life without laying out a pattern of identification. The NGOs studied here promote tolerance in all that they do, be they religiously oriented (like CEOSS) or secular (like the Ibn Khaldun Center). High levels of tolerance and acceptance within all sectors studied have been the standard.

To come back to Kymlicka's idea of competing identities, the schools of identity provide a framework for the possible points of identity reference, and the range of competing identities. Religious identity is not the only category of identity for a person or group, but it is certainly an important one in Egyptian society. Arab and not Western, Mediterranean and not Asian, Pharaonic and not Phoenician; these are all possible assertions of identity that an Egyptian might make in different contexts. In the national context, identities might be progovernment versus opposition, urban versus rural, and certainly Muslim and Christian. All of these are possible identities, either competing or compound.

It should be clear that religious identity is a primary identity and an important factor in public discourse, whether forthright or latent. Religious identity has had a special primacy in the context of the upsurge of particularly Islamic ideologies and movements in the past few decades. Not only has this resurgence had an impact on the centrality of religious identity and contributed to members of each community setting themselves apart from each other, but it has also had the opposite effect. In the assertion of unique and separate religious identity, a number of actors in public leadership positions have worked diligently to ensure that separate religious identity does not lead to increased sectarianism; and beyond that, they have worked to ensure that better relations are fostered. While the upsurge of Islamic identity and sociopolitical activism by Islamists has caused concern among the Christian community, members of both the Muslim and Christian communities have seized the opportunity to lessen this impact and strengthen relationships.

While religious identity is a primary but not exclusive identity, social boundaries are set with other lines as well. Barth asserts that with greater interaction between groups, distinguishing differences are less likely to persist. In this study, a high level of interaction has been demonstrated both in deliberate attempts to highlight commonalities and in efforts to cooperate in other areas of mutual interest. With such interaction, confrontation is less likely. Barth's framework seems to be applicable in Egypt at the levels of sociopolitical interaction between Christians and Muslims. By engaging together in a variety of areas, Egypt's Christians and Muslims seem to live out Schirch's idea that the rehumanization of the Other helps to reduce conflict, at least among those who are farther toward toleration on Walzer's continuum, as stereotypes are broken down.

Word and Work—Discourse and Practice

The actors examined here have set the bar high in their demonstrated tolerance and acceptance. It is important, though, to return to the question of rhetoric and actual behavior. What important difference is there between an actor's words and actions? Throughout this study, the statements and rhetoric of various actors—government, official religion, political parties, and NGOs—have been analyzed. In each case, their statements are shown to merit a reasonable level of credence.

Walzer (1997, xi) makes an important distinction between tolerance and toleration: tolerance is an attitude and toleration is the practice. Here, it is less possible to make clear determinations on the level of exhibited tolerance than on the levels of toleration. In a sense, this semantic distinction is an alternate way of posing the dichotomy of rhetoric and action. However, rhetoric being a form of practice, it falls under the category of toleration just as action does. Walzer's suggestion can be affirmed, that is, toleration is practiced in many settings to ensure a degree of social harmony, but toleration in no way has abolished the "us" and "them" (Walzer 1997, 92). Toleration in contemporary Egypt exists on the various locations of Walzer's continuum of toleration from acceptance to endorsement, but it is also the case that intolerance exists in varying degrees.

In the case of the government, it has demonstrated its obligatory function of maintaining a prevailing degree of conflict-free relations between Christian and Muslim neighbors. A vibrant Christian community that remains committed to making commercial, social, and political contributions to the country evidences this status. There has not been any kind of serious movement, in words or in deed, to establish a Christian enclave within Egypt, even though naturally there are higher concentrations of Christians in some places than others. Neither has there been an inordinate degree of Christian emigration from Egypt, even though Christians may have better access to the diaspora. While the Egyptian Christian communities in the United States, England, and Australia are very strong and politically active in their respective places of residence, it does not seem that the Christian population in Egypt is diminishing relatively or absolutely. Of course, it is difficult to be certain of this assertion quantitatively, since there are no reliable census figures or other sources by which to give an accurate demographic picture, either comparatively over time or at the current instant. However, indicators such as the 1976 census compared with 1997 estimates given by the government (10 percent) and by the churches (up to 20 percent) do not indicate a radical shift in demographics (Wagner 1997).

The government has been very strong in cracking down on Islamic radicals, which should help to put Christians at ease. It has also revoked the requirement that the president himself must approve requests for church construction or repair, placing that authority instead in the hands of the provincial governors. Some feel that this delegation of authority has simplified the application process for church construction or renovation by requiring less time and bureaucratic process to gain approval. Some also feel that local relations play a more important role, and indeed local Christian leaders do foster relationships with local government authorities. On the other hand, some fear that the removal of authority from the president himself means that local authorities, who may have leanings to a kind of political Islam, would be less willing to approve such application than the president normally would and would have less accountability.

The government's rhetoric has been clear: a message of national unity and the indivisible nature of the Egyptian populace. That is to say, in the eyes of the government, all citizens, whether Christian or Muslim, enjoy full rights and bear full responsibilities. Even so, one must recognize the fact that very few Christians have held cabinet-level positions. Obvious exceptions in modern history are Butros Butros Ghali, who served as deputy prime minister, Yusif Butros Ghali as minister of finance, and Mona Makram 'Ebeid as minister for the environment.

In the instance of a conference on minorities in the Middle East, the government helped to make its convening in Egypt very difficult. This kind of pressure and influence reflects two intentions. The first is to maintain the idea that Egypt's Christians and Muslims are two components of the Egyptian fabric. The implication that one is somehow different than the other is divisive in itself. That such extensive debate took place over the issue in Egypt also shows that the government has been, to some extent, willing to allow public discussion and discourse on such a potentially divisive matter. The extent of that willingness, however, is uncertain, as the second intent of keeping the conference off of Egypt's soil was perhaps to minimize the divisiveness of the matter.

In a second case, that of the violence in al-Kusheh, many questions were raised at the time about the complicity of the state in the deaths, centering mostly on the fact that security officers in the village did little or nothing to prevent the massacre. Does this mean that the government was looking the other way? Does it mean that the local security officers were? Much suspicion has been raised around these questions.

Official religion seems to have taken both rhetorical and practical initiatives to advance the cause of tolerance and acceptance. From the

Christian side, it is clear that the numeric minority group has an interest in being proactive in fostering good relations with Muslim neighbors. What is important is that these have been received with good feelings and reciprocated. Muslims have been proactive in the area of dialogue and good relations, not just within Egypt but internationally as well. In terms of action, efforts are made by the instrumentalities of official religion to bridge social gaps through social programs and interaction.

In the area of political parties, at least some members of the two parties examined in chapter 5 have "talked the talk" of good relations between Christians and Muslims. The Labor Party has gone through significant internal debate about its nature (secular or Islamic), and while the debate still may not be resolved it is clear that Christians and Muslims both have felt an identity with the Labor Party, to the extent that Christian candidates are on the party ticket. In the proposed Hizb al-Wasat, the founding members come from both faith communities and, while highlighting an Islamic culture, assert the role of both Christian and Muslim in achieving its agenda. In its work in the political party and NGO realms, there is a clear expectation that Hizb al-Wasat's words and actions are true to its basic philosophy of inclusion.

In the area of nongovernmental organizations, the rhetoric is more easily checked by action. In the two cases of CEOSS and the Ibn Khaldun Center, the foci of the work—community development and dialogue in the case of CEOSS, and research and intellectual development in Ibn Khaldun's case—reflect a very active, if not vocal, agenda that clearly demonstrates that acceptance and good relations are a necessary priority. The Ibn Khaldun Center has been controversial in more than one activity, and its closing in 2000 perhaps had something to do with its criticism of the government's religious education curriculum; it certainly was linked to its criticism of the government's handling of elections and, at least on the surface, the source of foreign contributions for its work. CEOSS works very deliberately and diligently in putting forth a discourse of cooperation through hosting interfaith panels and open lectures. In its more expansive development work, CEOSS demonstrates this discourse through nondiscriminatory programmatic activities in communities that may diverge from Egypt's overall Christian-Muslim demography.

Rhetoric and action, therefore, have a degree of parallelism that indicates that the talk is not just that but is a rather authentic expression of outlook. Even if rhetoric is not supported by action, if strong rhetoric is translated into passivity in other areas, the rhetoric then carries its own weight as it is communicated to people throughout the country and even throughout the world. Negative action is more problematic in light of positive rhetoric, though. In the cases examined here, the positive rhetoric of harmony and unity does not seem to contradict the actions of the same actors; words and actions seem to be consistently positive.

The Role of Religious Dialogue

Tarek Mitri's three proposals for an agenda of dialogue between faiths were "the role of religion in the present conflicts between, and within, nations"; human rights and their indivisibility; and "the future of the world and the role of religions" (1999, 84–85). Mitri proposes that dialogue be one of conversation and exploration, theological and academic; and also one of life, that is, that the kind of relations that exist in everyday patterns of life constitute a form of dialogue that is just as important, if not more so, than high-level discussions.

Mitri's first reference, as it applies to the context of Egypt, is the role of religion in national sectarian conflict. Based upon the findings and discussion of this book, an assumption can be made that a degree of conflict does exist. Even if, as Mitri points out, the conflicts are not religious, or are religious in only some aspect,

> Christians and Muslims are called to join efforts toward their resolution. More particularly, they need to seek ways of preventing the use of religious sentiments and symbols as weapons. . . . People of faith should, instead of competitively taking pride in their scriptures, collaborate in drawing inspiration from them in order to combat the idolatrous perversions of ultranationalism, ethnicism and communalism. (Mitri 1999, 84)

In the case of Egypt, this exhortation seems to corroborate what the representatives of official religion identified here are attempting to do. They have been working to base an ethic of cooperation and tolerance upon their own scriptures and sacred texts, and to communicate their understanding in one form or another to the people of their own—and the other—communities. The question of the efficacy of "trickle-down" religion has been rightly raised, but it is significant that the leadership is engaged.

The second agenda item Mitri proposes concerns human rights. Mitri states the problem as such:

> Despite the emphasis on their universality, [human rights] can be implemented selectively and the call for implementation can be reflective of a double standard. . . . Moreover, human rights advocacy is confined, at times, to solidarity with victims from one's own community. It is therefore crucial that Christians and Muslims uphold together the indivisibility of human rights, reconcile individual rights with those of the community and seal a common outlook through practical cooperation. (Mitri 1999, 85)

This same principle as applied to the idea of citizen rights (not foreign to human rights) has recurred numerous times throughout this study of Egypt's citizenry. The debate over equality of rights for non-Muslims in an Islamic state (culturally and legally, as defined by Egypt's constitution) has been vibrant, and it has been clear how important it is for Muslims to advocate for the equality of rights (and responsibilities) of Christians. In the case of Egypt, members of the numeric Muslim majority have made strong efforts to uphold the rights of Christians, defining them not as *dhimmi* but as equal citizens under the law. Actors in various sectors have reiterated this equality: government officials, the *shaikh* of al-Azhar, party members, and civil society actors in the NGO realm. By working together in these areas, the indivisibility of rights as a principle is strengthened, and opportunities for dialogue and cooperation are also fostered.

The third area is the role of religion and the future. Mitri proposes that "it is often said that the next century will be, in some way, religious. . . . But others predict, in a way that awakens the self-righteous conquering Christianity, that religions will define the 'bloody borders' among people. The impact of such a discourse about the future could not be underestimated, as it may function in certain situations like a self-fulfilling prophecy" (Mitri 1999, 85).

Those who claim that Egypt has been embroiled in a *fitna ta'ifiyya* for the past decade would say that a religious definition of "bloody borders" has already been realized in Egypt. Their adversaries in the debate, however, claim that indeed religion has a role, but it is one that can contribute to a better society in Egypt. The advocates of a positive role for religion struggle to promote cooperation and tolerance among a population in which fears of a more antagonistic vision have taken hold.

For many in Egypt, the issues of the nature of citizenship and the nation are still unresolved. The question of the defining role of religion is organically wrapped up in these issues. It has been noted that some Christians are concerned about the rise of an Islamic party to power in Egypt, either legally through the process of democratization or through a usurpation of power by other means. Some Christians support the continuation of the state's emergency laws for just that reason: to ensure that politically aspirant extremist Muslims are controlled and held at bay. Maintenance of such mechanisms appear to assist in the maintenance of authoritarian rule, however, with all that is entailed by that for all citizens, and constrains the possibility of a more fully vibrant civil society. Opposition, critique, and popular expression are all stymied, whether they are religious in nature or not. The process of political reform suffers as a result. In this situation, some do benefit to be sure, but others (perhaps many or most) are suppressed in expressing their true political preference.

At the same time, if all controls were lifted and a radical expression of religion were to emerge in a position of institutional state power, there is concern that a similar suppression of many or most would take place: Christians fear that they would become second-class citizens, *dhimmiyyin* in the classical Islamic sense of protected non-Muslims, or even worse than that; and moderate Muslims who do not agree in the more extreme interpretation of Islam would also find no place for expression.

Neither case is entirely preferable; this is the conundrum faced in many Middle Eastern and other countries that wish (or are pressured) to follow a path of either political or economic reform, or both. Such is a minimal argument for the encouragement of a vibrant civil society in which many of these discussions can find voice. In terms of Christian-Muslim relations in Egypt, the previous chapters have helped to identify state and nonstate actors that are engaged in this kind of discourse. Religion, as it has been demonstrated, is an active participant in civil society through religious expressions of both official religion and nonofficial religion (aspirant and existent political parties, and religious and secular NGOs).

Egypt and Civil Society

The religious issue has become a response to a call; the national issue is unity. Having focused on the national issue and the sociopolitical realm in which the discourse takes place, an evaluation of what has been learned in terms of the viability and applicability of the concept of civil society in Egypt today is important.

Accepting that a vibrant civil society exists to some extent in contemporary Egypt, the differentiation between civil society and state is recognizable in the Lockean model in which political and civil society is distinguished from the state (Mitri 1999, 85). Social and political debate can and does take place outside the realm of the state. 'Ashmawi asserts that liberal values do exist in Egypt—they are not inconsistent with Islam or its *shari'a*—and accepts the idea that citizenship is part of Egypt's legal, political, and social culture. Debate over the place of Christians vis-à-vis Muslims in the Egyptian context surely takes place, if not in private then in the public sphere. Even if the debate is somewhat controlled in the public sphere, that is, in newspapers and other media owned, operated, or otherwise subject to state parameters, this control has not been complete. While the government sets the parameters of newspapers or magazines by publishing, censoring, or banning them, it has been relatively easy for the owners of banned media to publish in other countries, such as Cyprus, and then get them into the country for sale to the public. Additionally, with the advent of satellite television and the Internet, the Egyptian public has access to news and debate over which the Egyptian government may have little or no control. Since Egypt is considered an important political and cultural center of the Arab world, there is much debate on news and talk shows about Egypt. Such access allows for opinions to be disseminated and points of view widely broadcast, thus breaching the control of the state.

In areas where the government has broader mechanisms for control, such as the regulation of political parties, even outlawed organizations such as the Muslim Brotherhood and other politicized Islamic organizations are able to find expression in legal political parties. Yet, much debate about the role of religion in politics is taking place within parties, as evidenced by the Labor Party's internecine conflict. The program of proposed parties is afforded space in the newspapers, as was the case of Hizb al-Wasat. Even when the party's application for legal status was first rejected, its ideas had been disseminated and debated. Its effort for legal license continues.

In the case of NGOs, even if a majority of the registered organizations are nonfunctional, a number have become quite effective in their work and mission. This efficacy has occasionally been a challenge to the government from the associational sphere, an affirmation of a nonstate actor's influence in society. The Lockean model of state and nonstate actors clearly exists in Egypt today.

The ongoing dialogue of state and nonstate actors around topics of communal relations is an example of the vibrancy of civil society. Associations deciding to apply for license to form a political party, such as Hizb al-Wasat, make a deliberate effort to resolve for themselves the role of the two religious communities in Egypt and the relationship they would ideally have. Similarly, the Muslim Brotherhood in its negotiations within its own leadership as well as electoral alliances must resolve this question. In the most recent election, by running as independents, the Muslim Brotherhood candidates were perhaps less beholden to such alliances, but they presumably held positions consistent with the organization of the Muslim Brotherhood on such questions. The ability of NGOs to take on sensitive matters in their daily work is a sign that the debate and discussion wants to find voice, and needs leadership. While the state still has much control, other segments of the sociopolitical realm can and do actively engage on such issues of vital importance for the citizenry. As Appleby (2000, 19) notes, "Building peace . . . 'calls for long-term commitment to establishing an infrastructure across the levels of a society.' "

A further consideration is that of the unit of analysis: the individual or the group. This study has leaned heavily toward an examination of group interaction, which is associated with public interaction. Public rhetoric and activity at the levels in question are certainly informed by individual attitudes, but they are tempered by the general realm in which they are presented and received. The ways in which individuals interact and the ways in which groups engage are characterized differently. As Seligman points out, the matters of agency and perception vary from the individual to the group levels and have significant bearings on the role of trust and risk in the interaction. Governments, religious institutions, political parties, and NGOs naturally are made up of individuals, but, in their actions and interactions, the corporate body is the operative unit. The Egyptian government, Muslim and Christian religious leaders, the several parties, and NGOs clearly function as and refer to groups. The Muslim and Christian communities are groups interacting with each other, as well as within the communities. In terms of citizenship rights, the assumption is that Egyptian society is comprised of Muslims and Christians and not citizens blind to their religion. This approach recognizes that religion is important to one's social and political status; indeed, religious affiliation is named on the national identity cards. The question of whether it is possible to consider Egyptian citizens without reference to their religion is only just beyond the scope of this study.

Various segments of Egyptian polity and society have exhibited tolerance toward the religious Other, even in times of heightened tension. The government and the institutions of official religion, political parties, and NGOs, through rhetoric and concrete action, have demonstrated a level of religious toleration that may be equated with cooperation. These expressions are significant, especially when a portion of the Egyptian community has chosen not to confer social citizenship upon another portion. Tolerance, toleration, citizenship, and civil society have been the axes around which the discussion has turned and have informed this consideration of the nature of intercommunal relations between Egypt's Muslims and Christians.

Finally, not only does social citizenship exist in Parsons' terms, but cooperation between Christians and Muslims can and does take place. This cooperation is a sign that religion and community defined by religious identity are not always divisive and need not be, but that they can be catalysts for productive development of interfaith relations and of society. All of this has important implications for the process of political reform, slowly emerging in Egypt. As the process of political reform continues, it will likely cause a degree of instability that could result in tensions that become manifest in sectarian ways. These examples of cooperation, even in the midst of conflict, demonstrate that potential conflict can be approached by many in positions of power, influence, and opinion making, to demonstrate a better way forward. Such efforts can help smooth the path of political reform, which will surely bring issues of religious identity and citizenship to the fore. No doubt, cooperation that takes place even in the presence of conflict is the most necessary if cooperation is to be appreciated and valued, thus moving beyond social citizenship and into an even more positive realm that might be called social collegiality. Such cooperation most effectively arises not in times of crisis but rather in calmer times, so that relationships can be fostered for proactive cooperation in many areas and called upon in times of increased tension to help manage and resolve crises. Pluralistic societies in Egypt and the Arab world do not need to struggle to enjoy their full fruits; religious diversity can contribute to vibrant civil society and indeed to peace making and in fact is doing so. In the clash of ideologies—conservative and exclusivist versus moderate and tolerant—seeking and modeling cross-communal cooperation among those who dream of more perfect social harmony can be important keys to reclaiming the discourse and the public debate.

Glossary

References

Index

Glossary

All terms are Arabic unless otherwise indicated.

ahl adh-dhimma (n.); **dhimmi** (adj.); pl. **dhimmiyun; dhimmiyyin:** protected people; an Islamic term referring to non-Muslim minorities protected by a Muslim polity

Aigyptos: (Gk.) Egypt

'alim; pl. **'ulama':** learned clergy in Islam

"Allahu akbar": literally, "God is greater"; an Islamic phrase, invoked most familiarly as part of the call to prayer

Dar al-Ifta': office of the mufti

da'wa: call; missionary activity

dawla: state, nation in the political sense

dhimma: protection

din: religion

diwan: court

fadila; pl. **fada'il:** virtue

al-fath al-islami: literally, "Islamic opening"; conquest by the Muslim armies and expansion of Islamic dominance of other peoples and lands, taking place primarily in the seventh century C.E. in what is now called the Middle East

fatwa; pl. **fatawa:** religious interpretative pronouncement on questions and issues, based on Islamic texts

fitna: sectarian tension or strife

gibt: (Gk.) Copt

hadith: body of sayings about the practices of the prophet Muhammad

hijra: literally, "emigration"; the basis of the Islamic calendar, dated from the first emigration of Muhammad and his community from Mecca to Medina in 622 C.E.

hiwar: conversation, dialogue

hizb: party; political party

'id al-fitr: celebration of the end of Ramadan, often lasting several days

iftar: meal after dusk during Ramadan to break the day's fast

infitah: literally, "opening"; an economic and political policy instituted by President Anwar as-Sadat

jama'a: (Egypt. **gama'a**) group

jama'at islamiyya: Islamic groups

jihad: struggle, religious striving

jizya: poll tax imposed on non-Muslims

khalifa: successor; head of the Muslim community, succeeding the prophet Muhammad

kifaya: literally, "enough"; the name of an opposition party in the 2005 presidential and parliamentary elections

mahjar: diaspora

Misr: Egypt

mufti: Islamic authority on interpretation of religious and legal texts, i.e., the Qur'an, the Hadith, and the body of Islamic jurisprudence, or *fiqh*

qibti; pl. **aqbat:** Copt

ra'is al-mu'minin: leader of the faithful

riba: usury; sometimes translated as interest

shaikh: elder

shaikh al-Azhar: rector and head of al-Azhar, Egypt's millennium-old Islamic university and historical authoritative office on Islamic learning

shari'a: Islamic law

ta'if: sect or religious community

ta'ifi (m.); **ta'ifiyya** (f.): sectarian

takfir: declaration of someone or something as antithetical or apostate to the Islamic faith

thawra: revolution; coup

umma: nation; people

'uzla: exile

wafd: delegation; also the name of an Egyptian political party

waqf; pl. **awqaf:** religious endowment

watan: state; nation-state

zabbal; pl. **zabbalin:** garbage collector

zakat: almsgiving; one of five pillars, or obligations, in traditional Islam

References

'Abd Allah, Zakariyya Muhammad. 1998. *Al-Barlaman al-misri (1976–1995): Dirasa tahliliyya li't-Tarkiba al-'ansuriyya.* Cairo: Markaz al-Mahrusa li'l-Buhuth wa'l-Tadrib wa'n-Nashr.

Abdel Fattah, Nabil. 1994. *Veiled Violence: Islamic Fundamentalism in Egyptian Politics in 1990s.* Cairo: Dar Sechat for Studies, Publishing, and Distribution.

Abou El-Magd, Nadia. 2000. "The Meanings of al-Kosheh." *Al-Ahram Weekly.* Feb. 3–9.

Abu-Nimr, Mohammed. 2003. *Nonviolence and Peacebuilding in Islam: Theory and Practice.* Gainesville: Univ. Press of Florida.

Al-'Adas, Muhammad. 2000. "Al-Azhar, Vatican Discuss Human Rights." *MECC News Report.* Autumn. Originally published in Arabic in *al-Liwa'*, July 11, 2000.

Al-Ahram. 1996. "Ad-Duktur Sayyid Tantawi Shaikhan li'l-Azhar." Mar. 28.

———. 2000a. "Shaikh al-Azhar wa'l-Baba Shenouda yu'araban 'an amli-himma." Jan. 12.

———. 2000b. "Sama'tu . . . wa qara'tu . . . wa ra'aytu." Feb. 1.

Al-Ahram Centre for Political and Strategic Studies. 1995. *Al-Hala ad-diniyya fi Misr.* Cairo: Al-Ahram Centre for Political and Strategic Studies.

———. 1998. *Al-Hala ad-dinyya fi Misr.* 2d. ed. Cairo: Al-Ahram Centre for Political and Strategic Studies.

———. 1997. *The State of Religion in Egypt Report.* Cairo: Al-Ahram Centre for Political and Strategic Studies. English-language summary of the 1995 edition of *Al-Hala ad-diniyya fi Misr.*

Al-Ahram Weekly. 2003. "Christmas for All." Jan. 9–15.

Al-Akhbar. 1995. "Naqaltu tahiyyat ar-ra'is Mubarak wa 'akadna ruh al-muhabba wa's-salam." Jan. 13.

'Ali, 'Abd ar-Rahim. 1996. "Lam natakhl 'an sh'ar al-Islam huwwa al-hall." *Al-Ahali.* Jan. 17.

Anderson, Benedict. 1983. *Imagined Communities: Reflections on the Origin and Spread of Nationalism.* London: Verso.

Ansari, Hamied. 1984. "Sectarian Conflict in Egypt and the Political Expediency of Religion." *Middle East Journal* 38, no. 3: 397–418.

Apiku, Simon. 2000. "Kosheh Storm Leaves Tension." *Middle East Times.* Jan. 13–19.

Appleby, R. Scott. 2000. *The Ambivalence of the Sacred: Religion, Violence, and Reconciliation.* Lanham, Md.: Rowman and Littlefield.

Arab Reform Bulletin. 2005. "Egypt: Parliamentary Election Results and Noor Trial." Dec.: 7.

Al-'Ashmawi, Muhammad Sa'id. 1989a. *Ma'alam al-Islam.* Cairo: Sina li'n-Nashr.

———. 1989b. *Al-Islam as-siyasi.* Cairo: Sina li'n-Nashr.

———. 1995. "Al-Aqbat laysa ahl adh-dhimma." *Rose El Yossef.* Mar. 13.

AUC Today. 1998. "Defending Human Rights: An Arabic Public Lecture Looks at Human Rights in Islam." Spring.

Al-'Awa, Muhammad Salim. 1998. *Azmat al-mu'assasa ad-diniyya.* Cairo: Dar ash-Shuruq.

———. 2000. "Al-Kusheh . . . ma al-'aml?" *Al-Ahram al-'Arabi.* Jan. 15.

Al-Banna, Ragab. 1998. *Al-Aqbat fi Misr wa'l-mahjar: Hiwarat ma' al-baba Shenouda.* Cairo: Dar al-Ma'arif.

Barth, Fredrik, ed. 1969. *Ethnic Groups and Boundaries: The Social Organization of Cultural Difference.* Boston: Little, Brown.

Bianchi, Robert. 1989. "Islam and Democracy in Egypt." *Current History.* Feb.:93–96.

Al-Birq. 1997. "Masihiyun wa muslimun sallu bi'l-uqsur sawiyyatan min ajl dahaya al-majzara." Dec. 4.

Bishri, Sami. 1998. "Al-Baba Shenouda yuqim ma'dat iftar al-wihda al-wataniyya." *Al-Ahram.* Feb. 2.

Al-Bishri, Tariq. 1988. *Al-Muslimun w'al-Aqbat fi itar al-jama'a al-wataniyya.* Cairo: Dar ash-Shuruq.

———. 1998a. *Bain al-Islam wa'l-'aruba.* Cairo: Dar ash-Shuruq.

———. 1998b. *Bain al-jama'a ad-diniyya wa'l-jama'a al-wataniyya fi'l-fikr as-siyassi.* Cairo: Dar ash-Shuruq.

Brinkman, Carl. 1927. *Recent Theories of Citizenship.* New Haven, Conn.: Yale Univ. Press.

Cairo Times. 2000. "Twenty Dead in Kosheh Clashes." Jan. 6–12.

Carter, B. L. 1986. *The Copts in Egyptian Politics.* London: Croom Helm.

Civil Society. 1998. "Egypt Asks Congress to Leave the Copts Alone." Mar.

Clarke, Paul Barry. 1994. *Citizenship.* London: Pluto Press.

Cohen-Almagor, Raphael. 1994. *The Boundaries of Liberty and Tolerance.* Gainesville: Univ. Press of Florida.

Coptic Voice: The Mouthpiece of the British Coptic Association. 1998. "Congressional Human Rights Caucus Briefing by Lord David Alton on the Persecution of Christians in Egypt." May.

Crecelius, Daniel. 1966. "Al-Azhar in the Revolution." *Middle East Journal* 20, no. 1:34–49.

Curtiss, Richard H. 1998. "Egyptian Copts Warn Against Congressional Pressure." *Washington Report on Middle East Affairs.* Sept.:71.

Cyprus Weekly. 1997. "Fear among Copts Intensifies in Egypt over Muslim Militants' Bloody Campaign." Mar. 28.

Ad-Dahabi, Edwar Ghali. 1993. *Mu'amalat ghair al-Muslimin fi'l-mujtama' al-islami.* Cairo: Maktabat Gharib.

———. 1998. *An-Namudhig al-misri li'l-wihda al-wataniyya.* Cairo: Maktabat al-Usra.

Dialogue. 2001. www.ceoss.org, updated April 1.

Early, Tracy. 1998. "Reports of Persecution of Egypt's Christians Are 'Overstated.'" *Ecumenical News International.* Mar. 26.

Egypt Human Rights Report. 2001. http://www.arabicnews.com/ansub/Daily/Day/010316/2001031631.html. March 16.

Egyptian Gazette. 2000. "Mubarak Praises Police Role in Preserving National Unity." Jan. 26.

Egyptian National Committee for Parliamentary Election Review. 1995. *Report of the Egyptian National Committee for Parliamentary Election Review.* Cairo: Ibn Khaldun Center for Developmental Studies.

Elbendary, Amina. 2005. "Neighbours Like Any Other." *Al-Ahram Weekly.* May 12–18.

Elghawaby, Amira. 2000. "Has the State Failed to Diffuse Sectarian Strife? *Middle East Times.* Jan. 13–19.

El-Ghobashy, Mona. 2002. "Antinomies of the Saad Eddin Ibrahim Case." MERIP Press Information Note 106. Aug. 15.

El Sawaf, Hassan. 1999. "Please Repeal This Provocative Law." *Civil Society.* July.

Farah, Nadia Ramsis. 1986. *Religious Strife in Egypt: Crisis and Ideological Conflict in the Seventies.* New York: Gordon and Breach Science Publishers.

Fathy, Ahmed. 2006. "Egypt Catholics Fault Pope." *Islam Online,* www.islam-online.net/English/News/2006-09/16/01.shtml. (Accessed Sept. 16.)

Fawzi, Samah, ed. N.d. *Mawdua'at muqtaraha li muqarrir id-din il-Massihi.* Cairo: Ibn Khaldun Center for Development Studies.

El-Feki, Mustafa. 1988. *Al-Aqbat fi's-siyasa al-Misriyya.* Cairo: Dar ash-Shuruq.

———. 1993. "Makram Ebeid: Politician of the Majority Party." In *Contemporary Egypt: Through Egyptian Eyes,* edited by Charles Tripp, 22–44. London: Routledge.

Fischer, Eric. 1980. *Minorities and Minority Problems.* Takoma Park, Md.: Erasmus House.

Fisher, Ronald J. 2001. "Social-Phychological Processes in Interactive Conflict Analysis and Reconciliation." In *Reconciliation, Justice, and Coexistence: Theory and Practice,* edited by Mohammad Abu-Nimr, 22–45. Lanham, Md.: Lexington Books.

Gabra, Gawdat. 1993. *Cairo, the Coptic Museum, Old Churches.* Cairo: Egyptian International Publishing House.

Gavlak, Dave. 1998. "Religious Rights Move 'May Make Matters Worse.'" *Cyprus Weekly.* June 5–11.

Al-Gawhary, Karim. 1996. "Copts in the 'Egyptian Fabric.'" *Middle East Report* 26, no.3:21–22.

Gellner, Ernest. 1983. *Nations and Nationalism.* Ithaca, N.Y.: Cornell Univ. Press.

Goldschmidt, Arthur, Jr. 1988. *Modern Egypt: The Formation of a Nation-State.* Boulder, Colo.: Westview Press.

Gopin, Marc. 2002. "The Use of the Word and Its Limits: A Critical Evaluation of Religious Dialogue as Peacemaking." In *Interfaith Dialogue and*

Peacebuilding, edited by David R. Smock, 33–46. Washington, D.C.: United States Institute of Peace.

Habib, Rafiq. 1990. *Al-Masihiyya as-siyasiyya fi Misr.* Cairo: Yaffa li'l Dirasat wa'n-Nashr.

———. 2000a. E-mail correspondence with author. May 12.

———. 2000b. Interview by author, Cairo, Jan. 19.

Habib, Samuel. Ca. 1993. Interview by author in Cairo.

———. 1994a. Introduction to *al-Fikr ad-dini wa'l-muwatanna.* Cairo: Dar El Thaqafa.

———. 1994b. Introduction to *al-Fikr ad-dini wa taqaddum al-mujtama'.* Cairo: Dar El Thaqafa.

———. 1995a. "Al-fikr ad-dini wa'l-musharaka fi al-haya wa'l-mujtam'a." In *al-Fikr ad-dini wa'l-musharaka.* Cairo: Dar El Thaqafa.

———. 1995b. "Ma' al-mufti fi'l-wilayat al-mutahada." *Al-Huda.* Jan.–Feb.

———. 1995c. "Rasalat al-mudir al-'am." In *al-Hay'a al-Qibtiyya al-Injiliyya li'l Khadamat al-Ijtima'aiyya: 45 'aman fi khidmat Misr (1950–1995).* Cairo: CEOSS.

———. 1997. Introduction to *al-Insan al-misri wa tahaddiyat al-qarn al-qadim.* Cairo: Dar El Thaqafa.

Halawi, Jailan. 2002. "Going Home." *Al-Ahram Weekly.* Feb. 7–13.

Halwa, Sa'id. 1998. "'Al-Sawm' yajma' al-Muslimin wa'l-Masihiyin 'ala ruh al-muhabba wa't-ta'atuf." *Al-Ahram.* Jan. 8.

Halwa, Sa'id, and Mushira Musa. 1997. "Ikhtilaf al-'aqa'id la yuwlid al-mukha-wif bal at-ta'awun." *Al-Ahram.* Dec. 18.

Halwa, Sa'id, and Suhaila Nazmi. 1997. "Al-Azhar wa'l-Awqaf jibha wahda li muwajihat tashwih surat al-Islam fi'l-kharij." *Al-Ahram.* Jan. 5.

Hammond, Andrew. 1996. "In the Name of the Son." *Middle East Times.* Jan. 28–Feb. 3.

———. 2001. "Though Nominal Winner, Egypt's Ruling NDP Party Embar-rassed in Parliamentary Elections." *Washington Report on Middle East Affairs.* Jan.–Feb.:31.

———. 2002. "Egyptian Appeals Court Orders Civil Rights Activist Ibra-him Released, Retried." *Washington Report on Middle East Affairs.* Apr.:36–37.

Hamzawi, Amr. 2005. "Interview with Abul Ila Al Madi, Founding Member of Egypt's Wasat (Center) Party." Translated by Jeffrey Poole. *Arab Reform Bulletin* 3, no. 10:3–4.

Hanna, Milad. 1998. *Qubul al-akhar.* Cairo: Dar ash-Shuruq.

Harb, Osama El-Ghazali. 2000–2001. "Democracy and Its Discontents." *Al-Ahram Weekly.* Dec. 28–Jan. 3.

Harbi, Muhammad. 1996. "Abu al-'Alaa Madi: Lassna hizban ikhwaniyyan lakin sha'aruna Islam huwwa al-hall." *Al-Wasat.* Jan. 22.

Hardin, Russell. 1995. *One for All: The Logic of Group Conflict.* Princeton, N.J.: Princeton Univ. Press.

Harel, Alon. 1996. "The Boundaries of Justifiable Tolerance: A Liberal Perspective." In *Toleration: An Elusive Virtue,* edited by David Heyd, 14–26. Princeton, N.J.: Princeton Univ. Press.

Hassan, Essam El Din. 1995. "Anxieties of Copts over the Upsurge in Islamic Fundamentalism." *Huqooq al-Insaan.* Apr.

Al-Hayat. 1996. "Misr: Qiyadi fi'l-ikhwan yansha' hizban yadumm Aqbatan." Jan. 12.

Hendriks, Bertus. 1987. "A Report from the Election Campaign: Egypt's New Political Map." *Middle East Report* July–Aug.:23–30.

Heyd, David, ed. 1996. *Toleration: An Elusive Virtue.* Princeton, N.J.: Princeton Univ. Press.

Hizb al-Wasat. 1996. *Awraq Hizb al-Wasat.* Cairo: Hizb al-Wasat.

Hodgson, Marshall G.S. 1974a. *The Venture of Islam: Conscience and History in a World Civilization.* Vol. 2, *The Expansion of Islam in the Middle Periods.* Chicago: Univ. of Chicago Press.

———. 1974b. *The Venture of Islam: Conscience and History in a World Civilization.* Vol. 3, *The Gunpowder Empires and Modern Times.* Chicago: Univ. of Chicago Press.

Horton, John. 1996. "Toleration as a Virtue." In *Toleration,* edited by David Heyd, 28–43. Princeton, N.J.: Princeton Univ. Press.

Hourani, Albert H. 1947. *Minorities in the Arab World.* London: Oxford Univ. Press.

Hudson, Michael C. 1996. "Obstacles to Democratization in the Middle East." *Contention* 5, no.2:81–105.

Huntington, Samuel P. 1993. "The Clash of Civilizations?" *Foreign Affairs* 72, no.3: 22–49.

Hurib, Khalid. 1997. "Nudafa' 'an al-Aqbat li-naghlaq fi wijh at-tadakhul al-ajnabi." *Al-Ahali.* Aug. 10.

Huwaidi, Fahmi. 1997. "A'tidhar ila kulli Qibti." *Al-Ahram.* Feb. 25.

———. 2000. "B'il-a'tidhar yabda' al-hall." *Wijahat nazr* 2:13.

Huwaydi, Amirah. 1997. "Islamists and Secularists to Publish New Weekly." *Civil Society.* Sept.

Ibn Khaldun Center for Development Studies. 1990. *Ibn Khaldun Center for Development Studies: An Overview of Goals and Activities.* Cairo: Ibn Khaldun Center.

Ibn Khaldun Center for Development Studies and the Minority Rights Group. 1994. *Bayan khitami 'an mu'tamar a'alan al-umum al-mutahida li huquq al-uqulliyyat wa shu'ub al-watan al-'arabi wa'sh-sharq al-awsat.* Limassol, Cyprus: Ibn Khaldun Center for Development Studies and the Minority Rights Group. May 12–14.

Ibrahim, Saad Eddin. 1993a. "Crises, Elites, and Democratization in the Arab World." *Middle East Journal* 47, no.2: 292–305.

———, ed. 1993b. *Humum al-uqulliyyat fi'l-watan al-'arabi: al-Taqrir as-sanuwi al-awwal, 1993.* Cairo: Ibn Khaldun Center.

———. 1995. "Civil Society and Prospects of Democratization in the Arab World." In *Civil Society in the Middle East,* vol. 1, edited by Augustus Richard Norton, 27–54. New York: E. J. Brill.

———. 1996a. *The Copts of Egypt.* London: Minority Rights Group.

———. 1996b. "Governance and Structural Adjustment: The Egyptian Case." In *Egypt, Islam, and Democracy,* edited by Saad Eddin Ibrahim, 135–81. Cairo: American Univ. in Cairo Press.

———. 1996c. "Islamic Activism and Political Opposition in Egypt." In *Egypt, Islam, and Democracy,* edited by Saad Eddin Ibrahim. Cairo: American Univ. in Cairo Press.

———. 1996d. "1995: A Year of Wavering Democracy." *Civil Society.* Jan.

Ibrahim, Saad Eddin, Marilyn R. I. Tadros, Mohammed Anwar El-Fiki, and Soliman Shafik Soliman. 1999. "History of Egyptian Civil Society." *Civil Society.* July.

Ibrahim, Youssef M. 1991. "Copts Are Targets as New Strife Roils Egypt." *New York Times*. Jan. 5.

———. 1993. "Under Muslim Assault, Egypt's Coptic Christians Wonder Where to Turn." *International Herald Tribune*. Mar. 17.

———. 1996. "Gunmen in Egypt Kill 18 in Attack at Tourist Hotel." *New York Times*. Apr. 19.

Independent Commission for Electoral Review. 1996. Statement Issued December 7, 1995. *Civil Society*. Jan.

Al-Isbu'. 1997. "Al-Kharijiyya tutlub at-tasadda l'maza'am itdahad al-Aqbat." Aug. 25.

Kafafi, Husain. 1998. *Al-Masihiyya wa'l-Islam fi Misr*. Cairo: Maktabat al-Usra.

Kandil, Amani. 1994. *Al-Mujtama' al-madani fi'l-'alam al-'Arabi*. Cairo: CIVICUS.

Kassem, Hisham. 2000. "The Illusion Solution." *Cairo Times*. Jan. 13–19.

Kazemi, Farhad. 2002. "Perspectives on Islam and Civil Society." In *Civil Society and Government*, edited by Nancy L. Rosenblum and Robert C. Post, 317–33. Princeton, N.J.: Princeton Univ. Press.

Kazemi, Farhad, and Richard Augustus Norton. 1996. "Civil Society, Political Reform, and Authoritarianism in the Middle East: A Response." *Contention* 5, no.2:107–19.

Kelsay, John. 2002. "Civil Society and Government in Islam." In *Civil Society and Government*, edited by Nancy L. Rosenblum and Robert C. Post, 284–316. Princeton, N.J.: Princeton Univ. Press.

Kennedy, Hugh. 1986. *The Prophet and the Age of the Caliphates: The Islamic Near East from the Sixth to the Eleventh Century*. New York: Longman Group.

Kepel, Gilles. 1986. *Muslim Extremism in Egypt: The Prophet and the Pharaoh*. Translated from the French by Jon Rothschild. Berkeley: Univ. of California Press.

———. 2002. *Jihad: The Trail of Political Islam*. Translated from the French by Anthony F. Roberts. Cambridge, Mass.: Harvard Univ. Press.

Khaleej Times Online. 2006. "Pope's Comments on Islam as Against Christ's Teachings." www.khaleejtimes.com/DisplayArticleNew.asp?xfile=data/middleeast/2006. Sept. 16.

Khalil, Ibrahim. 1996. "Ghata' al-aqbat li hizb al-ikhwan." *Rose El Yossef*. Jan. 22.

Khalil, Nevine. 1998. "Storm in a Teacup?" *Al-Ahram Weekly*. May 21–27.

Khattab, Azza. 2000. "A Question of Faith." *Egypt Today*. Jan.

Kheir, Nagy A. 1998. *An Open Memo from the Spokesman of the American Coptic Association*. May 14.

Al-Kiraza. 1997. "Shuhada'una fi Abu Qorqas." Feb. 28.

———. 2000. "Shuhada'una fi al-Kusheh." Jan. 21.

Kramer, Gudrun. 1998. "Dhimmi or Citizen? Muslim-Christian Relations in Egypt." In *The Christian-Muslim Frontier: Chaos, Clash, or Dialogue?* edited by Jorgen S. Nielsen, 33–50. London: I. B. Taurus.

Kymlicka, Will. 1996. "Two Models of Pluralism and Tolerance." In *Toleration: An Elusive Virtue*, edited by David Heyd, 81–105. Princeton, N.J.: Princeton Univ. Press.

Lane, Edward William. 1973. *An Account of the Manners and Customs of the Modern Egyptians.* 5th ed. New York: Dover Publications.

Langohr, Vickie. 2000. "Cracks in Egypt's Electoral Engineering: The 2000 Vote." MERIP Press Information Note 39. Nov. 7.

———. 2001. "Frosty Reception for US Religious Freedom Commission in Egypt." MERIP Press Information Note 53. Mar. 29.

Lebib, Hani. 1998. "What Is on Rifaat al Said's Mind?" *Civil Society*. June.

MacFarquhar, Neil. 2002. "Egyptian Court Frees Rights Advocate and Orders Retrial." *New York Times*. Dec. 4.

Mahjub, Muhammad 'Ali. 1994. Transcript of presentation, *al-Fikr ad-dini wa'l-muwatana*. Cairo: Dar El Thaqafa.

Mainardus, O. F. 1977. *Christian Egypt: Ancient and Modern*. Cairo: American Univ. in Cairo Press.

Al-Majalla. 1996. "Abu al-'Alaa Madi li'l-Majalla: Hizbuna wada' al-hukuma fi ma'zaq." Jan. 28–Feb. 3.

Makiya, Kanan. 1995. "Toleration and the New Arab Politics." *Journal of Democracy* 6, no.1: 90–103.

Malaty, Tadros Y. 1993. *Introduction to the Coptic Orthodox Church*. Alexandria: St. George's Coptic Orthodox Church.

Mansfield, Peter. 1969. *Nasser's Egypt*. Middlesex: Penguin Books.

Al-Mawla, Sa'ud. 1996. *Al-Hiwar al-Islami-al-Masihi: Darurat al-mughamara*. Beirut: Dar al-Manhal al-Libnani.

McClure, Kristie M. 1990. "Difference, Diversity, and the Limits of Toleration." *Political Theory* 18, no.3:361–92.

Middle East Report. 1987. "Egyptian Political Parties." July–Aug.

Miller, Richard B. 2002. "Overview: The Virtues and Vices of Civil Society." In *Civil Society and Government,* edited by Nancy L. Rosenblum and Robert C. Post, 370–98. Princeton, N.J.: Princeton Univ. Press.

Ministry of Religious Endowments (Egypt). 1991. *Samahat al-Islam wa huquq ghair al-Muslimin.* Cairo: Ministry of Religious Endowments.

Mitri, Tarek. 1999. "Reflections on Confrontation and Dialogue." *Studies in Interreligious Dialogue* 9, no.1:76–86.

Morcos, Samir. 1997. "Al-Istratijia al-gharbiyya hiyal masihii Misr." *An-Nahar.* Sept. 16.

———. 2000. *Al-Himaya wa'l-'aqab: al-Gharb wa'l-mas'ala ad-diniyya fi'sh-Sharq al-Awsat.* Cairo: Dar al-Misriyya li't-Taba'a.

Mubarak, Suzanne. 1998. Introduction to "Reading for All." Back cover of Hussain Kafafi, *Al-Masihiyya wa'l-Islam fi Misr.* Cairo: Maktabat al-Usra.

Muhammad, Anwar. 1993. *Al-Islam wa'l-maihiyya fi muwajihat al-irhab wa't-tatarruf.* Cairo: Dar Am li'n-nashr wa't-tawzi'a.

Al-Mujtam'a al-madani. 1999. "Hujum Zalim 'ala markaz Ibn Khaldun." June.

Musa, Bishop. 2000. Interview by author at Coptic Orthodox Youth Bishopric, Papal Center, Cairo, Jan. 22.

Naguib, Adib, and Ashraf Zaghlul. 1989. "Sanuwat fi khadmat al-mujtama'." *Risalat an-nur.* March.

Naguib, Fathi. 1999. Transcript of remarks at public lecture, *Haqq al-ikhtalaf.* Cairo: Dar El Thaqafa.

Naguib, Makram. 1994. "Laqa'una al-yum . . . da'wa ila siyaghat 'aql al-umma." Remarks at public lecture, *al-Fikr ad-dini wa taqaddum al-mujtama'.* Cairo: Dar El Thaqafa.

An-Nahar. 1997. "Al-Anba Shenouda: Nuhall mashakilana bi hudu' wa ma nashara asa' suma'at misr." Nov. 7.

Napoli, James J. 1998. "Egypt's Coptic Christians, While Struggling to Maintain Their Heritage, Decry U.S. Anti-Persecution Act." *Washington Report on Middle East Affairs.* July–Aug.:29.

"Naqaltu tahiyyat ar-ra'is Mubarak wa 'akadna ruh al-muhabba wa's-salam." 1995. *Al-Akbar.* Jan. 13.

Norton, Augustus Richard. 1993. "The Future of Civil Society in the Middle East." *Middle East Journal* 47, no.2:205–16.

Pennington, J. D. 1982. "The Copts in Modern Egypt." *Middle Eastern Studies.* Apr.:158–79.

Pickthall, Muhammad Marmaduke, trans. *The Meaning of the Glorious Koran: An Explanatory Translation.* New York: Dorset Press.

Post, Erika. 1987. "Egypt's Elections." *Middle East Report.* July–Aug.:17–22.

Post, Robert C., and Nancy L. Rosenblum, eds. 2002. *Civil Society and Government.* Princeton, N.J.: Princeton Univ. Press.

Pranger, Robert. 1968. *The Eclipse of Citizenship: Power and Participation in Contemporary Politics.* New York: Holt, Rinehart and Winston.

Qolta, Yuhanna. 2000. Interview by author at Patriarchate of the Coptic Catholic Church, Cairo, Jan. 14.

Queller, Donald E. 2001. *The World Book Encyclopedia,* s.v. "Crusades." Chicago: World Book.

Qur'an. *See* Pickthall, Muhammad Marmaduke.

Ar-Rafa'i, 'Abd ar-Rahman. 1999. *Thawrat 1919.* Cairo: Maktabat al-Usra.

Ragab, Samir. 1995. "Ghadan: Misa' jadid." *Al-Misa' al-isbua'iyya.* Jan. 14.

Ramih, Tala'at. 1997. *Al-Wasat wa'l-Ikhwan: al-Qissa al-kamila, al-watha'iq, li'akhtar sira'a siyassi fi'l-tasa'iniyyat.* Cairo: Markaz Yaffa l'il-Dirasat wa'l-Abhath.

Rashid, Yasir. 1997. "Shaikh al-Azhar wa'l-mufti li'l-Ahali: La jizya 'ala'l-Aqbat." *Al-Ahali.* Apr. 24.

Rizk, Samuel. 1996. "The Coptic Evangelical Organization for Social Services." *Civil Society.* May.

Rose El Yossef. 1997. "Nurfud at-tadakhul al-Amriki fi shu'un Misr bi-hijjat ad-difa'a 'an al-Aqbat!" Nov. 10.

Sachs, Susan. 2001. "A Tree Drooping with Its Ancient Burden of Faith." *New York Times.* Dec. 26.

———. 2003. "Egypt Clears Rights Activist Whose Jailing Drew World Protest." *New York Times.* Mar. 19.

Said, Mohamed El-Sayed. 2001. "Bothered and Bewildered." *Al-Ahram Weekly.* June 7–13.

Salah, Muhammad. 1996. "Rafiq Habib: al-Hukuma mutitarrifa wa la 'alaqa li'l-Wasat b'il-Ikhwan." *Al-Hayat.* Jan. 20.

Salama, Adib Naguib. 1993. *Al-Injiliyun wa'l-'aml al-qawmi.* Cairo: Dar El Thaqafa.

Salama, Nabil Naguib. 1995. "Hafalat al-iftar ar-Ramadani wa mua'id ash-sha'ab al-wahid." *Risalat an-nur.* Mar.

Salama, Usama. 1994. "Al-Aqbat fi Misr." *Rose El Yossef.* May 2.

———. 1997. "Al-Azhar yarfud tatbiq ash-shari'a al-islamiyya 'ala'l-Aqbat!" *Rose El Yossef.* Nov. 3.

As-Sammak, Muhammad. 1998. *Muqadimma ila al-hiwar al-Islami-al-Masihi.* Beirut: Dar al-Naffas.

Al-Sayyid, Mustapha K. 1993. "A Civil Society in Egypt?" *Middle East Journal* 47, no. 2: 228–42.

Schiller, Norbert. 2000. "Kosheh Investigation Begins." *Cairo Times.* Jan. 13–19.

Schirch, Lisa. 2001. "Ritual Reconciliation: Transforming Identity/Reframing Conflict." In *Reconciliation, Justice, and Coexistence: Theory and Practice,* edited by Mohammad Abu-Nimr, 145–61. Lanham, Md.: Lexington Books.

Schwedler, Jillian, ed. 1995. *Toward Civil Society in the Middle East?* Boulder, Colo.: Lynne Rienner.

Seligman, Adam B. 1997. *The Problem of Trust.* Princeton, N.J.: Princeton Univ. Press.

Ash-Sharq. 1998. "Al-Fatican wa'l-Azhar shakkala lajnat hiwar Islamiyya-Masihiyya." May 29.

Sid-Ahmed, Mohamed. 2000. "A no win situation." *Al-Ahram Weekly.* Jan. 20–26.

———. 1982. Interview in *Merip Reports.* Jan.:18–23.

Singer, Hanaa Fikry. 1990. "The Socialist Labor Party: A Case Study of a Contemporary Egyptian Opposition Party." M.A. thesis. American Univ. in Cairo.

Smock, David R., ed. 2002. *Interfaith Dialogue and Peacebuilding.* Washington, D.C.: United States Institute of Peace.

Spinner, Jeff. 1994. *The Boundaries of Citizenship: Race, Ethnicity, and Nationality in the Liberal State.* Baltimore: Johns Hopkins Univ. Press.

Stacher, Joshua A. 2002. "Post-Islamist Rumblings in Egypt: The Emergence of the Wasat Party." *Middle East Journal* 56, no. 3, 415–32.

Sulaiman, Mustafa. 1997. "Shaikh al-Azhar: Maza'am itdahad al-Aqbat batila wa mughrada." *Al-Isbu'a.* Sept. 1.

Suraya, Usama. 2000. "Qadaya misriyya fi hiwar ra'is al-wuzura'." *Al-Ahram al-'arabi.* Jan. 22.

Tantawi, Muhammad Sayyid. 1994. "Al-Fikr ad-dini wa taqaddum al-muj-tama'." Presentation at *al-Fikr ad-dini wa taqaddum al-mujtama'*. Cairo: Dar El Thaqafa.

———. 1995. "Al-Fikr ad-dini wa'l-musharaka." Presentation at *al-Fikr ad-dini wa'l-musharaka*. Cairo: Dar El Thaqafa.

———. 1997. Written response to questions posed at an interview by author at al-Azhar. Aug. 27–28.

———. 2000. Interview by author at al-Azhar. Jan. 24.

Tariq at-tahaddi: Qissat hayat ad-duktur al-qiss Samuel Habib. 1999. Cairo: Dar El Thaqafa.

at-Tawijri, 'Abd al-'Aziz bin 'Uthman. 1998. *Al-Hiwar min ajl at-ta'ayush*. Cairo: Dar ash-Shuruq.

Twine, Fred. 1994. *Citizenship and Social Rights: The Interdependence of Self and Society*. London: Sage Publications.

United Arab Republic. 1962. *The Charter*. 1962. Cairo: United Arab Republic Information Department.

United Nations Development Programme. N.d. "Programme on Governance in the Arab Region: Elections-Egypt." www.pogar.org/countries/elections.asp?cid=5.

Vatikiotis, P. J. 1985. *The History of Egypt*. 3rd ed. Baltimore: Johns Hopkins Univ. Press.

———. 1991. *The History of Modern Egypt*. 4th ed. Baltimore: Johns Hopkins Univ. Press.

Virtue, David W. 1996. *A Vision of Hope*. Cumbria: Regnum Books.

Wagner, Don. 1997. "Egypt's Coptic Christians: Caught Between Renewal and Persecution." *Washington Report on Middle East Affairs* Oct.–Nov.:87–88.

Walzer, Michael. 1997. *On Toleration*. New Haven, Conn.: Yale Univ. Press.

Al-Wasat. 1996. "Ma'mun al-Hudaybi li'l-Wasat: Hizb Abu al-'Alaa la yumath-thil al-Ikhwan." Jan. 22.

Weaver, Mary Anne. 2001. "Egypt on Trial." *New York Times Magazine*. June 17.

Williams, Bernard. 1996. "Toleration: An Impossible Virtue?" In *Toleration: An Elusive Virtue*, edited by David Heyd, 18–27. Princeton, N.J.: Princeton Univ. Press.

Yunis, Muhammad. 1997. "Ad-adyan bari'a min martabak il-hadith il-irhabi bi'l-Uqsur." *Al-Ahram*. Nov. 29.

Zeghal, Malika. 1999. "Religion and Politics in Egypt: The Ulema of Al-Azhar, Radical Islam, and the State (1952–94)." *International Journal of Middle East Studies* 31, no. 4:371–99.

Zubaida, Sami. 1992. "Islam, the State and Democracy: Contrasting Conceptions of Society in Egypt." *Middle East Report*. Nov.–Dec.:2–10.

———. 2001. "Islam and the Politics of Community and Citizenship." *Middle East Report*. Winter:20–27.

Index